WOMEN
AND
HUMAN RIGHTS

WOMEN AND HUMAN RIGHTS

Editor
Jyotsna Mishra

KALPAZ PUBLICATIONS
Delhi-110052

WOMEN AND HUMAN RIGHTS
(Women Studies, Human Rights)

ISBN: 81-7835-005-X

Published in 2000 in India by
Kalpaz Publications
C-30, Satyawati Nagar
Ashok Vihar Phase-III
Delhi-110052
E-Mail: kalpaz@hotmail.com

Laser Typeset at A.S. Printers
Printed at Mehra Offset Printers, New Delhi

Contents

Preface

Women consists half of the human population have been treated as weaker sex in all societies of the world. Hence crime against women, rape and molestation, emancipation of women, identity crisis, discrimination and many more phrase-like problems have been widely discussed and debated.

Violence affects the lives of millions of women worldwide, in all socioeconomic and educational classes. It cuts across cultural and religious barriers, impeding the right of women to participate fully in society. Violence against women takes a dismaying variety of forms, from domestic abuse and rape to child marriages and female circumcision. All are violations of the most fundamental human rights.

Governments agreed to adopt and implement national legislation to end violence against women and to work actively to ratify all international agreements that relate to violence against women. They agreed that there should be shelters, legal aid and other services for girls and women at risk, and counselling and rehabilitation for perpetrators.

The meaning of gender and sexuality and the balance of power between women and men at all levels of society must be reviewed. Combating violence against women requires challenging the way that gender roles and power relations are articulated in society. In many countries women have a low status. They are considered as inferior and there is a strong belief that men are superior to them and even own them.

Changing people's attitude and mentality towards women will take a long time—at least a generation, many believe, and perhaps longer. Nevertheless, raising awareness of the issue of violence against women, and educating boys and men to view women as valuable partners in life, in the development of a society and in the attainment of peace are just as important as taking legal steps to protect women's human rights.

Editor

1

Women and Human Rights

Violence affects the lives of millions of women worldwide, in all socio-economic and educational classes. It cuts across cultural and religious barriers, impeding the right of women to participate fully in society. Violence against women takes a dismaying variety of forms, from domestic abuse and rape to child marriages and female circumcision. All are violations of the most fundamental human rights. In a statement to the Fourth World Conference on Women in Beijing in September 1995, the then United Nations Secretary-General, Boutros Boutros-Ghali, said that violence against women is a universal problem that must be universally condemned. But he said that the problem continues to grow.

The Secretary-General noted that domestic violence alone is on the increase. Studies in 10 countries, he said, have found that between 17 per cent and 38 per cent of women have suffered physical assaults by a partner. In the Platform for Action, the core document of the Beijing Conference, Governments declared that "violence against women constitutes a violation of basic human rights and is an obstacle to the achievement of the objectives of equality, development and peace."

The Work of the Special Rapporteur

The issue of the advancement of women's rights has concerned the United Nations since the Organisation's founding. Yet the alarming global dimensions of female-targeted violence were not explicitly acknowledged by the international community until December 1993, when the United Nations General Assembly adopted the Declaration on the Elimination of Violence against Women.

Until that point, most governments tended to regard violence against women largely as a private matter between individuals, and not as a pervasive human rights problem requiring State intervention. In view of the alarming growth in the number of cases of violence against women throughout the world, the Commission on Human Rights adopted resolution 1994/45 of 4 March 1994, in which it decided to appoint the Special Rapporteur on violence against women, including its causes and consequences.

As a result of these steps, the problem of violence against women has been drawing increasing political attention. The Special Rapporteur has a mandate to collect and analyse comprehensive data and to recommend measures aimed at eliminating violence at the international, national and regional levels. The mandate is threefold :

— To collect information on violence against women and its causes and consequences from sources such as governments, treaty bodies, specialised agencies and inter-governmental and non-governmental organisations, and to respond effectively to such information;

— To recommend measures and ways and means, at the national, regional and international levels, to eliminate violence against women and its causes, and to remedy its consequences;

— To work closely with other special rapporteurs, special representatives, working groups and independent experts of the Commission on Human Rights.

Incest, Rape and Domestic Violence

Some females fall prey to violence before they are born, when expectant parents abort their unborn daughters, hoping for sons instead. In other societies, girls are subjected to such traditional practices as circumcision, which leave them maimed and traumatised. In others, they are compelled to marry at an early age, before they are physically, mentally or emotionally mature.

Women are victims of incest, rape and domestic violence that often lead to trauma, physical handicap or death.

And rape is still being used as a weapon of war, a strategy used to subjugate and terrify entire communities. Soldiers deliberately impregnate women of different ethnic groups and abandon them when it is too late to get an abortion.

The Platform for Action adopted at the Fourth World Conference on Women declared that rape in armed conflict is a war crime and could, under certain circumstances, be considered genocide.

Former Secretary-General Boutros-Ghali told the Beijing Conference that more women today were suffering directly from the effects of war and conflict than ever before in history. "There is a deplorable trend towards the organised humiliation of women, including the crime of mass rape," the Secretary-General said. "We will press for international legal action against those who perpetrate organised violence against women in time of conflict."

A preliminary report in 1994 by the Special Rapporteur, Ms. Radhika Coomaraswamy, focused on three areas of concern where women are particularly vulnerable: in the family (including domestic violence, traditional practices, infanticide); in the community (including rape, sexual assault, commercialised violence such as trafficking in women, labour exploitation, female migrant workers (etc.); and by the State (including violence against women in detention as well as violence against women in situations of armed conflict and against refugee women).

In the Platform for Action adopted at the Beijing Conference, violence against women and the human rights of women are two of the 12 critical areas of concern identified as the main obstacles to the advancement of women.

Governments agreed to adopt and implement national legislation to end violence against women and to work actively to ratify all international agreements that relate to violence against women. They agreed that there should be shelters, legal aid and other services for girls and women at risk, and counselling and rehabilitation for perpetrators.

Governments also pledged to adopt appropriate measures in the field of education to modify the social and cultural patterns of conduct of men and women. And the Platform called on media professionals to develop self-regulatory guidelines to address violent, degrading and pornographic materials while encouraging non-stereotyped, balanced and diverse images of women.

Defining Gender-based Abuse

The Declaration on the Elimination of Violence against Women is the first international human rights instrument to exclusively and explicitly address the issue of violence against women. It affirms that the phenomenon violates, impairs or nullifies women's human rights and their exercise of fundamental freedoms.

The Declaration provides a definition of gender-based abuse, calling it "any act of gender-based violence that results in, or is likely to result in, physical, sexual or psychological harm or suffering to women, including threats of such acts, coercion or arbitrary deprivation of liberty, whether occurring in public or in private life."

The definition is amplified in article 2 of the Declaration, which identifies three areas in which violence commonly takes place :

— Physical, sexual and psychological violence that occurs in the family, including battering; sexual abuse of female children in the household; dowry-related violence; marital rape; female genital mutilation and other traditional practices harmful to women; non-spousal violence; and violence related to exploitation;

— Physical, sexual and psychological violence that occurs within the general community, including rape; sexual abuse; sexual harassment and intimidation at work, in educational institutions and elsewhere; trafficking in women; and forced prostitution; and

— Physical, sexual and psychological violence perpetrated or condoned by the State, wherever it occurs.

The importance of the question of violence against women was emphasised over the last decade through the holding of several expert group meetings sponsored by the United Nations to draw attention to the extent and severity of the problem.

In September 1992, the United Nations Commission on the Status of Women established a special Working Group and gave it a mandate to draw up a draft declaration on violence against women.

The following year, the United Nations Commission for Human Rights, in resolution 1993/46 of 3 March, condemned all forms of violence and violations of human rights directed specifically against women.

The World Conference on Human Rights, held in Vienna in June 1993, laid extensive groundwork for eliminating violence against women.

In the Vienna Declaration and Programme of Action, governments declared that the United Nations system and Member States should work towards the elimination of violence against women in public and private life; of all forms of sexual harassment, exploitation and trafficking in women; of gender bias in the administration of justice; and of any conflicts arising between the rights of women and the harmful effects of certain traditional or customary practices, cultural prejudices and religious extremism.

The document also declared that "violations of the human rights of women in situations of armed conflicts are violations of the fundamental principles of international human rights and humanitarian law," and that all violations of this kind—including murder, systematic rape, sexual slavery and forced pregnancy—"require a particularly effective response."

Kinds of Violence against Women

Domestic Violence

Violence against women in the family occurs in developed and developing countries alike. It has long been considered a private matter by bystanders—including neighbours, the community and government. But such private matters have a tendency to become public tragedies. In the United States, a woman is beaten every 18 minutes. Indeed, domestic violence is the leading cause of injury among women of reproductive age in the United States. Between 22 and 35 per cent of women who visit emergency rooms are there for that reason. The highly publicised trial of O. J. Simpson, the retired United States football player acquitted of the murder of his former wife and a male friend of hers, helped focus international media attention on the issue of domestic violence and spousal abuse.

In Peru, 70 per cent of all crimes reported to the police involve women beaten by their husbands. In Pakistan, Prime Minister Benazir Bhutto strongly defended a 35-year-old mother of two who was severely burned by her husband in a domestic dispute.

"There is no excuse for such a behaviour," the Prime Minister declared after visiting the hospitalised victim. "My presence here is to send a message to all those who violate Islamic teachings and defy laws of the land with their inhuman treatment of women. This will not be tolerated."

According to the Human Rights Commission of Pakistan, in the 400 cases of domestic violence reported in 1993 in the province of Punjab, nearly half ended with the death of the wife.

According to the Special Rapporteur's report, many governments now recognise the importance of protecting victims of domestic abuse and taking action to punish perpetrators. The establishment of structures allowing officials to deal with cases of domestic violence and its consequences is a significant step towards the elimination of violence against women in the family.

The Special Rapporteur's report highlights the importance of adopting legislation that provides for prosecution of the offender. It also stresses the importance of specialised training for law enforcement authorities as well as medical and legal professionals, and of the establishment of community support services for victims, including access to information and shelters.

Traditional Practices

In many countries, women fall victim to traditional practices that violate their human rights. The persistence of the problem has much to do with the fact that most of these physically and psychologically harmful customs are deeply rooted in the tradition and culture of society.

Female Genital Mutilation

According to the World Health Organisation, 85 million to 115 million girls and women in the population have undergone some form of female genital mutilation and suffer from its adverse health effects. Every year an estimated two million young girls undergo this procedure. Most live in Africa and Asia, but an increasing number can be found among immigrant and refugee families in Western Europe and North America. Indeed, the practice has been outlawed in some European countries.

In France, a Malian was convicted in a criminal court after his baby girl died of a female circumcision-related infection. The procedure had been performed on the infant at home. In Canada, fear of being forced to undergo circumcision can be grounds for asylum. A Nigerian woman was granted refugee status since she felt that she might be persecuted in her home country because of her refusal to inflict genital mutilation on her baby daughter. There is a growing consensus that the best way to eliminate these practices is through educational campaigns that emphasise their dangerous health consequences. Several governments have been actively promoting such campaigns in their countries.

Son Preference

Son preference affects. women in many countries, particularly in Asia. Its consequences can be anything from foetal or female infanticide to neglect of the girl-child over her brother in terms of such essential needs as nutrition, basic health care and education.

In China and India, some women choose to terminate their pregnancies when expecting daughters but carry their pregnancies to term when expecting sons.

According to reports from India, genetic testing for sex selection has become a booming business, especially in the country's northern regions. Indian gender-detection clinics drew protests from women's groups after the appearance of advertisements suggesting that it was better to spend $38 now to terminate a female foetus than $3,800 later on her dowry.

A study of amniocentesis procedures conducted in a large Bombay hospital found that 95.5 per cent of foetuses identified as female were aborted, compared with a far smaller percentage of male foetuses.

The problem of son preference is present in many other countries as well. Asked how many children he had fathered, the former United States boxing champion Muhammad Ali told an interviewer: "One boy and seven mistakes."

Dowry-related Violence and Early Marriage

In some countries, weddings are preceded by the payment of an agreed-upon dowry by the bride's family. Failure to pay the dowry can lead to violence. In Bangladesh, a bride whose dowry was deemed too small was disfigured after her husband threw acid on her face. In India, an average of five women a day are burned in dowry-related disputes—and many more cases are never reported. Early marriage, especially without the consent of the girl, is another form of human rights violation. Early marriage followed by multiple pregnancies can affect the health of women for life.

The report of the Special Rapporteur has documented the destructive effects of marriage of female children under 18 and has urged governments to adopt relevant legislation.

Violence in the Community

Rape

Rape can occur anywhere, even in the family, where it can take the form of marital rape or incest. It occurs in the community, where a woman can fall prey to any abuser. It also occurs in situations of armed conflict and in refugee camps.

In the United States, national statistics indicate that a women is raped every six minutes. In 1995, the case of a Brazilian jogger raped and murdered in New York City's Central Park drew international attention once again to the problem. The incident occurred only a few years after an earlier sensational jogger-assault case in which the victim— an American assaulted in the same general area of the park —barely survived after her assailants left her for dead.

Relations between residents of the Japanese island of Okinawa and American GIs were thrown into turmoil in 1995 after two marines and a sailor allegedly kidnapped and raped a 12-year-old girl. The Special Rapporteur's report underlines the importance of education to sensitise the public about the special horrors of rape, and of sensitivity training for the police and hospital staff who work with victims.

Sexual Assault within Marriage

In many countries sexual assault by a husband on his wife is not considered to be a crime: a wife is expected to submit. It is thus very difficult in practice for a woman to prove that sexual assault has occurred unless she can demonstrate serious injury. The report of the Special Rapporteur noted that light sentences in sexual assault cases send the wrong message to perpetrators and to the public at large: that female sexual victimisation is unimportant.

Sexual harassment in the workplace is a growing concern for women. Employers abuse their authority to seek sexual favours from their female co-workers or subordinates, sometimes promising promotions or other forms of career advancement or simply creating an untenable and hostile work environment. Women who refuse to give in to such unwanted sexual advances often run the risk of anything from demotion to dismissal.

But in recent years more women have been coming forward to report such practices—some taking their cases to court. In her report, the Special Rapporteur stressed that sexual harassment constitutes a form of sex discrimination. "It not only degrades the woman," the report noted, "but reinforces and reflects the idea of non-professionalism on the part of women workers, who are consequently regarded as less able to perform their duties than their male colleagues."

Prostitution and Trafficking

Many women are forced into prostitution either by their parents, husbands or boyfriends—or as a result of the difficult economic and social conditions in which they find themselves. They are also lured into prostitution, sometimes by 'mail-order bride' agencies that promise to find them a husband or a job in a foreign country. As a result, they very often find themselves illegally confined in brothels in slavery-like conditions where they are physically abused and their passports withheld. Most women initially victimised by sexual traffickers have little inkling of what awaits them. They generally get a very small percentage of what the customer pays to the pimp or the brothel owner. Once they are caught up in the system there is practically no way out, and they find themselves in a very vulnerable situation.

Since prostitution is illegal in many countries, it is difficult for prostitutes to come forward and ask for protection if they become victims of rape or want to escape from brothels. Customers, on the other hand, are rarely the object of penal laws. In Thailand, prostitutes who complain to the police are often arrested and sent back to the brothels upon payment of a fine.

The extent of trafficking in women and girl children has reached alarming proportions, especially in Asian countries. Many women and girl children are trafficked across borders, often with the complicity of border guards. In one incident, five young prostitutes burned to death in a brothel fire because they had been chained to their beds. At the same time, sex tours of developing countries are a well-organised industry in several European and other industrialised countries. The Special Rapporteur has called on governments to take action to protect young girls from being recruited as prostitutes and to closely monitor recruiting agencies.

Violence against Women Migrant Workers

Female migrant workers typically leave their countries for better living conditions and better pay—but the real benefits accrue to both the host countries and the countries of origin.

For home countries, money sent home by migrant

workers is an important source of hard currency, while receiving countries are able to find workers for low-paying jobs that might otherwise go unfilled. But migrant workers themselves fare badly, and sometimes tragically. Many become virtual slaves, subject to abuse and rape by their employers. In the Middle East and Persian Gulf region, there are an estimated 1.2 million women, mainly Asians, who are employed as domestic servants.

According to the independent human rights group Middle East Watch, female migrant workers in Kuwait often suffer beatings and sexual assaults at the hands of their employers. The police are often of little help. In many cases, women who report being raped by their employers are sent back to the employer — or are even assaulted at the police station.

Working conditions are often appalling, and employers prevent women from escaping by seising their passports or identity papers. The report of the Special Rapporteur draws attention to the fact that there are many international instruments that can be used to prevent abuse against migrant women and suggests some measures to protect the human rights of migrant women.

Pornography

Another concern highlighted in the Special Rapporteur's report is pornography, which represents a form of violence against women that "glamorises the degradation and maltreatment of women and asserts their subordinate function as mere receptacles for male lust."

Violence Perpetrated or Condoned by States

Custodial Violence against Women

Violence against women by the very people who are

supposed to protect them—members of the law enforcement and criminal justice systems—is widespread.

Women are physically or verbally abused; they also suffer sexual and physical torture. According to Amnesty International, thousands of women held in custody are routinely raped in police detention centres worldwide.

The report of the Special Rapporteur underlines the necessity for States to prosecute those accused of abusing women while in detention and to hold them accountable for their actions.

Violence against Women in Situations of Armed Conflict

Rape has been widely used as a weapon of war whenever armed conflicts arise between different parties. Women and girl children are frequently victims of gang rape committed by soldiers from all sides of a conflict. Such acts are done mainly to trample the dignity of the victims. Rape has been used to reinforce the policy of ethnic cleansing in the war that has been tearing apart the former Yugoslavia. The so-called 'comfort women'—young girls of colonised or occupied countries who became sexual slaves to Japanese soldiers during the Second World War—have dramatised the problem in a historical context. Many of these women are now coming forward and demanding compensation for their suffering from Japanese authorities. "Such rape is the symbolic rape of the community, the destruction of the fundamental elements of a society and culture—the ultimate humiliation of the male enemy," the report by the Special Rapporteur noted. It stressed the need to hold the perpetrators of such crimes fully accountable.

Violence against Refugee and Displaced Women

Women and children form the great majority of refugee populations all over the world and are especially vulnerable to violence and exploitation. In refugee camps, they are raped and abused by military and immigration personnel, bandit groups, male refugees and rival ethnic groups. They are also forced into prostitution.

In her report, the Special Rapporteur proposes the following measures to be taken for the protection of women and girls in refugee camps: improvement of security, deployment of trained female officers at all points of the refugees' journey, participation of women in organisational structures of the camps and prosecution of government and military personnel responsible for abuse against refugee women.

Legal Steps to Criminalise Violence against Women

In recent years some countries have taken significant steps towards improving laws relating to violence against women. For example :

— In July 1991, Mexico revised its rape law in several important ways. A provision was eliminated that allowed a man who raped a minor to avoid prosecution if he agreed to marry her. Now judges are required to hand down a decision regarding access to an abortion within five working days.

— On 9 June 1994, the Organisation of American States adopted the Inter-American Convention to Prevent, Punish and Eradicate Violence against Women (also called Convention of Belam do Para), a new international instrument that recognises all gender-based violence as an abuse of human rights. This Convention provides an individual right of petition and a right for non-governmental organisations to lodge complaints with the Inter-American Commission of Human Rights.

— In Australia, a National Committee on Violence

against Women was established to coordinate the development of policy, legislation and law enforcement at the national level as well as community education on violence against women.

— In 1991, the government of Canada announced a new four-year Family Violence Initiative intended to mobilise community action, strengthen Canada's legal framework, establish services on Indian reserves and in Inuit communities, develop resources to help victims and stop offenders, and provide housing for abused women and children.

— In Turkey, a Ministry of State for Women was established whose main goals are, among others, to promote women's rights and strengthen their role in economic, social, political and cultural life. Legal measures are being adopted towards the elimination of violence against women. The establishment of special courts to deal with violence is envisaged. Psychological treatment for abused women is also planned, along with the establishment of women's shelters around the country. Specially trained female police officers could provide assistance to victims of violence.

— In Burkina Faso, a strong advertising campaign by the government as well as television and radio programmes on the unhealthy practice of genital mutilation were launched to educate and raise public awareness about the dangerous consequences of such an 'operation'. A National Anti-Excision Committee was established in 1990 by the present head of State. Today, the practice of genital mutilation has been eliminated in some villages of Burkina Faso. In others, there has been an incredible drop in the number of girls excised: only 10 per cent of the girls are excised compared to 100 per cent 10 years ago.

— Some countries have introduced police units specially trained for dealing with spousal assault. In Brazil, specific police stations have been designated to deal with women's issues, including domestic violence. These police stations are staffed entirely by women.

Ensuring that Laws are Obeyed

These examples illustrate some steps taken at the national level towards the eradication of violence against women. Combating and eradicating this scourge require enhanced and concerted efforts to protect women at the local, national and international levels. States have tended to adopt a passive attitude when confronted by cases of violations of women's rights by private actors. Most laws fail to protect victims or to punish perpetrators. Passing laws to criminalise violence against women is an important way to redefine the limits of acceptable behaviour.

States should ensure that national legislation, once adopted, does not go unenforced. State responsibility is clearly underlined in article 4 of the Declaration on the Elimination of Violence against Women, which stipulates that "States should exercise due diligence to prevent, investigate and, in accordance with national legislation, punish acts of violence against women, whether those acts are perpetrated by the State or by private persons." Any approach designed to combat violence must be twofold, addressing the root causes of the problem and treating its manifestations. Society at large, including judges and police officers, must be educated to change the social attitudes and beliefs that encourage male violence.

Challenging Traditional Attitudes

The meaning of gender and sexuality and the balance of

power between women and men at all levels of society must be reviewed. Combating violence against women requires challenging the way that gender roles and power relations are articulated in society. In many countries women have a low status. They are considered as inferior and there is a strong belief that men are superior to them and even own them.

Changing people's attitude and mentality towards women will take a long time—at least a generation, many believe, and perhaps longer. Nevertheless, raising awareness of the issue of violence against women, and educating boys and men to view women as valuable partners in life, in the development of a society and in the attainment of peace are just as important as taking legal steps to protect women's human rights.

It is also important in order to prevent violence that non-violent means be used to resolve conflict between all members of society. Breaking the cycle of abuse will require concerted collaboration and action between governmental and non-governmental actors, including educators, health-care authorities, legislators, the judiciary and the mass media.

2

Violence and Insecurity

The modern ideals of democracy, freedom and equality kindle young people's desire to be 'somebody' in the world. Yet the hierarchy and inequality built into the global economy and society shut out most youth from occupations that provide self-esteem and dignity. In the absence of serious efforts to ease these global inequalities, the experience of young people around the world will be defined increasingly by scarcity, unemployment, anxiety, anger, despair and powerlessness. Increasing numbers of people struggling to survive in the informal economy by engaging in crime, prostitution and other forms of the skin trade have little or no stake in the status quo.

In a world culture which glamorizes war and violence via Rambo movies and where weapons are easily bought and sold, angry and confused youth devoid of future prospects are easily lured into joining armies, armed insurgencies, gangs and other violent enterprises. Violent and destructive behaviours are not inherent in the animal nature of human beings as assumed by the likes of Hobbes and Malthus. Rather, such behaviours tend to occur where supportive social structures are absent and people are engulfed in fear and anxiety.

Commodity production and the extension of techno-bureaucratic control over people's lives have undermined community, family and cultural integrity, resulting in greater competition and individualism. Weakening family and community ties in the modern era have not been replaced with alternative modes of human commitment and social organization. As psychologist Mary Clark notes, the denial of human emotional needs such as bonding, trust, affection and a shared spiritual orientation to life in the modern world has resulted in a plethora of pathological behaviours ranging from "greed, dominance, wife-beating, child-abuse, drug abuse, callousness and violence to obsessive needs for attachment to sports teams, nations, and leaders who project an image of strength. Indeed, the root-lessness and alienation produced by technological and capitalist expansion and human emotional need for acceptance and belonging underlie the popularity of extremely violent, often self-destructive sects, militias, ethno-nationalist and religious fundamentalist movements in the world today.

The global refugee problem is another manifestation of the insecurity and destitution created by the combined effects of militarism, poverty and environmental destruction. There are currently about 27 million refugees in the world. While millions of people remain displaced in their own countries, millions of economic, political and environmental refugees spill into other countries, contributing to the stresses and conflicts of international migration. Malthusian calls to halt migration into the rich North overlook the roots of the refugee problem situated in global political and economic structures. It is estimated that by the year 2000 more than half the people in the world will be under the age of 20. As Malthusians often point out, increasing numbers of young dispossessed and angry youth in the Third World constitute a great threat to global peace and security. Indeed, they are the ones carrying the guns and doing much of the actual killing in the world. Although a lowering of the size of the global population may ease the competition, it will not eliminate the inequalities, insecurities and the violence located in the global capitalist, patriarchal and white supremacist social system. To understand escalating global violence and insecurity and threats to democracy, we need to understand how this world order of domination is maintained by militarism. Psychological colonization was essential to the maintenance of white supremacy and imperialism, as articulated eloquently by writers such as Frantz Fanon and Albert Mermmi. Yet the sense of racial superiority achieved through western education, Christianity, the colonial state and the capitalist economic system could not have been maintained without the use of organized violence.

Superior military power as well as cunning and deception enabled the Europeans to colonize 85% of the earth by the end of World War I. As a native of the Solomon Islands put it, "Nothing much is said about the sufferings on our side. Yet we fought with spears, clubs, bows and arrows. The foreigners fought with canons, guns and bullets." Like military superiority, collaboration with native elites was a precondition of colonial rule. Resistant native rulers were killed or their positions and titles given to others more amenable to colonial control. Indeed, not knowing the physical and social terrain, including the languages and customs of the natives, the foreign rulers were compelled to rely on a vast array of local administrators and to reward them amply for their services. These features of imperialism have continued in the post-independence, neo-colonial period.

Although Cold War ideology was formulated in terms of East-West competition, control of Third World resources and suppression of social revolutions were the major imperatives of western imperialism during the post-war, neo-colonial era as they had been during the era of classical colonialism. Even nuclear deployment was not an exclusively super-power issue.

Managing people

As capitalism expanded in the Third World, a huge infrastructure of dependency developed, spreading external control into state bureaucracies and universities and the managerial, technical and intellectual elites. But techno-bureaucratic authority was not sufficient for managing people or the environment. Expansion of export production and market liberalization often required violent repression rather than democratic government. Third World elites continued to be a collaborator class of imperialism in the neo-colonial period. But unlike in the earlier classical colonialist period, as the wielders of state power they had the right to use force against their populations. Without the support of outside military powers, however, most Third World dictatorships could not have survived against the opposition of local people. Both super-powers invoked Cold War ideology in seeking to extend their control and influence in the Third World through maintenance of client states, arms exports, armed intervention, as well as covert operations. In accordance with the Cold War national security doctrine articulated by George Kennan and others, the US provided arms, equipment and services to 'friendly governments'. Between 1950 and 1979, the United States provided foreign governments a total of $107.3 billion under military aid programs such as the MAP (Military Assistance Program), IMET (International Military Education and Training), FMS (Foreign Military Sales), EDA (Excess Defense Articles) and ESF (Economic Support Fund). During this period, the US also trained nearly 500,000 foreign military personnel under the MAP and IMET programs. A good number of the thousands of Latin American military officers trained at the US Army School of the Americas during the last 50 or more years have been responsible for 'serious acts of lawless violence' against populations in their countries.

The United States was directly responsible for turning Third World regimes into brutal and corrupt military dictatorships, as, for example, in Nicaragua under Somoza, the Philippines under Marcos, Haiti under the Duvaliers. The United States also installed and maintained dictators in the name of anti-Communism after overthrowing the demo-cratically elected regimes of Mossadeq in Iran in 1953, Arbenz in Guatemala in the same year and Allende in Chile in 1973 because they posed challenges to US corporate interests in those countries. Many of the armed conflicts in the Third World involved super-power military interventions in national liberation struggles.

The United States intervened either overtly or covertly (through the CIA) in Korea, Guatemala, Cuba, the Dominican Republic, Iran, Vietnam, Angola, Nicaragua, El Salvador, Afghanistan, Libya and Grenada, among other countries. The Soviet Union intervened in Angola, Ethiopia, Korea, Yemen and Afghanistan. For much of the Third World, the so-called 'Cold War' was not an "unprecedented half-century of global peace" as assumed by most Western analysts and the public. Rather, it was a period of actual wars and tremendous violence, suffering and insecurity. Despite global fears of nuclear war, the arms build-up and the arms race during the Cold War primarily involved conventional weapons for use in the Third World. Defense analysts Michael Klare and Cynthia Aronson have described this vast trade in weapons as the "international repression trade. As a result of this lethal trade, regions like Central America and the Horn of Africa, which are not weapons producers themselves, became some of the most militarized religions in the world. In at least a few countries, such as the Philippines, Nicaragua and El Salvador, resistance took the form of left wing insurgencies seeking to overthrow repressive regimes and establish Communist or socialist states. But even in the few instances where such movements came into power, as in Nicaragua after the overthrow of the Somoza regime, they did not succeed in establishing autonomous paths of development. Through the imposition of an economic embargo and continued military assistance to the pro-Somoza forces, the United States ensured that the Nicaraguan revolution did not succeed.

Counter-insurgency strategies were also used by the FBI and other US government surveillance institutions in domestic imperialist policies against Black, Native American, working-class as well as peace and justice movements in the US. In fact, many civil rights activists suspect that the Black American leaders Malcolm X and Martin Luther King Jr may have been killed with the knowledge of the FBI. Not all wars in the Third World during the Cold War were proxy wars of the super-powers. The global arms arsenal built up in the name of the super-power struggle militarized the Third World, encouraging all manner of armed conflicts by brutal military regimes and often equally violent opposition movements. In many Third World countries, repression has taken the form of "a systematic counter-insurgency strategy that is waged on a number of levels: ideological, social-psychological, political and military". The result has been widespread disappearances, torture, death squad activities, killings and other human rights violations.

The full extent of the devastation caused during the Cold War by wars in the Third World, euphemistically referred to as 'low intensity conflicts', will probably never be known. According to official estimates alone, about 40 million people, over 75% of them civilians, died as a result of civil and international wars fought with conventional weapons in the so-called Cold War period. Between 25 and 30 million people were also turned into refugees by these wars. Anywhere from 1 million to 3 million people died at the hands of the Khmer Rouge in Cambodia between 1975 and 1979. Over a million people died in the decade-long Iran-Iraq war in the 1980s and over 100,000 people were killed and 40,000 disappeared in the Guatemalan army's counter-insurgency campaigns between 1970 and 1990.

Land mines—a profitable part of the global arms trade-continue to kill and maim civilians long after the end of wars. According to 1994 UN estimates, in Cambodia; there is still one mine in the ground for every two people in the country and these kill or disable 300 people each month. Indeed, casualties of war have never been restricted to the millions killed. Population control was a major plank of Cold War ideology and the global management strategy of the United States. Not only was Third World population growth seen as a major threat to US national security, but the initiative for international population control came from the military, particularly men like General William Draper, General William Westmoreland, General Maxwell Taylor and Vietnam war era Defense Secretary Robert MacNamara. It was MacNamara, subsequently the President of the World Bank, who initiated World Bank activism in global population control. Given this military connection, it is not surprising that, as discussed earlier, many population control programs have also been run on a military model as a war against Third World 'over-population'.

Massive dumping of conventional arms by super-powers during the Cold War has been followed by political destabilization in many parts of the world at the end of the Cold War. Dismantling of nuclear warheads since the end of the Cold War could make available as much as 40,000 A-bombs worth of plutonium in the coming decade, threatening efforts to curb nuclear proliferation. Global military expenditures and military expenditures of the 'developed' countries have dropped in the post-Cold War period of the so-called 'New World Order'. But arms production, arms exports and military intervention continue to be the ultimate basis for managing and controlling global resources and populations.

Many industrializing Asian countries now openly attack democracy and human rights as western concepts, endorsing political authoritarianism as being more conducive to competitiveness in the world market. The US, on the other hand, increasingly justifies its trade relations with oppressive regimes such as China using the rationale of 'market democracy'. It claims that international trade alone will move these regimes towards greater democracy. But aggressive arms peddling and arms exports by the US and European countries belie alleged western commitment to global peace and democracy. In 1993, the Clinton administration allocated $1.3 trillion to the US military for the next five years, which was only a 5% reduction of the allocation of the previous Bush administration. This allocation represent about a $14,000 defense expenditure for every household in the US. As the US military continues to be the biggest 'public works program' in the world, providing regular paychecks to over 9 million people, the rationales, huge advertising budget, lobbying and of course arms production, exports, military construction, 'logistics support' and training around the world continue. In addition to maintaining existing weaponry, new weapons for international and domestic use are continuously being designed and marketed by the Pentagon and the defense companies. An example is a class of weapons known as 'mini-nukes', that is, nuclear weapons below 5 kilotons, designed to be used against developing countries.

Women, Children and War

While arms producers, arms dealers, lobbyists, military and government officials, insurgent army and mafia leaders profit from the murderous arms trade, Third World youth are using imported weapons to kill each other, often for causes they hardly understand. Countries such as Rwanda and Sri Lanka, which have suffered and continue to suffer greatly due to war, are not weapons producers themselves.

One wonders whether arms exports are a form of population control coming from the North. Indeed, the same governments led by the United States that are pushing population control are pushing weapons into the Third World as well. Children are the major victims of war. They are also increasingly the perpetrators of wars as well. Lacking alternative means of employment and social status, it is often boys from the poorer classes who are compelled to join armed forces and lose their limbs and lives in wars which essentially benefit a small international and local elite. In today's global gun culture, the anger, idealism and naivety of the young are easily manipulated by arms traders and power-hungry men seeking recruits to bear arms for violent and extremist movements.

As armies and guerrilla forces exhaust the supplies of available men, they are turning more and more to children and young women to replenish their forces. Military leaders are finding children to be extremely pliable and effective soldiers: "In wartime, a commander wants total submission. You get that only from a child." Girls are found to make especially obedient combatants. Of the 200,000 or so children involved as combatants in wars around the world today, about 10% are estimated to be girls.

As UNICEF has pointed out, in many contemporary Third World war zones children do not voluntarily join armed factions; frequently they are forcibly conscripted.

> ... boys, 11 years old or even younger... have been abducted and compelled to carry arms and others... have been forced to kill members of their own family, or have been used as 'cannon fodder' to cross enemy lines or minefields.

Quite often, children are drugged, as for example in Liberia, where teenage gangs controlled by various war lords have apparently been roaming the country killing civilians indiscriminately. In the more calculated killings by the Liberation Tigers of Tamil Eelam (LTTE), the separatist Tamil movement in Sri Lanka, both male and female children are conscripted, trained and widely deployed as suicide bombers. These children are also trained to wear cyanide capsules around their necks to be taken in case of capture." Allegedly, the girls are made to wear two cyanide capsule's instead of one, as a symbol of their greater patriotism. In patriarchal societies, men unleash their aggression on children, considered to be their property, and on women, considered to be the weaker and more docile sex. In the contemporary period of generalized global violence and war, gender norms and sexual violence are taking more and more virulent forms.

Patriarchy and war

Male dominance in the family may have been the origin of war. In patriarchal culture, power is equated with aggression and masculinity; weakness with compassion and femininity. Women are supposed to bear male oppression silently and meekly. Where they fail to do so, they are branded as 'loud', 'hysterical', 'crazy' and frequently punished with rape and physical assault. As feminist analysts suggest, male desire to dominate and conquer may result from a deep psychological insecurity stemming from men's inability to give birth to life.

The erotic fascination that many men have towards the hunt and war and their need to express their aggression could be derived from this primordial insecurity and fragility of the male ego. However, much of this weakness may also be culturally and historically created rather than biologically determined. For example, armed aggression has been used as a means for proving the power of the US by successive Presidents of the US. This was clearly visible in the case of the Gulf War, when President Bush vowed to "kick ass" in place of compromise or negotiation with Iraq. As political scientist Cynthia Enloe has written in her essay "The Gendered Gulf", "men's sense of their own masculinity, often tenuous, is as much a factor in international politics as the flows of oil, cables, and military hardware".

Rape of the enemy's women has been a common aspect of war. As women become active in social movements, politically motivated rape is increasingly being used as a form of 'low-intensity warfare' against women. Many women in Chiapas, Mexico, have been attacked and raped by Mexican soldiers and other unknown assailants for alleged support of the Zapatista Army of National Liberation (EZLN) since the start of the rebellion in Chiapas in 1994.

However, most women subjected to rape during wars are not necessarily political activists: their crime is often simply being women or belonging to an 'enemy' group, as has been the case of widespread rape of women in Bosnia and Rwanda. More than 250,000 women were raped during the civil war in Rwanda; many were also sexually mutilated and tortured. These traumatized women—mainly widows—and their children born of rape are now outcasts without any social or economic protection from their communities or the larger world. Rape was a common occurrence during recent anti-Muslim riots in India as well. As an analysis published in the *Bulletin of the Committee of South Asian Women states:*

> ... after anti-Muslim riots following the demolition of the mosque at Ayodhaya, thirteen Muslim women were raped under flood-light in Surat and the rapes recorded on video. Seven of the women were then burnt alive. It is worth recalling that the Nazis also took pictures of their victims.

The increasing identification of women with violent ethnic and religious fundamentalism portends not liberation but increased victimization of women. In order to sustain conflicts, hatred has to be inculcated and enemies created even where they did not previously exist.

The proliferation of weapons militates against the development of non-violent strategies for conflict resolution. In order to maintain and expand the military status quo, armed conflicts have to be continued. As the Communist enemy has now been defeated, the ethnic 'other' has become the main enemy in the post-Cold War world.

Women and fundamentalism

Cultural nationalism tends to rely on patriarchal authority to invoke a stable and secure past. In challenging the forces of modernization, right-wing fundamentalism attempts to restrict women to the private sphere and the wife and mother roles. In countries such as Algeria and Afghanistan, women are being targeted and even assassinated by fanatical male supremacist, Islamic groups for the 'crimes' of simply working outside the home and not wearing the veil. Yet, frequently, nationalist and fundamentalist movements also rely on women's participation in the public sphere for the achievement of their objectives.

The result is often contradictory expectations of women. An example is the veiling of Islamic women. As Leila Ahmed and other scholars have shown, the veil has been both a symbol of anti-imperialism and cultural self-assertion and an expression of women's subordination. It has both been voluntarily adopted by women and been imposed upon them by religious and state authorities. Despite their subordination in most nationalist movements, women have been an important element in even in the more belligerent, fascist variants.

The worsening global economic and social crisis is driving many women to join the women's wings of such extreme movements. Thus women, who have traditionally disavowed violence, are increasingly resorting to bomb- throwing and murder as the only means of self-assertion and empowerment. For young women joining such movements, as for their male counterparts, carrying a gun and fighting for a cause provide a sense of dignity and self-esteem they otherwise lack. As some observers have commented, it is often women who come from lower social classes and who have experienced little in the way of social status and self-esteem who tend to be the most militant and virulent in dedication to their cause. As Sri Lankan journalist Rita Sebastian has reported, participation in the violent struggle of the LTTE has brought about a massive transformation of the roles of women. The woman suicide bomber responsible for the assassination of the Indian Prime Minister, Rajiv Gandhi, symbolises the extent of that transformation, Women on motor-bicycles, with automatic weapons slung across their shoulders, or at the wheel of heavy trucks are a common sight. . . No different from their male counterparts, they have adopted the gun as the symbol of their liberation. Faced with a shortage of young and able-bodied men, the Sri Lankan government is also seeking to increase recruitment of young women into the armed forces.

However, ultimately the gun and the suicide bomb symbolize not liberation but destruction of the 'other' as well as the self. This is brought to light for example in a report on LTTE torture camps issued by a human rights group in Sri Lanka. Based on information gathered from escaped prisoners, it documents use of young Tamil women as torturers of other Tamil women imprisoned for allegedly serving as informants and accomplices for enemy groups.

The utterly harsh and inhumane treatment meted out by young women, sometimes mere children, to other women who could well be their mothers, sisters or grandmothers bespeaks not women's liberation but delusion, insecurity and depravity. If more sane life-enhancing options are not made available to young men, women and children, the world will become an even more dangerous and insecure a place than it already is. Instead, Third World conditions are multiplying everywhere.

The strategies of global free market authoritarianism make corporations increasingly "freer to exploit workers, consumers, and the environment, North and South, East and West". As companies demand more labor repression, curtailment of environmental activism and punishment of terrorist activities and as social conflicts and turmoil increase, many people in the North are also succumbing to racism and fundamentalism as means to cope with uncertainty and fear. A recent report of the US justice Department's Bureau of Justice Statistics shows that "even as the number of teenagers has declined" teenage violence with guns has steadily risen since 1985, thus making one question the Malthusian proposition that violence is inherently related to the increase in the number of angry young men. Apparently, 135,000 students bring guns to school every day and there are over 200 million handguns in the United States today. For many young men without economic opportunities and who are lured by media violence, manhood is associated with joining a gang and carrying a gun. Much of inner city violence in the US is inter-personal and random.

Teenagers kill each other at school and on the streets over petty rivalries and even over consumer items such as brand name sneakers and jackets. Every day, innocent bystanders are killed in crossfire and also because of police brutality. In the United States, inner city crime, drug- and gang-related deaths rival and sometimes surpass those of Third World 'low-intensity' conflicts. In 1987, the US had a homicide rate of 21.9 per 1,000 men aged 15-24, thus making the country "the unchallenged killing champion of the world".

A young Black man from Harlem may be less likely to reach age 40 than a young man in Bangladesh. One in every three Black men in their 20s in the US today is imprisoned, on probation or on parole. A much greater proportion of Blacks are arrested, prosecuted, convicted and imprisoned than are whites in the US. The war on drugs in the United States has been waged largely against Blacks. Although Black men constitute 13% of all monthly drug users, they represent 35% of all arrests, 55% of all convictions and 74% of all prison sentences for drug possession. As many criminologists have pointed out, these racial biases in law enforcement explain the sharply divergent views of Blacks and whites on the acquittal in the O.J. Simpson murder trial. Everywhere women are the victims of sexual assault and family violence, these being the fastest growing crimes in the US. According to the American Medical Association, in the US, 700,000 women are sexually assaulted each year, one every 45 seconds. Some 61% of female rape victims are under age 18.

There seems to be little anguish that young boys are raping women who could well be their own relatives. Often the victims themselves are blamed for walking alone in the dark and castigated as a prostitutes while the rapists brag about their manliness and sometimes even their mothers defend them. Tired and angered by male violence frequently directed at them, many young women are also seeking to assert themselves violently. Isolated acts of violence and participation in armed gangs in inner cities such as Los Angeles are increasing among young women.

Films and advertising glorifying violence are making more women equate power and liberation with aggression. Seeking new markets for guns, gun manufacturers and their powerful lobby, the National Rifle Association, are promoting guns as the symbol for women's liberation while companies in the fashion industry are promoting clothes which allow women to carry concealed weapons. What is urgently needed in the US is not a domestic population control policy, but a gun control policy. Instead, the production of sophisticated weapons that kill more efficiently is increasing. Winchester-Olin's new Talon bullet, targeted especially at the domestic market, is an example. The superior performance capability of this new bullet has been extolled in the *Handgunning Magazine:*

> . . . the cuts made by the tips of the 'blades' promoted further tearing along the length of the wound. The actual measured surface area of the permanent wound channel is therefore hugely *greater than the mere tubular track left by any conventional hollow point bullet.* (emphasis in original)

More and more states in the Unites States are also passing increasingly lax policies for gun possession while at the same time they are building more and more prisons to house criminals. The overwhelming response to social turmoil in the US, as elsewhere in the world, continues to be calls for population control, more weapons and 'law and order' rather than justice and social change. The number of prison inmates in the US has tripled over the past 20 years and prison building has emerged as one of the country's fastest growing 'industries'.

The cost of building prisons rose from $6.8 billion a year in 1980 to $30 billion a year in 1995, according to the US justice Department's Bureau of justice Statistics. As the number of prison guards has increased even faster than the number of prisoners, prison guards' unions are emerging as a major political force in states such as California. Where prisoners are disproportionately people of color and the guards largely white, racial tensions can easily be inflamed.

Today, many of the problems of poverty and crime are being blamed on the Gypsies, their large families and welfare dependence by state officials, intellectuals and ordinary citizens alike. A return of the brutality and genocide visited on the Gypsies during the Nazi era cannot be ruled out. The racism people express towards each other cannot be understood merely at the demographic and psycho-biological levels. It needs to be examined in relation to the generalization of the militaristic model of conquest and domination into all sectors of life.

The confluence of the forces of technology, capitalism and militarism has alienated people from each other, from nature and the deeper aspects of self. It has bred pessimism and cynicism and an acceptance of poverty, ecocide, genocide, violence against women, children and ethnic others as inevitable. It encourages ignorance, greed, fear and hatred; not wisdom, generosity, courage and compassion. Neo-Malthusian analysts see Third World population, growth as threatening democracy and enlightenment in the West and giving rise to anarchy and fascism in the Third World. But our investigation reveals that the roots of global militarism and repression lie largely in the industrialized countries in the North where population growth rates are actually declining. Malthusian focus on Third World 'overpopulation' diverts attention from the intensification of fascistic tendencies in the North. Moreover, as noted in earlier sections of this book, the collusion between population control interests and right-wing movements such as the anti-immigration movement encourage the spread of eugenicist and fascist ideologies of white racial and ethnic superiority.

Capitalism and right-wing fundamentalism may seem to be contradictory social forces: the former representing secular modernism; the latter religious tradition. But these two forces are increasingly converging to undermine democracy worldwide. This is particularly the case with Christian fundamentalism in the US, which derives its power from the 'dictatorship' of the right represented by the merger of big business and the state. Corporations and wealthy individuals in the

US control the political candidates and agendas and policies of politicians in office, whether Republican or Democrat, making a mockery of democracy in the country. Large corporations, especially defense corporations, exercise a tremendous influence on politicians and the electoral process in the US.

The issue of abortion continues to separate most Democratic politicians from most of their Republican counterparts. Still, the 1996 US elections revealed increasing social class convergence of the two parties in upholding corporate business interests over the interests of the poor, the immigrants, the environment, and so on. Candidates who are the most skilled at fund- raising and manipulating the media usually win. Once in office, staying in power seems to be the primary objective of most politicians in the US and everywhere else. The alienation of ordinary citizens from electoral politics is so great that many do not vote at all in US Presidential, Congressional or local elections.

During the process of increased globalization and restructuring of production which has been taking place since the early 1970s, women's economic subordination and poverty have deepened. Even when women and children are given paid employment in export production, for example in lacemaking in India or carpet weaving in Iran, their labour has been considered domestic labour and has remained unpaid or terribly under-paid. These developments reinforce the dualism of the male as the bread- winner and the female as the dependent housewife. Although globalization of production is increasingly female led and it is estimated that between 70 and 90% of new jobs in manufacturing are held by women, women's work in the formal labour force is relegated to relatively less paid, so-called 'women's work'. In South-East Asia, where feminization

196 Women, Population and Global Crisis of manufacturing is most advanced, only 17% of administrative and managerial workers in 1990 were women. With the increasing shift of manufacturing overseas and deindustrialization in the North, women in the North are being pushed more and more into the relatively low-paid, insecure service sector jobs in clerical work, domestic work, food service and retail work, the so-called 'women's jobs'.

Even when women do the same work as men, on average they receive 30-40% less pay worldwide. For example, in the 'newly industrialized countries' of Korea and Singapore, women's average wages in manufacturing in 1990 were 50% and 55% of men's wages, respectively. While women working for transnational corporations are paid higher wages than those working for local firms, the average wages for women workers in TNCs range from 50 to 75% of male wages in 'comparable occupations'. Indeed, the 'feminization' of manufacturing which has accompanied global economic restructuring has been built upon the 'flexibility' of women's labour, that is, lower wages and the supposed 'docility' of women.

Corporate restructuring is built not only upon increased exploitation of women's labour, but also upon increasing exploitation of child labour. For example, in Bangladesh, 20% of the labour force in the garment industry is estimated to be children under 12 years of age, some as young as 7 or 8. These child workers are crucial for the country's exported production and their families' survival. In Brazil, workers under the age of 18 represent 11.6% of the labour force and the use of child workers is still growing because employers want to avoid paying job benefits to adult workers.

The use of cheap child labour, whether it be by local employers or by transnational corporations, does not help improve the lives of poor children. It does not help bring down fertility rates in poor countries either. The suffering inflicted upon child export workers was recently brought to light by the case of the Pakistani child labour activist, Iqbal Masih, who received a Reebok human rights award, only to be brutally murdered soon thereafter. Notwithstanding low wages, exploitative working conditions, and absence of labour rights to organize, regular employment in the formal sector is considered a privilege in most countries.

The reason for this is massive unemployment and underemployment. Unemployment is far greater among women as a group than men globally, and particularly so in the poorer countries. As a result, large numbers of women are forced to migrate in search of work or attempt to survive in the informal sector doing poorly paid, menial work as petty traders, prostitutes, and so on. These issues will be discussed further later in this chapter in relation to the worsening global social crisis and new dimensions of women's poverty. Since corporate restructuring of the global economy in the early 1970s, foreign investments in the South have shifted increasingly from traditional areas such as resource extraction and manufacturing to services such as finance, insurance, communi-cations, advertising and the media.

During the last decade, the export income of the South fell sharply due to steadily declining commodity prices as well as trade protectionism in the industrialized countries. This, coupled with commercial banks' aggressive lending policies, led to increased borrowing by Third World countries. As investment markets in the North were saturated, banks looked to the Third World to recycle their petrodollars after the oil crisis in 1973. While only 25% of US investments in the industrialized countries were in banking, finance and insurance, 40% of US investments in the Third World were in these areas. In 1990, US investments in finance, banking and insurance in the Third World were $43 billion, that is, one-third more than US investments in manufacturing. But as financial analysts have pointed out, when overborrowing led to 'overheating' of Third World economies, the North cut off loans drastically in 1982, thus giving rise to the debt crisis.

At the beginning of 1989, developing nations owned foreign creditors trillions, that is, "just over half their combined gross national products and two-thirds more than their export earnings." The annual debt service bill approximated $200 billion, and the debt and interest on it continue to grow. In 1985 some African countries were spending as much as 50% of their export earnings on debt service payments. In 1990, Peru was being required to pay $ 100 million a month just to keep up with interest on the foreign debt.

According to the UN *Human Development Report* of 1992, the debt of Sub-Saharan Africa in 1992 was around $150 billion, that is, 100% of its GNP. The percentage of foreign investment located in the 'underdeveloped' countries has also been declining: from 30.6% in 1967 to 26.1% in 1973 to 22.0% in 1980 to 19.2% in 1989. Owing to these trends in investment and debt service, the South is today a net exporter of financial resources rather than a net recipient. While in the past the South received more from the North, since 1983, the resource flow has changed in the opposite direction. The United States received over $60 billion in resource transfers from the developing world in 1990 alone, a substantial amount of these transfers being debt service payments to banks domiciled in the US." According to the estimates of Susan George, between 1982 and 1990, the 'less developed countries' transferred $418 billion to the North, "the equivalent in today's dollars of some six Marshall Plans provided by the South to the North". As she points out, such a colossal "financial drain" was not achieved under direct colonialism; the Third World increasingly pays for its own oppression under neo-colonialism. As George also argues, although huge in comparison to the income of the Third World, the Third World debt is "relatively insignificant" when compared to the "Savings and Loans bailouts, BCCI scandals and astronomical federal budget and trade deficits in the United States itself all numbering in the hundreds or thousands of billions"."

Anne-Marie Beulink and other analysts have also pointed out that there is enough money in the world "to put an end to the debt crisis if the creditors were to see an advantage in that arrangement". But the commercial and political advantages of the creditor countries, mostly the Group of 7 and the IMF and the World Bank working on their behalf, lie precisely in the continuation of the debt. In 1995, the Third World debt was estimated at $1.7 trillion and of this 17% or $278 billion was owed to the World Bank and the IMF.[5] Naturally, these institutions put enormous pressure on the Third World to pay back the debt.

Impact of adjustment on women

According to the Report of the Commonwealth Expert Group on Women and Structural Adjustment and studies by feminist scholars, the effects of adjustment policies have been more severe on women as a group than on men. SAPs aggravate women's poverty in many different ways: by limiting women's access to services; by decreasing food production; by reducing access to jobs;

by shifting women into low-wage export sector jobs, and so on.

The problem is not simply that SAPs ignore their effects on the conditions of women. Rather, as Peggy Antrobus of the international feminist network Development Alternatives with Women for a New Era (DAWN) has argued, structural adjustment has been built upon the very exploitation of women:

> The problem with structural adjustment policies is not that they assume women are outside of development and need to be brought in (via accompanying compensatory programs) but that they are actually grounded in a gender ideology which is deeply, and fundamentally exploitative of women's time/work and sexuality. In the earlier periods of colonial capitalism, exploitation of women's labour was largely based on their roles as subsistence producers and reproducers of labour.

However, in the contemporary period of global economic liberalization and restructuring, capital accumulation is built increasingly on both the subsistence and wage labour of women. As noted earlier, global manufacturing and the service economy increasingly favour the cheaper labour of women over that of men. WID programs also integrate women into commodity production while reinforcing their traditional unpaid work as wives and mothers in the home. Likewise, SAPs increase the double burden of women in the paid and unpaid sectors. Cutbacks in social services have forced women, who are the primary nurturers and caretakers of families, to extend their own resources and that of their families.

Slashes in health care have required that women spend more time in caring for sick and elderly family members, thus increasing their 'invisible' and unpaid labour. The shifting of resources into export production has threatened women's subsistence production and ability to feed their families. Adjustment has also aggravated women's already low economic position by decreasing their earnings and increasing their work-loads.

The jobs being cut in state services, such as teachers, nurses and administrative staff, are usually held by women. When dismissed or having their wages cut, women are forced to seek additional work, often in the informal sector as vendors, prostitutes, and so on, and to rely on the support of family and friends. Where new jobs are available in the formal sector, they tend to be low-paid positions with little security or future, such as assembly-line work in free trade zones or migrant work as domestic workers. As public resources become scarce and incomes fall, women tend to work harder to provide for families, putting their own food and health needs last. As the Report of the Commonwealth Expert Group on Women and Structural Adjustment revealed, due to IMF/World Bank adjustments, female nutrition and health have declined in many Third World countries, especially in Sub-Saharan Africa.

Adjustment programs have exacerbated the conditions of high fertility by undermining women and children's health and education; in other cases, they have led to poverty induced fertility transitions. Moreover, economic hardship induced by adjustment policies frequently leads to marital conflicts and violence against women by men. The vast system of global political and economic inequality created by imperialism is maintained by militarism. Arms exports (including military and police gear, intelligence systems, torture devices and related hardware) and military intervention constitute the ultimate bases for imperialist control of global resources and populations. As we discuss in the next chapter, the global arms trade is a main factor fuelling political instability and violence across the world. We show that while arms sales are vital to western economies, they exacerbate global income disparities, cut into social welfare expenditures, drive down living standards and aggravate the problems of poverty and insecurity.

Cold War rhetoric made defense the leading sector of the global economy with a trillion dollar annual allocation by the end of the 1980s. Despite declining military expenditures by both the developed and developing countries in the post-Cold War era, global military expenditures continue to be enormous.

The total global military expenditure of $815 billion in 1992 equalled the income of almost half of the worlds population. Not withstanding expressions of intent to observe rules of restraint in arms sales to volatile regions, all the five permanent members of the UN Security Council continue to be concerned more with protecting the comparative advantage of their respective arms industries and export markets than with preventing arms proliferation. These five countries the—Russia, France, Britain and China—together account for over 80% of all global arms trade. When Germany is added to this group, they account for 90%. For the most sophisticated and expensive equipment, these five and Germany are the only exporters. In the post-Cold War period, the US has been the world's leading arms exporter, accounting for nearly 50% of global conventional weapons exports.

Impact on poor women and children

The burden of budget deficits, growing militarism and social welfare cuts have been borne mostly by the poor. According to the US Bureau of the Census, in 1993,

33.1% of Blacks, 30.6% of Hispanics and 12.2% of whites fell below the poverty line (the poverty threshold was $14,763 for a family of four in 1993).110 The percentage of children under the age of 18 living below the poverty line increased from 15.1% in 1974 to 22% in 1995. In 1993, 17% of white, 45.9% of Black and 39.9% of Hispanic children in the US lived in poverty. These statistics alone should cause one to question whether the US is the most advanced and exemplary nation in the world. However, white male analysts like Patrick Moynihan have tended to blame the alleged matriarchy of women-headed households for poverty, crime and other problems in the Black underclass, while Malthusian analysts frequently blame these problems on teenage pregnancy. Feminization of poverty, female-headed households and homelessness are not problems peculiar to women in the Third World. They are global phenomena located in the expansion of the capitalist economy and patriarchal culture. Increasing numbers of educated career women in the North are also having children outside of marriage and creating alternative households.

Evidence suggests that, globally, women heads of households provide better nutrition and education for children than do male heads of households. Yet, owing to deep-rooted sexism, female-headed households tend to be disproportionately poorer than male-headed households across the world. Although more and more women are working, they are in low-skilled, low-paying jobs and as such do not make enough to support themselves and their families adequately.

According to a 'women's social health index' developed by the Fordham University Institute for Innovation in Social Policy, women's social health declined from 78 points in 1974 to 38 points in 1988. According to this index, which is based on poverty, violence, health coverage and the income gap between men and women, in 1988, one in seven women was poor; one in six was living without health coverage and one in three of all female-headed families lived below the poverty level.

In some very poor urban and rural areas within the US, infant mortality actually increased during the early 1980s. Infant mortality rate is particularly high among the homeless population because 30% of homeless women do not receive prenatal care. Infant mortality among them is 25 deaths per 1,000 as compared to 17 per 1,000 for other poor women. As noted earlier, poverty, infant mortality and high fertility are closely correlated.

We can argue, then, that like IMF/World Bank policies in the Third World, 'adjustment' policies in the US, too, may have had a pronatal impact' in that they have increased, poverty, especially the poverty of women. When income is lowered individuals and families attempt to survive by increasing the "number of family members in the labour force and by working longer hours". There are indications that as economic restructuring and 'free market' policies such as privatization, deregulation and dismantling of the welfare state advance across the North, more and more countries will experience increasing income inequality, worsening poverty and political turmoil. ' When women fall below the poverty line, children fall with them, and when children are turned into a 'surplus' population, they frequently, turn to crime and violence as desperate attempts at survival.

The welfare state is not the ultimate answer to the problems of poverty and the global social crisis. Yet, it is important to recognize the important role that state social spending has played in reducing poverty in both industrialized countries and Third World countries and states such as Sri Lanka and Kerala. In a number of industrialized countries, such as the UK, France, Germany and Sweden, public benefits have acted as a form of income redistribution and poverty alleviation. In these countries the percentage of the total population in poverty before public benefits is estimated to be greater than that in the US. It is the extensive provisions made available by the state in the form of health, education, labour and income security policies, and so on, that have helped reduce the percentages of the populations in poverty in these countries much below the percentage of those living below the poverty level in the US. But now, as more and more European governments adopt conservative economic policies similar to those in the US, the social gains won through labour and other struggles are eroding.

A close parallel can be observed between the policies starting with the Thatcher regime in the UK and the Reagan-Bush regime in the US in the 1980s. Due to privatization of state sectors, cutbacks in the social welfare state, harsh suppression of labour unions and increased spending on defense, and so on, income disparities and poverty increased in the UK. In 1989, 400,000 people in the UK were officially classified as homeless, of which 40% were single-parent families with young children. As elsewhere in the world, most single-parent families in the UK tend to be headed by women. It is likely that the concentration of economic power within the European Community could strengthen the collective power of capital over that of individual states. This could result in a slashing of state benefits, a reduction of labour rights and increases in class, gender and racial inequalities in Europe.

The recent labour strikes in France and violence directed at immigrants in most European countries reflect growing economic insecurity and social discontent associated with rapid social changes taking place in contemporary Europe. The social dislocations and economic inequalities associated with restructuring and integration of the former USSR into global capitalism seem to be even worse. As a number of analysts point out, while the IMF imposed economic program upholds the narrow interests of the new, often corrupt, merchant class, it represents an instrument of 'Third Worldization' for the majority of people in the former Soviet Union. Under the former Communist regime there was full employment and poverty was absent; now open unemployment and poverty are said to be serious problems. In 1991, according to the UN Human Development Report, there were 100 million people below the poverty line in the Russian Federation and Eastern Europe. Evidence from contemporary Eastern Europe and the former USSR indicates that economic restructuring may be leading to a process of feminization of poverty there as well.

Although women in this region previously enjoyed the highest rates of female employment, as state social welfare supports are cut and women lose employment, they seem to be increasingly defined by their reproductive roles. As women get left out of jobs in the formal sector they become economically marginalized and forced to survive in the growing informal economy doing mostly odd jobs. As economic insecurity and poverty increase in Russia, more and more men are abdicating their parental obligations altogether and the number of women-headed households is soaring. As Noeleen Heyzer, the Director of UNIFEM, observes, as have many other feminist analysts and activists, the brunt of globalization and economic and social crises is borne disproportionately by women. This is clearly visible in deepening poverty in the contemporary period and desperate survival strategies being adopted by the poor.

Women's poverty and global crisis

Not only is women's work in the home unremunerated, but global economic growth and technological advancements, including the so-called contraceptive revolution', have not resulted in greater sexual equality or leisure time for women. In some of the countries in the South worst hit by the current economic crisis, some very poor women are now forced to work an average of 60 to 90 hours a week just to maintain their living standards of a decade ago. As United Nations and other studies show, the economic ravages of recent years have also contributed to widening the gap in hours worked by men and women. Almost everywhere, in their multiple roles as income earners, family caretakers, educators, health promoters, and so on, women work more hours a day than men. Gender inequalities in hours worked are greatest among the poor.

In Nepal, for example, among men and women over the age of 15, women are estimated to work an average of 77 hours per week as opposed to 56 by men. In Bangladesh, in the same age group, women do an estimated average of 31 hours of housework per week as opposed to five hours by men. Environmental destruction and the increasing scarcity of resources have increased the time women spend on household maintenance, obtaining water, fuelwood, and so on. Women of colour are the beasts of burden in the world. Their social and economic subordination and the long hours worked affect health and nutrition, fertility patterns and the general quality of their lives.

The disparity in male and female lives is also evident in relation to personal expenditures. Evidence shows that even in the poorest households men tend to keep a personal allowance for such luxuries as cigarettes, alcohol, gambling and socializing outside the home. Just as most women are self-sacrificing, most men are selfish. Although women living alone or with other women may find a sense of relative freedom from the daily psychological and physical abuses of domineering men, evidence shows that in female-headed households women tend to be even poorer and more overworked. As economist Diane Elson has observe.

The core of gender subordination lies in the fact that most women are unable to mobilize adequate resources (both material and in terms of social identity) except through dependence on a man. Women are not counted as heads of households unless they are living alone or unless there is no adult male in the household. Male-biased data collection methods underestimate the extent of female-headed households. Still, these estimates show that up to 30% of households in the world today are headed by women. At least one-fourth of households not counted as female-headed also rely for more than 50% of their total income on women's earnings.

More and more women are having children outside of marriage and the number of female-headed households is soaring across the world. As increasing numbers of men move away from the role of providers, women are forced to play both the traditional male and female roles. This further increases women's burdens and their ability to compete in a labour market beset already with very high unemployment. Although many women emigrate in order to avoid physical violence, it is the structural violence of poverty which most explains the rising numbers of women migrants across the world.

In many poor countries, like the Philippines and Sri Lanka, female labour export constitutes a main source of foreign exchange, if not the main source. Many of the women who emigrate to work as nannies and housekeepers in the oil-rich countries in the Middle East and the newly industrializing countries in South-East Asia are mothers themselves, but they are forced to leave their own children behind in order to earn money to support them, This has been the sad reality for many poor women historically in class-based societies. Migrant women workers have no labour rights or legal protection. Quite often, they are turned into virtual house slaves by their employers. Not Wily are many sexually exploited and physically attacked, but at least a few have died at the hands of their employers.

The case of Flor Contemplacaion, a Filipina who was executed in Singapore for killing another Filipina maid and a Singaporean boy, brought to light the extremely difficult working conditions endured by many migrant women workers. Still, many poor women choose to emigrate for lack of alternatives in their own countries. Emigration to the US or Europe does not always lead to social and economic improvement either. Many women and men find themselves working in thoroughly exploited jobs and living under oppressive conditions as 'illegal aliens'. Until recently, children provided a means for survival for immigrants in the North. But now, as children born in the US and Europe are not automatically given citizenship and as social benefits to children are cut, this survival option is being closed to many poor immigrant women.

As the migration option is closed, as the degraded natural environments can no longer provide subsistence, and as traditional community and family structures weaken in the process of capitalist development, more and more poor people are forced to turn to the informal sector in order to survive. Micro-enterprises in the informal sector such as small-scale production and petty trading tend to be glorified as the solution to poverty, especially women's poverty, by liberal theorists in the North. But they fail to see that corporate expansion is inherently inimical to the long-term success of micro-enterprises and that illegal trades such as sex, drugs and weapons characterize the burgeoning informal sector. Constrained by the lack of viable economic options, many men, women and children are forced to adopt survival strategies ultimately destructive to themselves and their families and communities. With nothing but their bodies and the bodies of their children to sell, more and more poor people enter the expanding sectors of the global economy known as the global skin trade. The skin trade, which constitutes the production and distribution of negative use values, is one the most profitable and fastest growing sectors of the global economy.

The global sex trade, which includes prostitution, sex tourism, mail order brides (the traffic in women as wives for foreign men) and pornography, is a billion dollar global enterprise. Young women are typically the prostitutes. The number of masseuses and prostitutes in Bangkok alone is said to be in the range 100,000 to 200,000, which may be an underestimate. Child prostitution and prostitution of boys are also on the rise in many Asian countries. Malthusian analysts typically blame population density and growth for the spread of diseases such as AIDS and the Ebola virus in Africa.

However, as many other analysts have shown, the spread of these diseases is 'socially determined The spread of AIDS is closely linked to poverty and sexism, especially male promiscuity and sexual irresponsibility in many countries and regions in the South like Thailand and Africa. Sex tourism in particular is considered to be a significant factor in the spread of AIDS in Thailand.

Many poor Third World women among the so-called bottom billion of the world population are forced to participate in the global child adoption industry, which sells their infants, mostly baby girls, to wealthy couples in the North. Although this may seem to be a short-term solution to the problem of poverty and 'overpopulation' in the South and wealth and widespread infertility in the North, in the long term it is physically and psychologically destructive to women, their children and their communities.

Despite the humane motivation of parents who adopt and the caring and prosperity experienced by many adoptees, it is difficult not to see international child adoption as a medium for appropriating the most precious resource—children from the South by the North. While many couples in the North assert their right to adopt, they fail to look at such developments as stringent population control policies and widening global inequality which force many poor women to give up their children in the first place. In China, orphanages are said to be competing fiercely for western clients who pay thousands of dollars in hard currency to buy babies, most of them abandoned girls.

Apparently, the prettiest and healthiest girls are groomed for adoption while the others are neglected and even allowed to die. There have been reports of the existence of 'baby farms', joint local and foreign enterprises in Sri Lanka where poor, young women who are pregnant and often destitute are maintained only to have their infants taken from them soon after birth for sale to foreigners for large sums of money. There are also designs underway by certain biogenetic corporations in the US to "supply" US clients with Mexican "surrogates" to bear them children.

Violence is neither in our evolutionary legacy nor in our genes. It is scientifically incorrect to say that humans have a 'violent brain'. While we do have the neural apparatus to act violently, it is not automatically activated by internal or external stimuli. Like higher primates and unlike other animals, our higher neural processes filter such stimuli before they can be acted upon. How we act is shaped by how we have been conditioned and socialized. There is nothing in our neurophysiology that compels us to react violently. It is scientifically incorrect to say that war is caused by 'instinct' or any single motivation.

The emergence of modern warfare has been a journey from the primacy of emotional and motivational factors, sometimes called 'instincts', to the primacy of cognitive factors. Modern war involves institutional use of personal characteristics such as obedience, suggestibility, and idealism; social skills such as language; and rational considerations such as cost-calculation, planning, and information processing.

The technology of modern war has exaggerated traits associated with violence both in the training of actual combatants and in the preparation of support for war in the general population. As a result of this exaggeration, such traits are often mistaken to be the causes rather than the consequences of the process. We conclude that biology does not condemn humanity to war, and that humanity can be freed from the bondage of biological pessimism and empowered with confidence to undertake the transformative tasks needed in this International Year of Peace and in the years to come.

Although these tasks are mainly institutional and collective, they also rest upon the consciousness of individual participants for whom pessimism and optimism are crucial factors. Just as 'wars begin in the minds of men', peace also begins in our minds. The same species who invented war is capable of inventing peace. The responsibility lies with each of us.

Researchers in the area of family violence in the United States have spent about 20 years in understanding the nature and the extent of the problem. After identifying major social factors associated with the problem of wife abuse they have advocated different coping mechanisms for the solution of the problem. Different researchers have given attention to develop programmes for the wife batterers, such as individual therapy marital and family therapy psychoeducational or psycho-therapeutic group approach; Anger control technique cognitive behaviour strategies and coordinated programmes involving group treatment and community intervention. In addition to research on batterers treatment programmes, researches have also suggested treatment techniques for the victims. Andersen *et al.* argue that separation of the abused wife from her husband is an important factor for the treatment of abuse and ultimately for her survival and yet when she leaves her husband, she exposes herself to an ever increasing risk of violence. Thus a wife must not leave her husband until she has the resources to stay away either permanently or long enough to facilitate significant change in the husbands behaviour.

Although different researchers in the United States have started working on the solution of wife abuse, yet they are unable to reach at a consensus because most of them are naive. There is high drop out rates in such programmes. After such programmes their battering ceases but psychological abuse heightens. Stordeur and Stille argue that patriarchal society will not change overnight and that men in society who are reaping the rewards of violence will resist relinquishing their domination, men who attempt to give up their violence will be faced with covert and overt pressures from other men to come back in fine with the attitude of masculine superiority. The procedures advocated by these researchers may not be applicable to the Indian cultural situation.

First, because the available knowledge regarding violence against wife is only anecdotal but there is also no consensus on the definitions of wife abuse. Additionally, no national sample survey has been conducted in India to find out the extent and the severity of the problem. Under these circumstances efforts should be made to assess the nature and the extent and the severity the problem as well as to identify the factors associated with wife abuse. Further, coping involves three sets of behaviour pattern. First, reactions to violent relationship; secondly, procedures adopted to deal with abusive relationship and thirdly, to develop mechanisms for countering violent behaviour pattern or getting freedom from abusive relationship. Because of above noted reasons this chapter is restricted to only the reactions of the victims to different forms of violence as well as the steps they take to deal with the situation.

Husband's violence against wife is not a continuous process but revolves around relative peace and violence. There would be certain periods when the partners exhibit complete sympathy, understanding and love for each other. On other occasions the relationship would be marred with violence.

Most of the women who are victims of their husbands violence are of the view that conflicting situation in their intimate relationship is transitory. It is perhaps with this false hope that they continue living in the abusive relationship. The perceptions of abuse by victims are likely to be different depending upon their training, life situation and availability or non-availability of alternatives. They, in turn, are likely to have ramifications on their reactions to their abusive situation. Further, their reactions are likely to be coloured by the presence or absence of other members in the household. In case, the conjugal violence takes place in the absence of other members of the family or outsiders, the victims are likely to react differently as compared with those victims who are abused in the presence of others.

Victims who are abused in the presence of others are more likely to feel humiliated as they may develop a feeling of having been let down in the eyes of others. The victims are likely to react sharply even to the, mildest form of abuse in case such abuse takes place in the presence of children and in-laws. In case of children, the victims may feel that their limited area of authority over children has been eroded.

On the other hand, if the abuse takes place before the in-laws and outsiders, the battered women are likely to feel that they have been let down in the estimation of their in-laws and outsiders. Such victims are more likely to develop a feeling of helplessness. Before taking into account the victims' reactions to their abuse it is therefore essential to know, in whose presence their abuse had taken place. Out of 187 cases of victims of violence, only 24 victims informed that their abuse took place in the absence of other members of the family or outsiders. It is only in these cases where violence can be labelled as a "private matter" between husband and wife. In a majority of cases their abuse took place in the presence of their children. Such a situation is likely to create a sense of powerlessness among the victims. Further it would have negative effect on the children.

A number of researchers are of an opinion that children who are brought up in violent families are more likely to become violent parents. It was only in 25 cases where women were abused by their husbands in the presence of outsiders. Such a situation is likely to create greater humiliation and shame for the victims. Approximately one-fourth of the victims were abused in the presence of their in-laws. Their abuse may be attributed not only to interference in the conjugal relationship by the in-laws but also depicts stronger ties with family of orientation of the husband than his family of procreation.

As the respondents were allowed multiple choices it was noticed that a number of victims told that they were abused in the presence of other members of the family as well as outsiders. These are the victims who are more likely to be depressed as the charm of their married life starts fading away. Studies conducted on wife abuse and victims- reactions report a high incidence of depression among the victims. Wife abuse has been claimed to produce reactions among the victims such as "paralyzing terror", "terrifying intimidation", "shame and degradation" and "humiliation and isolation". A number of clinical studies report a high incidence of depression and anxiety.

The literature on psychological problems of battered women consistently report depression, anxiety and somatic problems. The samples of the battered women in these studies are exclusively the samples of women who come forward and seek help, hence are not the representative samples of the abused wives. It is quite probable that there may be psychologically troubled and more anxious abused wives who have not sought such help. Keeping in view the methodological shortcomings and the small size of the sample and lack of comparison group, it becomes difficult to draw any generalization with regard to reactions of the abused women. Further, it is not known whether they have been abused on single occasion or repeatedly.

Additionally, psychological distress experienced by battered women was initially thought to be responsible for their battering. Recently researchers have proposed that depression, anxiety and somatic disorders reported by battered women are the consequences of their being abused rather than a cause. Based on Second National Family Violence Survey in the United States, Gelles and Harrop examined the effects of violence against women as per the information provided by 3002 female respondents. Women who reported experiencing violence also reported higher level of depression, anxiety and somatic disorders. Such a situation has prompted these battered women to contemplate suicide and a higher percentage of them had reportedly made suicidal attempts in comparison to non-battered women. The battered women may also develop a feeling of helplessness as they may find themselves unable to check the violent behaviour of their husbands as well as they find that social definitions are unsupportive in helping them to come out of the abusive relationship.

The abused women often suffer from, what Walker calls "Learned helplessness", in that the victims come to the conclusion that no relationship exists between their actions and the outcomes. After trying and failing to prevent the abuse of their husbands they give up. In addition, learned helplessness is more likely, when the victims of abuse attribute the abuse to internal, stable and global causes. There is, however, another side to this learned helplessness.

The helplessness on the part of the victims is created by their perpetrators of violence. It is in this context that Kipnis opines that battering males may induce guilt in their victims by blaming them for the abuse, until they come to blame themselves. Blaming the victims is frequently used to justify use of coercive power. Further, the battering men arouse fear in the victims by frightening them with threat of abandonment and of physical violence and by actual physical violence of varying severity.

Additionally, the victims are forced to develop a feeling of powerlessness and helplessness because they find that social support system would not come to their rescue, hence they continue to suffer humiliations in silence with the hope that things may improve. There would be a few cases who may not accept a victim's role and as a consequence of being abused by their spouses, they may develop a feeling of hatred and may also become vengeful. Keeping in view the cultural ethos and status of women in India, where a wife is expected to treat her husband as God (*Pati Parmeshwar*) few victims of such abuse may develop a feeling of hatred against their husbands. In the present study an attempt was made to find out the reactions of the victims to their abuse. It was expected that most of the victims would give their reactions which would be self-directed rather than directed against the perpetrators of violence, i.e., their husbands.

Keeping in view the reactions of the victims of different types of violence in the conjugal relationship it was noted that a majority of the cases had developed a feeling of depression. The results of the present study support the findings of Gelles and Straus and Gelles and Harrop that high level of depression was a consequence of their being abused by their husbands. Further, a number of respondents assumed the responsibility of provoking their husbands to be violent and hence, started blaming themselves for their abuse.

These cases developed a feeling of guilt in them and indirectly endorsed the contention of their abusers that they had "asked for it". A number of researchers have also come to this, conclusion in their studies in which the victims assumed the responsibility of provoking their husbands to be violent a and suffered from the feeling of guilt. Additionally, a few respondents became afraid after having been abused by their husbands. These were the cases who have been threatened of dire consequences by their husbands if they did not act according to their dictates. As a consequence of their abuse they became very fearful and hence, their conjugal relationship was marked with fear rather than mutual love and understanding. As expected, a few victims blamed their husbands for their violent acts. There were only 11 cases who developed 117 hatred against their husbands because of their violent behaviour pattern against them and three cases as an outcome of their being abused developed animosity and hostility to such an extent that they became vengeful and would like to take up some action against their perpetrators of violence. It can, thus be assumed that these cases who have developed hatred and enmity against their abusive spouses are likely to seek intervention from the formal agencies so that they could teach a lesson to their abuseis.

The above description regarding the reactions of the victims helps in concluding that in spite of being abused by the husbands, the women in India suffer in silence and do not develop a feeling of hatred against their spouses. It does not, however, mean that they have not reacted to their abuse but their reactions were self-directed rather than directed against the abusers. The strategy an individual adopts depends upon ones perception of the abusive situation. The analysis of the reactions of the victims to their violence indicated two types of reactions.

However, keeping in view one's training, socialization, life situations and the possibility of getting help from kin and others, one would act accordingly. It is further, envisaged that marital relationship is marked both by mutual sympathy and conflict. When two persons interact there may be a number of issues on which they think alike as well as have difference of opinion. Keeping in view the quality as well as the permanency of relationship, some incidents of dispute between the partners or sporadic incidents of conflict or violence may be accepted by the partners as part and parcel of their intimate relationship. As stated earlier conjugal relationship is not marked with continuous conflicts and fights but there are occasions when such conflicts stop and partners have cordial relationships.

Hence, the conjugal relationship revolves around love and conflict and there is a tendency on their part to overlook certain sporadic incidents of disputes. The basic assumption of exchange theory that human interaction is guided by the pursuit of reward and avoidance of punishment is not applicable to the husband wife relationship particularly in the Indian society. The following writers Homans and Blau, Gelles believe that an individual who provides a reward to another thereby places him or her in debt, so that the second individual must furnish benefits to the first in return.

The interaction will continue if rewards come equally to both the parties, if not, it will be broken off. However, intrafamilial relations, particularly, husband-wife relationship, cannot be broken off easily. As a consequence, when a partner perceives injustice or is abused, the individual may become angry but keeping in view, the social definitions and societal reactions a person may think twice before initiating any step which would permanently break off the relationship. Each victim of abuse is likely to work out her own strategies to deal with abusive situation in the conjugal relationship. It is only when violence becomes recurrent and individual strategies fail to bring about change in the violent behaviour pattern of the spouse, the victim may feel quite helpless. It is this helplessness on the part of the victim which would force her to seek some assistance from other persons.

Frieze *et al.* found that members of the wife's family are more likely to be sought out help to end battering than any other informal help source. Among the formal agencies police were likely to be approached than other formal sources. Almost similar conclusions were drawn by Pagelow with regard to use of formal sources. Based on indepth interviews of the victims Bowker came to know about different techniques used by the women, to get their husbands to stop battering. These techniques were clustered into three types:

— personal strategies, including talking, promising, threatening, hiding, passive defense, aggressive defense and avoidance;

— use of informal help sources, including family members, in-laws, neighbours, friends and shelters; and

— formal help sources, including the police, social service agencies, lawyers and district attorneys.

It is expected that the victims would first use informal help sources before seeking formal help in case she is not able to check the violent behaviour of their husbands. Further, the help from the informal sources would not imply asking them to intervene but by sharing one's experiences with them and seeking their advice for dealing with the abusive relationship. It was in this context that the victims were asked, whether they shared their abusive experiences with their relatives and close friends? It is interesting to note that a majority of the victims did not share their abusive marital relationship experiences even with their relatives and close friends but preferred to rely upon their own strategies to deal with the abusive situation. It needs an independent study to find out the reasons as to why these cases have not shared their experiences with their informal sources for seeking their advice to tackle the abusive situation as well as the reasons why they are continuing to stay in the abusive relationship. As the scope of the present study was limited to finding out the coping behaviour pattern of the victims, the description would be limited to only those cases who have sought informal and formal help to deal with the situation.

Out of 187 victims of violence, only 50 cases shared their experiences with their informal help sources, i.e., kin and close friends. Out of these 50 cases, 36 cases were the victims of physical violence of their husbands and 6 victims were adopting "passive" and "aggressive-defence" mechanisms. In the remaining 14 cases, they were free from physical violence but were the victims of verbal and psychological violence of their husbands. When the victims own strategies to deal with violent situation fail, they are likely to approach their informal group to seek advice to face the situation. As the victims themselves have failed, they seek their advice with the hope that by acting on their advice, they will be better equipped to change the behaviour pattern of their husbands so that they could have cordial relations with their spouses.

Whenever there is a conflict between husband and wife and this conflict is brought to the notice of informal group of the conjugal unit, there would be certain persons who would show sympathy to the victims and others may take the side of the husbands. Depending upon the nature of the abuse, the reactions of the informal group are likely to vary. Further, some members of the informal group may advise the victims to patch up for the purpose of saving their marriage whereas others may simply lend lip-service but would not give any concrete advice.

Still others, are likely to advise the victims either to seek help from formal agencies or to break off the abusive relationship. Data reveal that in a majority of the cases, the members of the informal group advised the victims to patch up with their spouses. Indirectly these members valued their continuation in the conjugal relations and advised them to reconcile to the situation for the purpose saving their marriage. As in the case of the victims, their informal group also endorsed the traditional values, wherein it is the wife who is expected to yield irrespective of the fact whether she is at fault or not just in opposition to this, 10 victims were advised to seek help from formal agencies and in 8 cases the members of informal groups even advised for breaking off marital relationships.

In addition to these, there were 15 cases where the victims found the attitudes of the members of their informal group not of much help because they showed indifference to their problem. After seeking the advise of the members of the informal group the victims are not likely to translate the advise into practice irrationally and immediately. They would re-evaluate their situation and would work out their own strategies to deal with the situation. To the marital partners the richest payoff of well managed conflict comes with yielding after a fight. Any intimate relationship implies some readiness to yield one's own self-interest when it clashes with that of a partner.

Give and take relationship between husband and wife also implies bending one's own will to the wishes of the other. Yielding, no doubt, involves loss of self-respect but those who value the relationship yielding is a small price so long as it leads to cessation of the conflict and an improvement in the quality of the relationship. Given the lower status of women in our society, as well as the stigmatized position of the single woman, the victims are likely to take the initiative of patching up the differences because they do not like to break off the relationship permanently. It does not, however, mean that it is only the women who move first in the direction of reconciliation. In the conjugal relationship both the partners are likely to patch up if they value the relationship.

The husband, the perpetrator may also realize his mistake and may become very apologetic over his behaviour pattern. It is, therefore, expected that both the partners would take the initiative for reconciliation, however, more wives than the husbands are likely to take the first step. The data indicate that in a majority of the cases both the partners take the initiative to patch up, i.e., sometimes the husband reconciles first and at other times, it is the wife who takes the initiative for reconciliation. Either husband or wife here means that whosoever realizes his or her mistakes first, takes the initiative for reconciliation.

Secondly, more wives than the husbands take the first step for reconciliation. Further, out of 33 husbands who tried to reconcile first after the quarrel, 78.79 per cent were also the initiators of the quarrel whereas in cases of 44 wives who tried to reconcile first, only 59 per cent had started the quarrel, but less percentage of husbands had tried to reconcile. On the other hand, less number of wives had started the quarrel but a higher percentages of them had taken the steps for reconciliation.

The results reinforce the dominant position of husbands in the conjugal relationship. In spite of reconciliatory approach of the wives to put an end to the conjugal quarrel, it might erupt again and again and might force them to seek help from some formal agencies. Their decision to involve formal agencies in the intimate relationships is not an abrupt or a spontaneous response to one isolated violent act on the part of their spouses. Their decision is an outcome of recurrent violent behaviour of the spouses as well as based on negative experiences over a period of time. It has been argued that the battered women are in a kind of "social trap" in which an immediate pay off obscures the violent events that precede it. In this process the relationship alternates unpredictably from periods of violence to periods of relative peace, thereby creating hope that things could be made to be alright if the women can just keep things running smoothly.

However, when the situation escalates and goes beyond their control only then, they would venture to seek the help from the outside sources. It, however, does not mean that all the victims of their husbands' violence would seek intervention from formal sources after having failed to control the abusive behaviour pattern of their husbands. A number of victims may be ignorant about the type of the formal help available or they have developed "learned helplessness" and reconciled to their fate or they may be afraid that such intervention instead of helping them may enhance the severity of abuse against them. This is an area which needs an independent study, particularly in Indian setting where research on conjugal violence is very much limited. After having failed in their personal strategies to deal with violent situation they seek help from the informal groups. In case such help also does not yield any result and violent situation persists as a natural consequence thereof, they may seek help from the formal agencies. It is, however, expected that few victims of husbands violence will seek intervention from formal agencies. It is in this context the victims were asked, "Had they sought help from the formal agencies for resolving the violent situation?" It is surprising to note that out of 187 cases of husbands violence only 16 victims had sought help from outside formal agencies. Nine victims sought the intervention of influential persons who could have some control over their husbands and seven victims sought the help of women organizations like Punjab Istri Sabha.

However, when such intervention failed to yield the desired results two victims had sought help from the legal counsellors and one case sought help from Crime Against Women Cell of the Police Department. It would be in the fitness of the thing to explain the background of such victims who have sought help from the formal agencies. Out of 16 such cases, 14 were the victims of their husbands' physical violence and among these 14 cases there were 5 victims who had also used 'defensive violence' against their violent husbands.

The remaining two cases were the victims of other form of violence. It is surprising to note that out of 67 victims of battering, only 14 battered women have sought help from-the formal agencies. The results of this study do not support the contention of Gelles that the greater the severity of battering, the more likely the victim would seek intervention from formal agencies. As to why the remaining cases have not sought such help can be the subject matter for another independent study. As the present study has been restricted to only those cases who sought help from the formal agencies, the subsequent analysis will be restricted to only those 16 cases. With regard to the educational background of the victims who sought help from formal agencies, it was found that either those respondents who were less educated or had high educational qualifications sought such help. Out of 16 cases, 9 had graduated and above.

On the other hand, 6 cases who were either illiterate or had education up to middle level sought such assistance. Although it is difficult to draw any generalization based on 16 cases yet it is safe to conclude that women who are highly educate or had lower level of education seek assistance from the formal agencies and women, who belonged to middle category.

The class background of their spouses was also checked and no distinction was found with regard to their class affiliation. These 16 cases were equally distributed in an the four social classes, however, with the exception of the victims of upperclass, the cases belonging to other three classes were the victims of physical violence of their husband and in the upper class out of four cases, only two were the victims of physical violence and remaining two cases were the victims of other forms of violence. In short, no clear cut association was found between the class background and seeking help from formal agencies. With regard to the type of help advanced by these formal agencies, it was noted that in 6 cases the women organizations provided them social or moral support implying thereby, listening to their problems sympathetically and assuring them that their injustices would be vacated. In five other cases, help in the shape of counselling was extended.

The foregoing analysis on the reactions to husbands violence and coping behaviour of the victims highlights subjective dependency of the Indian women to their marital relationship. This subjective dependency is the outcome of their socialization, life situations, social definitions, values and norms and lack of alternative support systems. Hence, the objective conditions not only influence the victims' reaction to husbands' violence but also their coping behaviour pattern.

3

Crime against Women

The report of the World Conference of the U. N. Decade for Women reads: While women represent 50% of world adult population and a third of official labour force, they perform nearly two-thirds of all working hours, receive only a tenth of world income and own less than one per cent of world property.' This is true more or less about India too. Women is the sufferer in the hands of men all over the world. Perhaps, women were free and equal in quite very old times. Gradually, the women were treated as inferior and moreover, they treated themselves inferior.

The lack of physical power leads to general timidity in women. During the middle ages, cruel and inhuman treatment was meted out to them. They followed the holy scriptures in which they were told to get, happiness by sumbissiveness. The women sacrificed everything including their lives. The higher the sacrifice, the higher the salvation became a motto for women. In reality, women rarely had an identity apart from that given to them as wives, mothers and daughters.

Although, they were worshipped as deities at home, they were treated as second class members of the family.

What was the reason for this? Some historians felt that it was because of the fire which tied the women to kitchen, while others-think that it was due to needed protection on foreign invasions. Another reason supported is the patriarchal system where girl is to leave her parent's place and go to her husband's place.

The girl being alone in the new family, it became easy to subject her with various atrocities. The ancient custom of 'Swayamvaram' choosing the husband was replaced by arranged marriages. Then the custom of dowry became the steelframe of marriage. The parents wished to have sons, who may fetch cash and dowry. On the other hand, the daughters were never welcomed and the mothers wished themselves dead and cursed on the birth of a female child. Infanticide was practiced and a law had to be passed to stop it.

The women were tortured physically as well as mentally in their own homes. The women were treated as slaves and idiots. The women were made to put on 'Purdah'. They could not own any property. She had no personality of her own. In India, it was worse. She was told to serve her husband and in-laws. She was to call her husband as 'Swami' and she the 'Dasi'. In literature, the woman was relished to cherish sex. In India, the pitiable condition continued in Muslim and early British period.

The cruelties were so much like infanticide, child marriage, bigamy, Sati, abduction and various other physical and mental cruelities, that the atmosphere forced for some reforms. Social reformers like Raja Ram Mohan Roy, Swami Dayanand and Swami Vivekanand and others took up cause of women and several laws were enacted to improve the position of women.

The marriage and family were not included in the

Constitution as done in Japan and other countries. Because of this, the women in India still suffer. She is put under brackets of being a Hindu, Muslim, Christian or Parsi women. In spite of fundamental rights, she has been discriminated in law. There was such a commotion that the Muslim Women Act, 1986 had to be passed. Miss Asha Goyal, a practicing Advocate applied for a post in the Department of The Judge Advocate General in 1972, her application was rejected on the plea that the post might necessitate attending Court Martial. Even the Supreme Court dismissed the petition. Miss C.B. Muthamma, a Senior Officer of IFS challanged the rules regarding resigning before marriage if she married a non-Indian.

The Supreme Court in its judgement remarked about the Constitution being neglected. Another leading case was of Air Hosteses about their services being terminated if they got pregnant. Only partial relief was allowed by the Supreme Court. The condition about termination of service on the first pregnancy of the Air Hostess was declared invalid. They were allowed in service till the age of 45 years. The crimes against women may be enumerated as:

Physical torture

i) Tests under the guise of directing congevital abnormality, female foetus is aborted after sex determination. If it is found that it is a female child, the pregnancy is terminated. It has become quite popular and several open advertisements to the effect can be seen in the newspapers and magazines. Thus the birth rate of women is decreasing. There should be some law against this.

ii) Neglect, Starvation, lack of immunization, no medical service and malnutrition of female child. A son is given the choicest food, milk, while the female child is not provided with.

iii) Infanticide-In spite of laws, it is still prevailing.

iv) Eve-teasing

v) Molestation

vi) Abduction and kidnapping

vii) Wife beating Wrongful confinement

ix) Fraudulent marriage

x) Adultry - Enticement of married women

xi) Cruelties on married women

xii) Rape

xiii) Outraging the modesty of a woman xiv) Defaming young girls

xv) Prostitution

xvi) Indecent representation of women

The rise in the rate of crime against women has been reported in all types of crimes-ranging from eveteasing to abductions and killings. The number of registered cases has also gone up alarmingly in the past few years. Although the actual number of cases reported is much more than the recorded ones.

Mental cruelties

i) Discrimination in male and female child.

ii) Married women debarred of employment in several organisations.

iii) Female generally having no say in her marriage.

iv) No equal remunerations.

v) Wife having no title in her husband's or in-laws property or home.

vi) the Dowry menance.

vii) Discrimination under law-

a) in Christian Law, ground for divorce for a man is adultry while for a women has to prove 'incestuous' adultry or adultry coupled with another matrimonial offence.

b) woman not a natural guardian of her children.

c) no community of property.

d) Hindu women not entitled by birth to a share in the co-parcenary property, nor she can ask for partition in ancestral property. Daya-Bhaga does not recognise the role of survivorship.

e) Generally the father wills away the property to the sons and the daughters do not get any right of inheritance. The father should not be allowed to will away the share of the daughter.

f) Application cannot be filed under Hindu Marriage Act where the wife lives.

g) Muslim Inheritance Law of giving half share to a daughter and the Parsi Law double the hare to a male.

h) Custody of Children.

i) Discrimination in employment.

j) The law of maintenance is unjust, cumbersome, wife has no right to the property of husband even if built with her efforts or contribution. An application for maintenance and alimony under section 24 and section 25 of the Hindu Marriage Act can be filed only in pending proceeding or at the time of passing the decree or subsequent there to. If a wife wants to file application for maintenance, she cannot do so. Under section 18 of the Hindu Adoption and Maintenance Act, on an application the wife was asked to pay ad-velorem Court Fee, which she was unable to do so. Under Section 125 of Penal Code, the amount of maintenance in proceeding is not adequate. It should be available to a woman from the moment she was deserted or thrown out and not from the date of application. The test of 1/5th of income of the husband is not just fair and reasonable. Further, the maintenance should be deducted at source immediately. How a woman can go to court and wait for years for the maintenance? If the law of bigamy is enforceable against a government servant, why not the maintenance be deducted form the husband's source of income. The wife should be able to file and application u/s 19 of Hindu Marriage Act at the place she lives and the law should be amended thereto.

k) The personal laws relating to Christians and Muslims should be changed wherever there are discriminations.

As per the guidelines for treatment of women in prisons, action should be taken. No women should be kept in prison with order from the court. Recently, the Supreme Court has laid guidelines for treatment of women in prisons, some of whom were in prisons in the State of Bihar not because they had committed but because they were needed to give evidence in cases in which were victims of crime. A Committee formed by the Government given its report on prisons and one can imagine the fate of women as prisoners.

Need for new measures

To prevent the atrocities on women some preventive measures are necessary. These may be-

i) *Socially redefining violence :* We have to redefine the concept of violence against women'. It means seeing the crimes like rape, abduction, wife beating, dowry death and murder as acts of violence motivated by power and authority. Violent acts can occur in many circumstances where people will not acknowledge them normally. Women have to say things publicly which they dared not say before.

ii) *Strengthening up the women organisations:* Voice of a single woman does not carry weight. If a group of women of like minded views join together, form an organization and raise their voice against the suffering of woman, they can make an impact. The social norms can be attached by the organisations only. The organisations should create an awareness among women to struggle against their oppression and to fight the persons who exploit, humiliate and torture the women. They may hold protest marches, demonstrations and public meetings in different areas and localities, provide emotional support to women victims, pressurize the police to act speedily, organize orientation camps for women for educating them about their rights and laws relating to these, file writ petition in courts, follow-up the cases and hold press conferences. In the recent past, the women organisations have brought to light several cases of women where they are ill-treated by the men, police or otherwise. Whenever some representatives of the women organisations speak and write to police, the police is bound to take up some action. The same way the women organisations help the women in distress in getting legal aid from the District Courts

Legal Aid and Advice Committee, State Legal Aid and Advice Boards. The women organisations help the women in getting admissions in Short Stay Homes and getting them wrestled in life. Women organisations have put in tremendous efforts and have been effective in getting several legislations or amendments passed by the Parliament.

iii) *The humanistic approach:* It is necessary to develop a humanistic approach to the victims of crimes against women. These may include rethinking of roles, rehabilitation of victims and evaluation of organisational procedures of police, courts, rescue homes etc.

iv) *Changes in criminal justice system:* There should be change in attitudes and values of judicial officials, the establishment of Family Courts, and a change in police attitude. Re-orientation of magistrates is necessary. Instead of raising technical points and acquitting the accused, the circumstantial evidence should be given importance.

v) *Role of Police :* The role of police is to uncover law violations and to bring to book those people who threaten the social order. It is upto them to identify an act as crime. The image of police has deteriorated due to irresponsibility and corrupt as well as unlawful practices. A Police Officer should give proper treatment to the complainant and seek his co-operation and confidence rather than ill-treating him/her. The role of police is very important as far the cases concerning cruelties on women are concerned. Each case is to be registered and investigated by the police and later challans are to be put up in the court. The role of police has been very poor in this regard. First of all, the police personnel are generally men. Whenever a woman goes to the Police Station or Police Post to lodge her complaint against her husband, in-laws, neighbourers, or any other person who has assaulted her cruelly, raped her, or done some other crime, police does not take any notice. Rather she fears to go to the Police Station and seek their help because it is said that once the women go to the Police Station to take some help, they would be harassed instead of getting any help. Police is never taken as a friend of the citizens. How the women can seek the, help of the Police? When she is mentally upset too much or is physically assaulted, she goes to the Police and Police does not care. When a woman reports that she was harassed or beaten by her husband or in-laws, the police says "It is your family affair, why have you come to us? The men are used to beat their wives." Further, women is not secure in the Police Station. There are many instances where women went to a Police Station for help and they were mentally and physically harassed. Anyhow, when the women organisations interfere and insist on registering the case, the Police does not like it. If a Women Organization reports against any police official, no action is taken. Somehow, if the case is registered with great difficulty, it is lodged under incorrect section. The investigations undertaken by a very junior officer. It is obligatory that an Officer of the rank of Assistant Commissioner of Police should investigate the crime against women. The junior officer, who is investigating the case, has many other cases to investigate. He has not much time to concentrate in a particular case. At the later stage, when the Challans are put up in the court, there is not enough proof or evidence for want of thorough investigation. Further, a case is supposed to be investigated at the earliest and not later than three months, but due to delay in investigation beyond three months and non-submission of Challans in time, the court either bails out the culprit or release them after three months because they cannot be kept in jail for more than 90 days. Once the culprit comes out of the jail, it becomes very difficult for the harassed women or their relatives. No police protection is provided to her. Thus, we find that out of 10 cases registered by the police, perhaps only one culprit is punished. It is suggested that a delinquent police officer should be prosecuted and punished. It is further alleged that the police is bribed at the lower level. Whenever there is a crime against women, the woman or her people do not get police help as the other party bribes the police heavily and the investigation of the case becomes very weak. Many a times, judicial officers have commented and noted that the case was very weak and proper investigation was not made. So, the inquiry should be made by a Gazetted Police Officer. I understand, the police of Japan is a close friend of citizens, especially to the women and the old. Our police should also adopt such attitudes so that they may also be treated friends of the citizens. The Crime Against Women Cell was created with an object to help the women in distress, but its establishment only seems to be a mockery as they have failed miserably to give justice to the women. The Police officers working in this Cell should be specially oriented to deal with the problems of the women humanly and with understanding. Instead the Police officers have a tendency to be rude and they pressurize the women to reconcile with the husbands. However, the job of the Women Cell is to register a case against the husband whenever a complaint is made by his wife. If there are chances for reconciliation or rehabilitation, the cases should be returned to the women organisations. It is pertinent to, point out that even the Stridhan is never returned by the husband and police takes a very lenient view of it and the articles are rarely returned to her.

If this Cell is working only to compete with the women organisations and to gather statistics to impress the Government, then the whole machinery of the Cell will collapse and no good will be achieved. The only solution is that the Women Cell should work in-close-co-ordination with the women organisations and create an atmosphere where women can come without fear to redress their problems.

vi) *Formation of specific institutions:* Specific Institutions e.g. Independents, Anti-Discrimination Board to look into the Dowry complaints, Anti-Discrimination Board, Equal Opportunity Commissions will have to b set up to implement the laws once enacted with power to

a) Investigate into specific complaints of discrimination on any ground, be it sex, community, class or religion,

b) do research into the discriminatory laws, customs and practices.

c) suggest detailed amendments in these laws and give its findings on the customary and factual discriminations.

d) give its decisions on specific cases which will have a binding force, subject to appeals as from Tribunals.

Action and Implementation Centres at grass-root levels is

of great importance as these Centres will act as Complaint/Education/ImplementationandClearing Centre.

vii) *Role of lawyers :* Sensitive lawyers can play a significant role in achieving equal legal status to women in India. It is their duty to challenge the discriminations. The lawyer works for the disadvantaged section of the society and aims to obtain relief for them.

viii) *Legal aid movement:* In the Legal Aid Movement, the women should be mobilized in co-operation with Voluntary Organisations and legal aid agencies for propagation and promotion of legal literacy. Knowledge of laws and access to the judicial system would strengthen the position of women and enable them to seek remedies and relief available under the law. It includes legal literacy, awareness about the machinery, providing legal assistance and actual litigation in court as well as in pre-trial stages. The work in this field must necessarily start with a programme of legal literacy of voluntary social workers and organisations and through them for women in their respective areas. Mass media and particularly the Press, All India Radio and Door Darshan have an important role to play in spreading legal literacy.

The crimes against women deserve a scientific study and the victims of crimes require an objective approach in our reactions and a more humanistic response in our dealings.

4

Dowry Death in India

The most dramatic form that violence against women has taken is what the Indian media labeled "bride-burning" until in 1978 or so, feminists cut out the alliterative fuzz by redesignating it quite baldly as "dowry murder." During the 1980s, urban north India has seen a growing number of murders of married women, variously called dowry murders or bride burnings. The burning of wives is neither an extension of nor culturally related to the notorious practice of *sati*, the voluntary immolation of Bengali widows on the funeral pyres of their husbands. The resonances are startling—the burning of women, the thin line between suicide and murder—but the differences are significant because they point to a serious further devaluation of women in present-day India in spite of a century of progressive legislation on women's rights.

Sati was socially countenanced suicide because the widow was perceived as having failed in her ritual duties to ensure the longevity of her husband by using her special female power or shakti; bride burning, however, is murder and equally culpable by social and legal standards. The method of dying or killing, that is, the immolation of women in both cases, is also a false parallel. The rituals that are prescribed for sati are adequately described elsewhere; suffice it to say that it was public act that generated social awe, status, religious merit, and even material gain for the woman's kin and affines and made her sati, or the virtuous wife in death. Burning a wife, a ritually auspicious person, is perhaps more appalling than the less sensational ways of doing her in (poisoning, drowning, strangling, shooting, or bludgeoning, among others) but is chosen chiefly for the forensic advantage it has over the others. It virtually destroys the evidence of murder along with the victim and can easily be made to look like an accident. It is also relatively simple to commit. It occurs in the kitchen, where the lower middle-class housewife spends a large amount of time each day.

Pressurized kerosene stoves are in common use in such homes; a tin of fuel is always kept in reserve. This can be quickly poured over the intended victim and a lighted match will do the rest. It is easy to pass off the event as an accident because these stoves are prone to explode, and the now ubiquitous but highly inflammable nylon sari easily catches fire and engulfs the wearer in flames. Signs of a struggle simply do not show up on bodies with 90 or more percent third-degree burns.

The bereaved widower, who has equipped himself with a cast-iron alibi, is soon in the marriage market again looking for a new bride with perhaps a more handsome dowry. Often it is the mother-in-law, with or without her son as accomplice, who will obligingly commit the murder. Dowry serves as the foundation on which explanation for discrimination against women have been built; it has the conceptual richness to satisfy a variety of analytical tastes over time. The colonialists stressed its cultural roots in a benighted Hinduism;

Marxists see it as an economic institution, feminists view it as gender discrimination for daughters did not traditionally inherit land. Today, the dowry system is seen as the prime motive for two other crimes akin to infanticide widely prevalent in the subcontinent. Female infant neglect reflected in the worst adverse female to male sex ratios in the world today, and the abortion of female fetuses made possible by the abuse of recent advances in fetal diagnostic technology. Until recently, billboard advertisements in Bombay, for instance, made an unabashed appeal to pregnant women to take the expensive and some what risky amniocentesis test. It importuned them to spend 500 rupees now on the test in order to save 50,000 rupees in the future on a daughter's dowry.

The cause of bride-burnings or dowry death in India was, indeed, dowry, and indubitably a cultural problem. This alleged fact has found wide support expressed in both detailed historical and anthropological analyses of female infanticide, the oldest and most widespread form of murder believed to be related, even in other cultures, to the practice of dowry. Dowry, an integral part of Hindu high caste culture, appeared to be a timeless and pernicious custom that constructs women as a financial liability to their natal homes as infants and in their marital homes as brides. Its ban, by an act of the Indian Parliament in 1961, seems only to have entrenched the custom deeper.

There were glaring contradictions in the explanations. Culture was blamed on the one hand, but so were Westernization, which brought in gross materialism, greed, and a desire for consumer goods and modernization, which put a cash value on everything and commercialized human relationships. Here was the puzzle: Was this violence against women related to the ancient custom of dowry or was it a product of acculturation to Western and modern culture? But why then in the West, where dowries were once common, had the practice all but disappeared? Clearly culture does change; what made the culture of dowry gradually disappear in the West and change for the worse in India? When examining the evidence, particularly the colonial evidence on infanticide, the explanation that had hoped only to deepen and endorse began to unravel.

Statistical evidence on sex ratios in the subcontinent point to a serious anomaly in the logic that underpinned the colonial verdict on the dowry system and made their figures suspect. On close inspection a startling fact emerged. Several families from Hindu lower castes and religions, such as Islam and Sikhism, which did not follow the practice of dowry and even received bride price (bride price is paid in cash and/or gods to the bride's family by the groom's family), were found guilty of committing infanticide, so it was awkward to insist on either dowry or upper caste pride (as pronounced in the case of Rajputs [powerful landowning and ruling castes in North India]) to be the cultural justification of so heinous a crime.

The convenient lie of branding dowry as the motivating culprit, or finding barbaric practices particularly among the upper caste Hindus, was begun by colonial bureaucrats in the mid-nineteenth century. Parliamentary inquires about the improverishment of the India peasantry had to be answered satisfactorily. It was expedient to lay the blame on culturally sanctioned "improvidence" and wasteful ceremonies and rituals, chiefly marriage celebrations and dowry, than to reverse the colonial land revenue policies that had uprooted the old system and transformed the basic relationship between peasants and their land. These official documents generated by colonial bureaucrats are laced with information that flatly contradicts their own assertions, and the net result was that the one clear fact about the nature of this timeless custom of dowry dissolved into a murky half-truth. The politics of the process of describing and attributing meaning to the cultures of the colonized became more important to understand than their unhappy social consequences. Dowry in its menacing form for some women, as we know it today, was patiently the artifact not of an organically unchangeable and permanently constituted Hindu or Sikh culture but of acculturation in colonial time and space. This change, fortunately, did not occur evenly across castes and classes, and today, the majority of Hindu families practice what might be seen as a precolonial form of dowry. It is this process of change—sporadic, uneven, and regrettably irreversible—that this study endeavours to reconstruct from the very documents that claim otherwise.

After a careful rereading of colonial sources, dowry could be called on of the few indigenous feminist institutions in an overwhelmingly patriarchal and agrarian society (since the term feminist is hotly contested, I do not insist on it). In the late nineteenth and early twentieth century, dowry was not the enemy but rather an ally of women, acting as an economic safety net in a setting where women always married outside their natal villages (village exogamy is still almost mandatory) and where they did not normally inherit land. This institution was invented by women for women and the resources that were given to women were substantially under their direct control. Items for a daughter's dowry were accumulated gradually for each daughter not just by her immediate family, but by the entire village, which shared in an intricate web of reciprocal obligations; very few items were purchased, since most of them were produced at home, bartered, or received as part of the reciprocal gift exchange among village families. Nor were daughters perceived as an economic burden. The dowry was the only independent material resource over which women had partial, if not total, control. It was viewed by a woman's natal family not only as a matter of pride but also as a means of securing for her the best possible match, while providing her with recourse in an emergency.

Dowry can be reckoned not only as the index of the appreciation bestowed upon daughters in their natal villages and the measure of their status in their conjugal villages, but the practical concern of familiar to unsecure for their daughters a husband from a comparable family in which her children would be raised. How then did such a strongly spun safety net twist into a deadly noose? The time span studied covers the mid-nineteenth century to the present.

The place is the Punjab, in the northwestern part of the subcontinent, a varying and often partitioned space. In 1851, the Sikh Bedis were found guilty of female infanticide. This discovery became political capital for the British and justified their two unsanctioned bitter and bloody wars against the Sikh ruler of the Punjab, Maharaja Ranjit Singh, that led to the annexation of the Punjab only two years earlier. The righteousness of British aggression was further underscored, in their own estimation, by the fact that Guru Nanak, the founder of the Sikh religion in the fifteenth century, was of the Bedi caste.

The present-day Indian states of Punjab and Haryana (which was part of the Indian Punjab until 1966) continue to have the most adverse female to male ratios, or 879 and 870 per 1,000 males respectively in the 1981 census. Female infanticide is treated as an aberration of the past because the British government set up a department to deal with it in 1870 and closed the department in 1906, claiming total success in their campaign to suppress the practice and make the Punjabis less improvident about dowries. They were wrong on both counts: Sex ratios have steadily worsened nationwide in the twentieth century. In 1901, there were 972 females for every 1,000 males, while in 1971 and 1991, the ratios have declined to 930 and 920 females per 1,000 males respectively.

The practice of killing female infants may have become less prevalent, but it was substituted by the less detectable practice of medical or nutritional neglect that achieved the same end more slowly. It was the current sex ratio in India and comparable ratios in Pakistan and Bengladesh that aroused my suspicion that female child mortality has little to do with dowry or Hindu culture, since the partition of the subcontinent had been on religious lines and removed Hindus from west Punjab and cast Bengal in 1947.

Since dowries do not figure prominently in Muslim culture, why were the sex ratios not all that much better in these two Muslim nations? This suspicion began the quest for a new culprit and the reappraisal of this intriguing cultural whodunit. The rest of the investigation was not startling. Female infanticide was found among all castes and classes of people and the rationale for it was to have a planned family with the right number of children of the two sexes, in a convenient birth order.

The bias in favour of boys was also universal, whether Hindu or Muslim or Sikh, and whether urban or rural. The British did not exactly manipulate the numbers to build the case against hypergamous, landowning castes; they merely ignored the numbers that contradicted that clean-cut explanation, which seemed to strike at the roots of the culture of the Hindu ruling classes, while their own policies strengthened the bias against women. By a careful rereading of colonial records not only on infanticide but also on variety of seemingly unrelated matters, such as land revenue, peasant indebtedness, and foreclosures of agricultural property, it is possible to establish that the meaning of dowry changed drastically in the colonial period in qualitative and quantitative terms and that is skewed gender inequalities further.

The records that indict the custom of dowry as the cause for killing female infants are littered with clues that lead to the history of a changing custom rather than the characterization of it as a practice frozen in time and supported by the ruinous extravagance and the tradition-bound behavior of a caste society. This gradual but radical transformation in the meaning, practice, and effects of the dowry system in the Punjab, and by implication elsewhere, was triggered by the changes in the colonial political economy and the extension of political and social control in areas where the practice existed. When the British encountered the practice of dowry in the Punjab, they collected opinions on the nature of the custom. None of the reports describe dowry as gifts that could be demanded by the groom's family. They found it to be a collection of voluntary gifts of clothes, jewelry, household goods, and cash bestowed on the bride by family and friends at the time of the wedding. In forty-nine separate volumes of customary law of an equal number of districts in the vast territory that constituted colonial Punjab-present-day Pakistan and Indian Punjab, Haryana, Jammu, Delhi and Himachal Pradesh - this definition of dowry has been reiterated as many times. Nowhere was it treated as the prerogative of the groom and his family to demand specific consumer goods and large sums of cash for the groom's business, education, or mobility; it was voluntary and depended on the pecuniary circumstances of the bride's parents. The British charge of "improvidence" was not based on the expense for dowry but on wedding celebrations. These latter costs were strictly itemized and evaluated in cash for three economic tiers in society and became part of the bureaucrats' handbook for enforcement. Wedding expenses did not mean only a daughter's wedding expenses; many cases cited as evidence of proficacy in the handbooks of refer to the weddings of sons.

Changes in dowry system

Yet the concerts about the escalating pressures of enhanced dowry in the late nineteenth and the twentieth centuries suggest that changes in this period affected the nature of this institution. The upward spiral in costs continued; cash and an ever-increasing range of consumer goods that became available in the Punjab as imports from Europe made the increase especially steep. Demands for cash at the time of betrothal, lavish feasting and entertainment of the wedding guests, gifts for the family of the groom, expenses for the celebration of annual fasts and festivals, and the birth of children and their naming and tonsure ceremonies changed in time the nature of the daughter-parent bond. This trend has steadily aggravated in the postcolonial period and in its extreme form it has been the cause for violence against women and, more recently, the burning to death of wives who brought inadequate dowries.

What we are dealing with is not just a dowry problem but a pathology or a syndrome rooted in history and gender inequality in a patriarchal society. Colonialism and patriarchal values became meshed in an alliance against women, even when the avowed purpose of legislative reform in this period was to uplift the status of women in Indian society. Because the issue of violence against women is not merely an academic puzzle, but a matter of life and death, a reexamination of contemporary evidence in the light that history and feminist theory shed, is urgently warranted. In other words although dowry is the centerpiece of this study, it cannot help but illumine the pervasive commercialization of social relations in general and the central event in women's lives—marriage—in particular. This will help in assessing the loss of women's economic power and social appreciation even as they gained in legal and political rights through the process of changes unleashed in this period. This complex interaction of local customs, such as dowry, and colonialism has hardly been suspected to exist, let alone been adequately analyzed.

The widely accepted denunciation of dowry undergirds a host of corollaries that have blurred the thinking on the triangular relationship among marriage, gender, and property, which needs to be discussed in some detail. It also pushes to the fore other, perhaps, bigger questions. Did colonial policies often create, or aggravate, the very problems they sought to ameliorate? "Social evils" was the common designation for Indian customs such as sati and thuggee (the practice of thugs, a criminal caste), "discovered" by the East India Company collectors and magistrates and described as part of the exotic and "barbaric" culture they encountered. Systematic legal and police measures were taken to eradicate these practices. It was in this context that Indian women and their status in Hindu society became a central preoccupation of the colonial powers. Were the social evils, such as accelerating chronic indebtedness, increasing drunkenness, and improvidence in the Punjabi countryside, the unwitting consequence of rules and regulations of the new regime rather than the consequences of Hindu or Muslim culture? What influence did the colonial codification of customary law (rivaj-i-am) and its implementation in the new colonial courts in the Punjab have on various customs, particularly on the definition of the rights of women and the notions of dahej (dowry) and stridhan (women's wealth)? These questions are explored in detail in the larger study to plumb the depths of social change and disruption under British rule. Now we have to explain the politics of two key terms, culture and colonialism and their interrelationship on which the arguments rest. Neither represents a permanently constituted entity; both are continually contested and negotiated sets of power relations, and history has constructed their meanings. Moreover, native and culture and British colonialism were in dynamic relationship with each other and not without mutual, albeit unequal, effect on each other. In other words, it would be as narrow-minded to construe Hindu culture or tradition as a timeless, frozen entity as it would to think of the more than 250 years of British rule in India as a fully imagined and executed vision that can be called British colonialism. Both continually changed in the process of interaction and acculturation.

Colonialism in mid-nineteenth century Punjab could not be mistaken for the ·colonialism that Bengal experienced when it was first overtaken in 1757; differing strategies produced different results in the two places. Colonial investment in the Punjab, although accomplished at little cost to the British, greatly expanded agriculture production. By building canals, communications, and railway lines, this ultrafertile grain-producing region was linked to a thriving international market.

The British extracted wealth from the countryside through heavy taxation and exports of wheat and other raw materials to Europe. Although this development was self-interested, it brought prosperity to this region along with enormous changes in the peasant's way of life. There was also an intensified colonial interest in understanding, describing, and ultimately reforming the varieties of cultures encountered among the subjugated people; this interest was not academic or philanthropic but political.

The stubborn tendency to interpret indigenous culture as an organic entity with immutable values, symbols, and belief systems was plainly self-serving. That the culture of the colonialists was dynamic and ever-changing and Indian culture was static, timeless, and inflexible were representations enable bureaucrats to devise means of social control in addition to political and economic domination. It was colonialism's professed mission to improve civilize, and regenerate Indian society, but this could be done only after the serious flaws in the culture were located. The abominable status of women became the ground on which this legitimacy was founded.

Anthropology was invented to study the unchanging structures (kinship patterns, marriage rules) for societies without history. When Bengal was the lofus of the colonialists' concern, vivid accounts of sati fulfilled this role admirably and fattened the volumes of the Parliamentary Papers in the late eighteenth and early nineteenth centuries. Descriptions of female infanticide made horrifying reading in subsequent years from the provinces annexed later.

The discovery of, and operations to control and abolish, female infanticide in the North-West Provinces Punjab and Oudh caught international attention through the same media. It goes without saying that their horror was genuine, as is ours, even while we endeavor to explain the political purposes the suffering of others often serves. What is extremely interesting is the construction of the crime as a cultural artifact, and how a colonial agenda was served by social reform.

Miller and Panigrahi accept the cultural construction unquestioningly. Miller goes further and says that culture provides the motivations for infanticide, whether they are seen by the people involved as ritualistic,...economic,...or ecological... It is culture that "invents" the reasons for which some children who are born are not desired. Second, it is culture that sketches the outlines of the group that is to be the target of infanticide: whether it is to be only boys, only girls, first sons, daughters beyond the first, children born on Thursday, children born with teeth, or children with crippling deformities. This argument involves a sleight of hand that conflicts material and ecological reasons under the rubric of culture and is therefore difficult to refute. Miller, in an uncritical application of the classic "work equals worth" argument, shows how the masculine sex ratios of the north and the balanced sex ratios of the south of India can be explained.

Swidden and wet rice cultivation, with a high demand for female labour in the south, leads to inclusion of females in property-holding and land being given as dowry, giving women the social advantages of being in the work force, which leads to an (emotional?) appreciation of daughters and balanced juvenile sex ratios. The opposite is true, in her view, in dry-field plow cultivation areas in the north, where women are excluded from production (which is patently inaccurate) and given dowries of movable property only.

The high cost of raising and marrying daughters leads to discrimination against them, which explains the masculine juvenile sex ratios. It is predicated mainly on census figures and data from postcolonial ethnographics, which have descriptions of marriage costs that shows have grown in response to the forces at work in the nineteenth and early twentieth centuries. In the Punjab, for example, bride price and dowry simply exist and it is therefore untenable to argue that women's work in the fields alone determines the mode of marriage payments. Briefly, what happened under colonial rule to the Punjab countryside is recorded in a succession of revenue settlement reports.

The British had pioneered the permanent settlement in Bengal presidency in 1793; its revolutionary feature was that it transformed land, in which all classes and castes of people had varying rights and shared unequally in its produce, into private property that could be bought, sold, or mortgaged. This created (very crudely and quickly) a class of zamindars with immense holdings on the one hand and landless peasants on the other. This is because the revenue payments were fixed in perpetuity and due on a certain fixed date every quarter. These amounts and dates had little sensitivity to seasonal variations in the quantity of produce or to delayed harvest times, both of which depended on the caprice of the weather. In a bad year, there would be no recourse but to mortgage or sell the land to meet government demand, which was set at a higher, more "efficient" level than the past rulers had deemed fair. This created absentee landlords, for traders and money lenders from Calcutta could now buy this land in government-sponsored auctions or foreclosures of mortgaged land. An army of landless peasants roamed the countryside for food, shelter, and wage labor.

The economic and social havoc this caused in Bengal has been adequately dealt with in the works of a large number of historians and economists. In the Punjab, which was conquerred after two aggressive wars between

1840 and 1849, the British tried to find a less disastrous revenue policy than the one they had perused in once-rich bengal. They settled on a ryotwari settlement by giving titles to the land directly to the peasants (ryots) who tilled it. This method might have been less disastrous except for except for two components: the fixed amounts and dates for payment of land revenue and the newly created ability of peasant proprietors, who were in this case more numerous with small holdings, to alienate their land through mortgage or sale. These components proved as disastrous as any attempt to "rationalize" customary man/land relations that the British had hitherto undertaken. Money landers in the past had advanced small loans, and the object was never to let a debt be paid off entirely, keeping the debtor as a permanent customer.

The new breed of truly avaricious money lenders, with a new appetite for appropriating the debtor's land rather than the repayment of the debt was also a creation of colonialism. With land as collateral and with prices of land rising, the peasant was able to borrow far more than he could ever before: up to 70 per cent of the value of his land. He borrowed either in a bad year or in a year when the harvest was late, chiefly to pay his taxes on time. Chronic indebtedness became the other side of the coin of prosperity for the vast majority of these small peasant proprietors.

The figures on foreclosures on the lands of the people who were not seen as the best cultivators, namely Rajputs, and of the self-exploiting jat, tell a painful story. Interests rates went up from an already high level around 18 to 24 percent to an exorbitant 24 to 40 per cent range, with various other tricks and deceits built into the loans secured with land titles to hoodwink the illiterate peasant. Prices of land went up too, particularly as monetization of the economy moved along apace with the building of canals, roads, railways, and market facilities, and the price of grain increased as exports rose. Apart from the colonial government, the grain merchant and the money lender, not the peasant, were the most direct beneficiaries of this trend. They no longer wanted to sustain the traditional symbiotic relationship with their peasant debtors; they now wanted as quickly as possible to foreclose on the mortgaged property and hire the former proprietor as an ill-paid day laborer.

The corresponding increase in holdings of bania and khatri (commercial castes) who were the money lenders and merchants was a dramatic overall 40 percent loss for the traditional peasantry within the first twenty years of the ryotwari settlement. Canals were not entirely beneficial either and brought two tragic consequences that were difficult to dealt with—malaria epidemics and infertility to irrigated lowlands due to an increase in the salinity of the soil.

The opening of the Western Jumna Canal in 1840-41, for example, raised the water table and made some of the contiguous eastern districts, such as Panipat and Karnal, a barren waste of water-logged, saline land that looked like "snow-covered fields". For thirty years, there was no resurvey or reassessment of land revenue, and appeals from the distressed peasants were not heeded. Acts of last resort—desertions, vagrancy, immigrating to a fertile district, and serving as bonded labour—became routine. This, eliminated the difference between the security of rights in land that sons inherited and the "movable property" that daughters inherited as dowry.

The dowry became a prize for men as much as their inherited rights in land had been. If anything, a dowry was the more versatile in a situation where land was barren. The other unfortunate effect of the canal was the spread of water- and vermin-borne diseases, such as malaria and typhoid, that claimed dark colonial plot—just tragic and unintended ecological and etiological disasters that undermined the ability of the peasants to pay their fixed dues. So, indebtedness and poverty grew in the midst of the new prosperity. A sample statement from the dozens of reports from revenue officials gives us a flavor of the peasant's lot in 1872-80, after three decades of British rule in the Punjab. A Mr. Sharer was dispatched to examine the complaints of the peasants in Karnal district. His investigations showed that the water table had risen sixty feet, barely two or three feet below the surface, causing the tract of land to become totally barren. Punjab and how it affected social exchange. This quiet desperation built pressure to exploit customary ways of obtaining cash or gold or silver to buy land elsewhere, or to replenish a herd—and dowry was a logical place to look.

The will to obtain larger dowries from the families of daughters-in-law, to demand more in cash, gold, and other liquid assets, becomes vivid after leafing through pages of official reports that dutifully record the effects of indebtedness, foreclosures, barren plots, and cattle dying for lack of fodder. The voluntary aspects of dowry, its meaning as a mark of love for the daughter, gradually evaporates. Dowry becomes dreaded payments on demand that accompany and follow the marriage of a daughter. Women appear to have resisted giving up their ornaments to the very last, when the situation became utterly dire. Jewelry would be the last thing a peasant had to offer when in arrears over revenue and had to save his land from the auctioneer's block.

The social effects of this indebtedness were enormous. It made the raising of daughters into a kind of economic burden that never existed before the new revenue settlements. Wedding expenses of both males and females could be curtailed and so could funeral expenses, but dowry became the lever that a woman's affines grasped with tenacity.

The ritual calendar and the harvest calendar in peasant society are intimately linked: betrothals, marriages, tonsure ceremonies, sacred thread initiation ceremonies occurred at "auspicious times" and were celebrated on the small profits of the harvest. British revenue policies never permitted capital accumulation, but kept the peasant at his wonted subsistence level. Inflexible British revenue payment timetables proved often not to synchronize with nature—a late monsoon would mean a late harvest and that would drive the marginal cultivators to deplete their savings or to the moneylender's door to meet their payment schedules. These short-term loans frequently became life-long debts because land as collateral gave the money lender the incentive to make his conditions of repayment as difficult as possible.

The next thing the peasant would need was a further loan to marry off his pubescent daughter because the profits of the harvest were now pledged to the money lender. What this spiral of events boils down to is that a daughter's marriage, which customarily could not wait too long past her puberty, became the last straw that broke the camel's back. A son's wedding cost as much as a daughter's wedding (and this is true even today in Punjabi urban and rural families), but a son's wedding could be postponed. While funeral expenses could be trimmed, wedding expenses that could be borne by the bride's family steadily climbed because of reasons that will emerge presently.

The crucial fact, however, was that neither daughter's weddings nor funerals could wait; other ritual events could be postponed, particularly the son's betrothal or wedding day. So it was not the cost of the wedding but the constraints of time that made a daughter's wedding an exploitable condition in early colonial times.

A daughter's wedding, therefore, necessitated a loan more often than a son's; and a possible demand for a bigger dowry from her in-laws would occasion an even bigger loan. In desegregating a farmer's debt, the amounts that pertained to a daughter's dowry were seen as inexcusable improvidence. This kind of circumstantial evidence against dowry finally indicated it as the killer. The British increasingly understood the devastating ramifications of their own revenue policies but they preferred to blame the culturally based dowry system, rather than their own rational reconstruction of the land holding and revenue system.

The notoriety about dowries quickly gained currency, and women were the lossers in both natal and affinal families. It can be asserted with confidence, because a plethora of evidence dots the journals, reports and other accounts of British officers, that in the colonial period the cost of a daughter's wedding went up as a result not just of higher tax levels but of other policy decisions as well.

The chief among these was the policy to reduce drastically the allowance that villages had customarily received for social expenses for the community. Although these were still collected as common charges for the village, several Settlement Reports describe a 90 per cent reduction in what the village elders or the headman received because this common fund customarily defrayed expenses on ritual occasions the colonial authorities deemed unnecessary or "improvident."

5

Violence against Women

Women are often terrorised so that they do not assert their rights. Violence against women manifests itself as rape, molestation, stripping eve-teasing, kidnapping and abduction, domestic violence including wife battering, dowry harassment, dowry death, cruelty to women driving them to commit suicide or other forms of murder like female, foeticide, female infanticide and sati. As is well-known reporting of such cases is very poor, generally for fear of social stigma, poverty of parents lack of evidence and so on. Although violence against women is a global problem, it is yet to be recognised as an issue of human rights abuse.

The major instrument for human rights for women is the UN Convention on the Elimination of all forms of Discrimination Against Women (CEDAW) adopted by the General Assembly in 1979. India has recently ratified the CEDAW. The incidence of crime is rising at a very fast rate in our country and crime against women is no exception. As per the report of the National Crime Records Bureau, namely Crime in India 1991, a total number of 10,410 cases or rape were reported in the country. Out of these 2,596 cases were reported in a single State, viz., Madhya Pradesh, followed by 1,417 cases in Uttar Pradesh. Andhra Pradesh, Bihar, Maharashtra and Rajasthan, have all registered more than 5000 cases each. These six States taken together account for nearly 70 per cent of the total rape cases reported in the country during 1991. Among the Union Territories, Delhi (erstwhile UT) tops the list with 214 90.7 per cent) cases while Lakshadweep has the distinction of having no reported rape case. Incidence of child rape (below 10 years) has multiplied manifold i.e. from 394 in 1990 to 1,099 in 1991.

The number of child rape cases in the age group 10-16 years was 2,630 in 1991. The number of cases registered in 1991 (provisional) for other crimes against women are, dowry deaths 5,157, molestation 20,611, kidnapping and abduction 12,3000 eve-teasing 10,283 and cruelly by husband and relatives 15,949. During the period from 1987 to 1991, the incidence of crimes increased as under:

rape	:	26.1%
molestation	:	26.5%
kidnapping and Abduction	:	36.4%
dowry deaths	:	169.7%

The highest rate of increase of crimes against women during 1987-91 was 28.23% in Pondicherry, i.e. an increase from 26 in 1987 to 760 in 1991. No dowry deaths were reported from Arunachal Pradesh, Goa, Manipur Meghalaya, Mizoram, Nagaland, Andaman & Nicobar, Islands, Dadra & Nagar Haveli and Lakshadweep. Out of these six states and UTs. have Scheduled Tribe majority in their populations. Crimes against women fell by 77% in Nagaland and 47 per cent in Himachal Pradesh during 1987-91.

Tendencies for committing violence atrocities and

injustices against women generally have social cultural and psychological bases. They are rooted in greed for money lack of trust, a false sense of superiority of man over a woman. Feelings of insecurity, bad habits like drinking, gambling, criminal or unsound mind, etc. Also make a person prone to inflict violence on others. General complexities of life and frustrations also lead to violence against women.

A fear of sharing of property by women is one of the main causes of atrocities inflicted on them. Rapes are known to occur due to power distortions and socio-economic inequalities. Similarly, growing consumerism and greed have aggravated the problem of dowry and associated crimes. Under Section 10 (1) (f) of the NCW Act, the Commission may take *Suo moto* notice of matters relating to deprivation of women's rights and non-implementation of laws enacted to provide protection to women and take up issues arising out of these with appropriate authorities.

In pursuance of these provisions in the Act, the Commission has been performing various types of functions ranging from informal counselling and advice to formal action to bring to book persons causing harassment and cruelty to women. It has been looking into a number of complaints made from different parts of the country. In some cases members of the Commission personally visited and inquired into the complaints and took up the cases with appropriate authorities. During the period under report, the commission received 246 complaints from different States and Union Territories relating to various types of atrocities and injustice. Since the office of the Commission is located at New Delhi, the maximum number of complaints were received from Delhi.

The complaints related to harassment for dowry

torture by police, refusal to register FIRs wrongful confinement of women in police lock-ups, lodging non criminal lunatic women in jail, domestic violence dowry deaths rape of grass root functionaries discrimination in employment, wrongful transfers deprivation of entitlement of widows from rightful employment, succession and pension, indecent representation of women desertion bigamy, torture and cruelty by husband and in-laws. Depending upon the nature of the case, the Commission took direct action or made interventions with the appropriate authorities. A statement regarding complaints from different States and Union Territories is given at Annexure V. Out of complaints looked into by the Commission, some illustrative cases are given below.

Cases in which Commission took Action

Smt. Bhanwari Devi, a Saathin of village Bhateri working under the women Development Programme (WDP) of the State Govt. Carried out a vigorous campaign against child marriage. This was resented by some of the villagers. On 22nd September, 1992 some men from the village raped Smt. Bhanwari Devi. They ties her husband to a tree and beat him up.

The victim's efforts to seek justice were futile because the culprits could influence the local police to be hostile to the victim. At the request of a voluntary organisation, Members of the Commission visited the village and investigated the case. They also held discussion with medical experts police offices and offers of WDP etc. They met the Chief Minister and urged him to take stringent action against the culprits. Women's organizations were justifiably agitated about the efforts from various quarters to shield the culprits and the inertia of the State law enforcement machinery.

The commission took up the matter for Human Resource Development. Based on the report of the

Commission who had investigated the case, the Prime Minister sanctioned Rs. 10,000/ as relief to the victim from PM's Relief Fund. The case was subsequently entrusted to CBI for investigation.

The Commission received a complaint from the father of an eight year old girl in Jabalpur that his daughter had been raped by a medical practitioner in the neighbourhood. The Supreme Court had sentenced him to 7 years imprisonment and fined Rs. 25,000. But the culprit had not been arrested even after 5 months of passing the sentence. The NCW vigorously pursed the matter with the State Govt. of Madhya Pradesh. Subsequently in February, 1993 that the medical practitioner had been sent to jail.

The commission took *Suomoto* notice of the gang rape of a pavement dweller Nehar Banu in Calcutta. She was picked up by a police barraks. She was raped in the police barracks by the constable who picked her up along with four other constables. The Chairperson and Members of the Commission visited Calcutta and intervened with the police authorities demanding action against the culprit. As a result of their efforts disciplinary proceedings were conducted against the police constables concerned. Apart from the above 13 more cases of molestation rape and other types of atrocities were also brought to the notice of the Commissioner of Police, Calcutta and I.G. Police, West Bengal by the Commission.

The minister of State for women and child Development referred the case of an 18 year old girl employed as a peon in Calcutta University to the NCW. The girl was raped by a senior level Assistant in one of the laboratories in the university. A Member of the Commission visited Calcutta to make on the spot inquiry to the incident and had discussions with the vice-

Chancellor Dean of Law and the Registrar of the University. It was found that no FIR was lodged with the police by the University authorities for investigation into the rape incident although the Assistant was chargesheeted and suspended from service pending completion of the disciplinary proceedings a against him.

The Member of the Commission insisted on launching criminal proceeding against the culprit. The member also met the Welfare Minister of West Bengal urging him to take action against the accused as well as for providing shelter and protection to the victim girl. The Chief Minister readily responded to the initiative taken by the Commission and appropriate measures were taken by the authorities. The accused was dismissed from service and the victim was suitably rehabilitated by the University authorities.

The Commission received a complaint in October, 1992 from the Chairperson of Kutra block, Sundergarh District Orissa that her modesty had been outraged by the Minister for Panchayati Raj of the Government of Orissa. Although she had field an FIR at Kutra Police Station, influential persons had tried to pressurize her to withdraw the FIR. On receipt of the complaint the Commission investigated the case by exercising its powers of a Civil Court vide Section 10 of the National Commission for women act. The proceedings continued beyond March, 1993.

In may, 1992 Commission received a compliant from an NGO that a sub-Inspector of Delhi Police had farmed false charges against a girl of threatening to kill her had kept her in the police look-up at Lajpat Nagar Police Station denied her food, water and toilet facilities besides denying contact with her young children aged 3 and 5 years, and had thereafter attempted to force her to join the flesh trade run by the gang of a notorious pimp.

While in look up and also afterwards he made overtures and obscene gestures to her and even got two goods into the Police Station to terrorise her. Due to the intervention of the Commission's Chairperson a vigilance enquiry was held by the police authorities and the Sub Inspector found guilty and dismissed from service.

On receipt of a compliant from a Member of Parliament, alleging that certain officials of the Central Fuel Research Institute, Dhanbad, had behaved in an indecent and obscene manner towards women scientists, NCW took up the matter promptly with the Director General, Council of Scientific and Industrial Research for an early investigation into the matter. As a result the Director General CSIR constituted a Fact Finding Committee which pinpointed the names of three staff members and they are suspended and charge-sheeted. An inquiry officer was appointed to hold inquiry into the charges framed against these officials. The Director General, CSIR assured the Commission that CSIR was constantly pursuing the case.

A young bride was tortured and murdered by her husband mother-in-law and her brother-in-law who was a police constable. The husband and the mother-in-law were arrested on the basis of an FIR field at the Police Station but the Police was reluctant to arrest the brother-in-law. The aggrieved party approached the NCW. The Commission took up the matter with the authorities concerned. The constable was arrested and suspended from service.

A minor girl named Shamim aged 7 years, resident of a jhuggi in Katwaria Sarai in South Delhi, was raped by a Chowkidar aged 50 years. Noting from newspaper report a Member of the Commission had the case thoroughly examined and checked with Hauz Khas Police Station whether FIR was registered under Section

376 of the IPC. The case was committed to the Sessions court—Court of the Metropolitan Magistrate, Patiala House Court, New Delhi. The accused was arrested.

A minor girl aged about 10 years a resident of Rampura, Delhi was raped by her teacher aged 38 years. On the basis of the report appearing in newspapers a member of the Commission vigorously pursued the case with the police and ensured that the police not only promptly registered FIR but also made a proper and thorough investigation the accused was charged under Sections 376 and 506 of the Indian Penal Code. A case was filed the accused arrested and no bail was granted to him.

A Member of the Commission visited the state government Home for Women at Panagaon at Nowgaon (Assam) and came across a very sad incident of a minor daughter being raped by her father in his drunken state. The victim girl, aged 14 years was lodged in the State Home and was found in a state of great depression compounded with fear. She appeared traumatised from the shocking experience. The member of the commission visiting the Home endured for her special attention to restore her mental and emotional stability with the result that the victim girl is now pursuing her studies in a school and being looked after by the Department of Social Welfare, Government of Assam for her future rehabilitation.

In our country, the governmental authorities at all levels have periodically expressed determination to eliminate violence against women. Certain actionable strategies have also been adopted in various States/ Union Territories. In addition to improving the existing mechanisms, new measures are also needed to protect the women and girl children. On the basis of

(a) the Commission's experience of looking into and redressing women's complaints and

(b) interaction and consultation with government and social workers from different regions,

The Commission have formulated the ensuing recommendations to eliminate violence against women.

District level bodies for reviewing/monitoring complaints of violence against women have been set up in some States such as Maharashtra and Gujarat. The composition of such a body called Mahila Suraksha Samiti or its equivalent varies from state to state. The committee usually consists of police officers (and magistrates in some States) in charge of the area, legal aid workers representatives of women's organisations counselling experts etc. These committees need not have uniform structure throughout the country. In fact, the composition and functions of such bodies should suit the local needs and conditions in each State/area. Recognising the significant role of these bodies and their immense potential we recommend that:

(a) Wherever a district level monitoring body exists it should be strengthened with more powers appropriate status and financial and staff support.

(b) In States where no district level mechanisms exist, suitable bodies should be created immediately.

It is an established fact that in most regions in India, it is the voluntary organisations that have pioneered and sustained the campaign to combat violence against women. Recognising the strengths and capabilities of voluntary organisations for generating public response to violence and social mobilisation, much greater support should be provided to the voluntary sector by the Central and State governments than hitherto.

The existing schemes of assistance to NGOs should

be modified to include a specific component for combating atrocities against women. The Govt. of Gujarat have a scheme for NGOs to reimburse travel costs, subsidise legal expenses etc. for NGOs when they take up cases of crimes against women. We recommend that:

— A special scheme be introduced by the Central Government to provide financial support to NGOs specifically for dealing with cases of violence against women.

In several metropolitan areas and cities in the country, Women's Cells (under different names such as "Crimes Against Women Cell" in Delhi) or All-Women Police Stations have been set up as a special mechanism to cope with violence against women. In some areas, these cells originated as anti dowry cells and their activities remain confined mainly to restoration of "Streedhan" and providing counselling in some cases. All-women Police Stations are more recent innovative creations. Inn States like Maharashtra and Tamil Nadu, such Police Stations are reported to be achieving commendable results.

The Cells/Police Stations are performing an important ad difficult task. There is an urgent need to set up such Cells/Police stations in all the urban areas. The present practice in the Police Department of marginalising such cells should give way to a more enlightened approach of providing more clout and staff support to the Cells/Stations. We recommend that:

— Women's Cells/Police Stations should be set up in every town having a population exceeding one lakh and should be given adequate powers, funds and staff.

Even today, as we approach the 21st century, violence against women is usually treated as a marginal issue by the law-enforcement machinery in our country, whether it be the police, the prosecutors or the medico-legal fraternity or often even the judiciary. It is essential to sensitize this entire machinery to gender issues, particularly violence against women. Often, the police and other personal are unaware of the police safeguards for women and the amendments to laws relating to such safeguards. We recommend that:

— A gender sensitization module should be incorporated in all the training programmes for the police, the prosecutors the magistrates, the forensic and medico-legal personnel and the judiciary.

Harassment of young brides within the matrimonial home is more horrendous ordeal than even atrocities by criminals outside the home. When cruelly on a defenseless women is inflicted by the husband/in laws who are the "swamy"/guardians to whose care she was entrusted by her parents the woman is both physically and emotionally shattered. It is obvious that tightening the legal safeguards (amendments to IPC, etc.) has not made by dent on this problem. We feel that the only effective remedy for the dowry death is financial deprivation or confiscation of property of the husband/in-laws. We recommend that:-

— A legal provision should be made to confiscate the property of the culprits (husband/in-laws) in every case of dowry death.

One of the functions of the commission as stipulated in the National Commission for Women Act is to take up special studies into specific problems of discrimination, atrocities against women. Social workers as well as Hon'ble Minister of Human Resource Development suggested that in view of the rising menace of sexual abuse of girl children, a study of the problem of "girl child rape" would be warranted. The Commission took up a first-hand study of several cases of girl child rape under investigation by the police or under trial in a court of law. After assessing the magnitude and complexities of the problem in the

Indian context, the Commission decided to organise a seminar on "child rape" to focus attention on the problem and to search for solutions.

The seminar was held on October 7-8, 1992. Eminent legal experts and jurists medico-legal experts specialists of mental health social workers women activities police officers and academicians participated in the seminar. The seminar was designed and structured to examine comprehensively various aspects of the problem of girl child rape such as: (a) the substantive law relatig to child rape; (b) procedural issues and required changes; (c) medico-legal aspects; (d) mental health of the victim; (e) rehabili-tation of the child victim etc.

The seminar achieved some of its objectives in ample measure. It received wide coverage in newspaper magazines and other communication network, thus generating tremendous awareness regarding the menace of girl child rape among parents teachers and other custodial authorities for children jurists, etc. Social Workers and even doctors aware surprised to discover that they themselves did not know enough about the medico-legal issues. The seminar recommended specific changes in the provision of laws and in procedures. These are cited in the ensuing paragraphs.

Recommendations of the Seminar

(1) Since marriage below the age of 18 years is prohibited under the Child Marriage Restraint Act, 1929, section 375 of the IPC should be amended so as to raise the a age specified in clause "Sixthly" from 16 years to 18 years and section 376 of the Code should be amended to raise the quantum of punishment for a man who rapes his wife aged 12 to 18 years.

(2) Section 354 of the IPC should be amended to provide for harsher punishment of five years in

cases where the victim is a female child below the age of 18 years.

(3) A distinct offense commonly known as "eve teasing of a female child below the age of 18 years should be incorporated in the IPC.

(4) The quantum of punishment of an accused should be relatable to the age of the victim as well as the accused should be punished with death sentence.

(5) Minimum punishment for child rape should be 10 years RI with discretion to award lesser punishment for reasons to be recorded in writing. For custodial rape, the minimum punishment should be imprisonment for life with discretion to reduce it to 10 years RI for reasons to be recorded in writing. For gange rape, the minimum punishment should be imprisonment for life.

(6) The offense of child rape should not be a part of general law should be separately dealt with by making a separate provision in the IPC or in a special law including there in enhanced punishment for the accused of custodial rape when the victim happens to be below the age of 18 years.

The separate provision or law should also provide for enhanced punishment for cases cover by sections 376 A to 376 D where the victim is below the age of 18 years.

On Procedural Law and Evidence

(1) Section 54 the Cr. P.C. regarding medical examination of an arrested person should be suitably amended to provide that whenever such arrested person happens to be a women, she should be examined only by or under the supervision of a female medical practitioner.

(2) The procedure for interrogation of a child victim

should be changed and the violation of the provision of the provide to section 160 of the Cr. P.C should be made punishable.

(3) Section 437 of the Cr. P.C. relating to release of person on bail should be made more liberal by providing that ordinarily a women should be released on bail unless there are special reasons to the contrary.

(4) Section 155 of the Evidence Act, 1872 regarding impeachment of the credit of witness should be suitably amended by permitting the accused to put questions of the past sexual intimacy between himself and the girl on prior occasion only and disallowing questions on any collateral sexual relationship between the girl and others.

(5) Section 309 of the Cr. P.C. provided for trial on day-to-day basis. However, in practice trial of a rape case prolongs for years. To overcome this, a time frame for trial of rape cases should be fixed. Alternatively, special courts to try rape cases should be established.

(6) Questioning of the child victim should be reduced to the minimum and such questioning should be done at the place of her residence in the presence of her parents or social workers of the locality. Non-compliance of this provision should be made punishable.

(7) Trial of rape cases should be by a lady judge, investigated by a lady police officer and, if possible, dealt with by lady advocates.

(8) Testimony of the child victim should be conclusive proof of the act of rape and no corroboration should be necessary.

(9) Appointment of jury from amongst respectable people (not being layers) should be considered to

assist speedy disposal of rape cases. In such jury, women should be given more representation.

(10) Police report under section 173 of the Cr. P.C. should include medical examination report of the victim of child rape.

(11) Investigation of custodial rape should be conducted some outside agency, namely CID, Anti-Corruption Bureau or CBI. Investigation should be conducted by an officer not below the rank of DSP.

(12) State government should prescribe rules for quick medical examination of the accused and victim and the manner of reporting results. The rules may also include that the doctor should record in the words of the victim the detailed narration of the incident which may be verified by physical marks.

(13) Proceedings of a rape case should be allowed to be published (section 327 of the Cr. P.C. to be amended). However names of the accused and the victim should be withheld.

(14) The state should deploy lady public prosecutors to conduct a child rape case in a court.

(15) Investigation by police in the cases of child rape should be done on priority basis and should be completed within a prescribed time limit.

(16) Female child below 18 years should not be detained in police custody but if her detention is considered necessary, she should be detained in a recognised remand home or recognised social institution working for family welfare. Such detention in police custody should be made punishment.

(17) Child cases should be given top priority and the courts should be required to dispose them within prescribed time limit.

On Medico-legal Psychological and Rehabilitation Aspects

(1) Government should provide facilities for formal as

well as practical training for the medical practitioners examining a child rape victim.

(2) There is a necessity of certain of a fund (Statutory or otherwise) for rehabilitation of rape victims. The fund should comprise the fine or other penalties imposed on an accused, donations from voluntary organizations and state contributions.

(3) The psychological trauma undergone by the child should be duly appreciated and every effort made to restore the mental health of the child by providing counselling and other health care, preferably within the family.

(4) Medical examination should be done not only of the child victim but also of the accused soon after the commission of the crime. Medical examination of the victim should be by a lady doctor.

(5) Efforts should be change the social perception of rape. This task should be taken up by the state urgently with the help of NGOs reach the people.

(6) A regular campaign for building awareness and public education on the problem of child rape and the measurement required for the rehabilitation of the victim should be launched through official and non-official media.

(7) Sex education may be included in the school curricula for students in the age group of 12 to 16 years.

(8) Law should be amended to enable the court to award compensation to the victim by offender.

(9) Social activities parents and the State should endeavour to impart sex education to the child. This observation was made in view of the opinion of experts that most child rape cases a re familial or the accused is invariably known to the child.

(10) State should set up vocational training centres to rehabilitate the victims and make them financially independent.

(11) Occurrence of child rape is rampant in slum areas. Government should give special attention to these areas.

During the period under review, the various recommendations made in the Seminar on Child Rape were being further examined by an expert group of women lawyers and activities.

Violence within Family

The process of socialization always aims at reenforcing the values justifying and strengthening the power relations in the social system. In India, women conforming to the society's ideals have been hailed as sitas and savitris. Those who dared to defy have been victimized, scandalized and at times murdered, our history is replete with struggles against capitalism, caste system, feudalism and patriachy but it seems that struggle against patriarchy is left out in all broad struggles e.g. one in class struggle, the men and women of different classes stand united against those of the other class.

However, the same men feel insecure when women talk of waging a war against partiarchy. Those who talk of eliminating classes don't accept the concept of eliminating partiarchy. Even the rebels, for a long time roused to accept as a fact the subjugation of women in the joint struggles of men and women. In Maharashtra, the first protest against violence on women was registered in the 19th century. Traditions like 'sati and 'keshavapan' (shaving women's hair after the husband's death) were attacked. Mahatma Phule and Savitribai Phule were the first rebels. Then followed the tradition of reformists like Agarkar, Lokahitavadi and the role of periodicals like sudharak', 'Subodh Patrika' and 'Kesari' of the earlier days which reached and influenced the elites of Maharashtra, The issue of 'Baljarath Vivah' could be focused and highlighted only due to the persistent efforts of these periodicals.

The debate on this issue revealed the brutality of rape within marriage. 'Sudharak' dated, Nov. 10, 1,890 carried translation of an article on this subject,, first published in 'Subodh Patrika'. It raises the question of age of marriage while highlighting thirteen cases of Bal-Jarath Vivah (four each of the age nine years, ten years and eleven-twelve years and one case of seven years of girls). The seven year old girl was married to a man 40 years of age, weighing fourteen stones (two hundred and eighty pounds).

The experience of intercourse was so painful for one young girl that she wept for three full days. Another one had to be hospitalised. However, the next day, the husband approached the doctor and demanded his wife as he wanted to 'use' her.

About a hundred years have passed since these debates were raised. Notwithstanding enormous socio-economic changes, question of violence against women in all spheres of life continues to evade solutions. It would continue to do so till the foundations of patriachy are smashed. The evolution of women's movement world wide has thrown open questions which reveal the true nature of the sacrament Institutions of marriage and family. It has also provided us analytical tools to understand the nature and causes of different forms of violence perpetrated over women and their interrelationships. In India, we have a unique situation of co-existence of all forms of violence, specially of elimination of women e.g. selective female foeticide, female infanticide, bride burning and sati. The incidence of violence of all forms within family has also gone up. So has the awareness about it. According to a study published by Peoples' Union for Democratic Rights (PUDR), the member of unnatural deaths of women has been rising in the last few years most of these are a result of bums. 90% of these cases were married.

During a period of 8 months in 1982, the area falling under the jurisdiction of just two police stations in Bombay reported one death of a women due to bums every fifth day. Five women's organisations in Bombay have been jointly monitoring the bum cases admitted to one of the municipal hospitals. The burns ward consist exclusively women.

A man may be admitted once in a month while a woman is admitted almost everyday in it. While the extent of burns (&hence the possibility of death) is quite low in case of men, most women have bums over 50% of their bodies. Experts feel that bums over 50% cannot be a result of accidents. Because in such cases, the victim and those nearby it would try to extinguish fire and hence would succeed in protecting a major portion of body from burns. What does the high incidence of women with more than 50% burns indicate, not down right murder? It is true that mostly women work in kitchens and hence have greater chances of catching fire. Still, one hardly hears cases of male cooks working in restaurants and eating places of getting burnt inspite of the fact that they are exposed to a greater occupational hazard in form of open, large 'Bhattis'.

The why it is the stove that explodes, it is the saree or dupatta that catches fire? Why are our kitchens such hazardous places? Even if we accept for arguments sake that all these cases are suicides, isn't such a large number of suicides an indication of a sick, decaying society? The statistics from a hospital in south Madras confirms this. During the period 1977-82 it reported threefold rise in cases of women committing suicide and two fold rise in women hanging themselves to death.

Mental violence: All these experiences revealed the true nature of the system of married and family in out society. The stereotype rules of men and women are rigidly defined. While the material gains brought by the man are for everyone to see, the inputs provided by the women being distant are often invisible. The amount of time, energy and labour spent by women in performing her duties go unnoticed. Often she has to pay in terms of sacrificing her likings, interests and skills, while the society offers man many opportunities to go out of house and share with others his joys and sorrows such opportunities are much less for a woman. This 'mental violence' agony of losing life's most precious treasures and the lack of opportunities to share it with somebody also stems out of our societal structure. In such violence, there are no visible body marks. But the wounds inflicted on the mind are difficult to heal.

The woman, right from the moment of stepping into the husband's home tries to forget her own identity and adjust everything according to the needs of the new place and the people living in it. Inspite of it, she is under a constant watch and is often criticised for anything under the sum e.g. for not bringing in enough money from her parents, for not being trained properly etc. She tends to overldook these facts because she has been 'trained' to do so.

The society, the religion, her parents and in-laws, everyone expects her to become her husband's shadow. The worst thing is that all these come as a rude shock to her after marriage, because the institution of marriage in our society is highly glamourized. Hence, for a woman 'the union of souls' turning into a nightmare is a truly horrifying and shattering experience.

The mental violence may be committed in such a subtle manner that others will never come to know of it. The woman in this case hailed from an educated, well-to-do family. She was bored of playing the role of a 'decorated doll and 'ideal housewife' and wanted to do something of her own. She had decided to take up the B.Ed. course. Nobody from the husband's family openly, opposed her proposal. But the workload within the house suddenly increased.

The number for servants was cut down. All other members became much more busy in their activities outside home and hence contributed even less to domestic work. The elder members embarked on an eight month 'Teerth-Yatra' Thus it become almost impossible for her to pursue her study. It was as if she was foolish to take such a decision.

Before the onset of women's movement, the question of domestic violence used to be pushed under the carpet. It was individualised and trivialized. Well some men do get violent. It's just the freaky nature of may be there are all psychic cases which need treatment was the reply. The character of domestic violence as a social phenomenon was first revealed and analyzed by the women's movement. It also branched further to evolve support groups to take care of individual cases of domestic violence, at the same time focussing this issue on a macro level. When a woman approaches a group like 'Women's Centre' for help she feels that she is the only victim of 'such violence. She blames her bad luck; she blames herself or other women for what she had to suffer each one thinks that of all others are leading decent lives whereas she is the only one who is suffering. The first thing we do is to make her feel that her is not an isolated case, Even in suffering, she is one of the several thousands or lakhs of women who are the target of domestic violence. We regularly organise get together of all women who approach us for help and initiate discussion on topics of everybody's concern.

We have discovered that the sharing of experiences results in a spirit of solidarity and women, no longer concerned only with their problem, reach out to help other women, This helps to explode myths which propagate and sustain domestic violence. It also provided examples of women who dared to defy society's norms and tried to lead independent lives. This gives courage to other women to fight back and solve their problems with their own initiation. A woman tortured and mistreated at the husband's home who wishes to step out of it faces several problems.

The parent's home may be far off and she may not have enough money to travel. Even after reaching there, the initial welcome may soon turn cold when the family realises that she has not come for a few days, but intends to stay on. There may be financial problems, constraint on space and privacy of family members. Above all is the fear of losing the 'Khandhan ki Izzat'. So attempts are made to convince her that her husband's home is the only paradise for her.

Denied support, both financial and emotional, what Options does such a woman have? Most women do not get access to education and hence to good living. Even these from the middle or upper classes who are privileged to receive high education abandon the studies or careers to suit their married lives. Because our society believe that marriage is the primary occupation, the only way of life for all women for all such women, it is very difficult to make a fresh beginning. Another important problem is of finding suitable shelter. This problem is more acute in cities and towns. It haunts women There are hardly any hostels and most of them do not accept women with children.

The women belonging to minority groups feel much more insecure. They are insecure when they live with the members of their own communities because they have defied the norms of conduct followed by other members of the community. On the other hand, they do not have much faith in members of other communities, specially the males. In order to tackle the Problem of women, specially those stepping Out of their homes, a conference on 'Women and Shelter' was organised in Bombay in December 1987. There are many problems which eat up the energy and drain the resources of women intending to lead dignified, independent lives.

The laws do not offer much relief because it is mostly men who make and implement laws. They often tend to Protect other man who violate Such laws. Moreover, the titled power balance in our society and the cumbersome legal procedures make justice almost impossible to achieve. Quite often women tend to give up their fight and go back to the husband's home. Such a compromise might ultimately result in murder of such a woman. It has happened with us and it is indeed a very shattering experience to see someone attached to us lying dead and when you know that you could not prevent it from happening. However, bow can one blame such women if they accept compromises? There may be too many tensions weighting on their minds. Sometimes it is the fear of losing one's children, sometimes it is the promise of material benefits and security from the husband which lures women away from their determination. In spite of heavy odds the women's movement provides the only hope against forces of violence growing in all fields of life.

The recent conference on 'Women Religion and Personal Laws' organised by 'women's Centre' shows that the women all over Asia are raising their voice against the existing laws which h are highly biased against women. They are facing a lot of opposition from the growing fundamentalist forces. It is because these forces as well as the State realise women's potential as a force against all types of violence. In some cases, the State is trying to co-operate, women's movement by showing sympathetic gestures towards it. In others there is confrontation between the State and Women's groups on many issues.

All these show that inspite of several limitations Women's movement has the ability to cross barriers of Caste. Class, community and even Nations. Sisterhood can be a bond which unites all women irrespective of their differences. We should never forget that the fight against the domestic violence is just a part of our wide battle against patriarchy. There is a link between female foeticide domestic violence, bride burning and Sati. We have to fight on all fronts, while we are engaged in providing support to needy women, we should not lose sight of the action on the macro level. There is no short cut to peace and equality. Domestic violence as a form of social problem and social issue is being increasingly discussed by social scientists, social workers and activist groups and is given attention by media. This has resulted in some legislative changes and directives have been issued to the police department regarding this issue.

In Pune city, 114 women met an accidental death (bums and poisoning) during were period of four months. Out of which 85% women were newly married and were in age group 18 to 35 years. These figures indicate only those' who could not escape death. Such kind of statistics is not merely statistics of accidents, but they are manifestations of malady in our socio-political system.

Depending on the analysis of domestic violence various voluntary organisations are evolving different programmes and Government is developing new schemes to tackle this issue. But inspite of this there seems no decrease in the incidences of Domestic violence. This paper attempts to analyse the wide spread phenomenon of domestic violence and various theorizations concerning causes of domestic violence and includes some experiences of' an activist group which is active on this issue. In last part of the paper some broad strategies have been suggested.

Domestic violence is violent victimization of women, within the boundaries of family; usually by men (or his family) to whom they are married or with whom they have marriage like relationship. Violence can be both physical and psychological. It indicates threat or aggressive behaviour towards her not only to her physical being but towards her self respect and self confidence. Psychological violence is carried out with psychological weapons (threats/insults/humiliating treatment/denial of human existence) rather than physical attack. Physical violence includes all types of aggressive physical behaviour by husband or his family towards the women's body (victim). Sexual violence could include both passive (denial) or active violence.

Patriarchy Denotes a social system characterised by mate dominance over women. In context of the family it becomes "a system originating in the household wherein the father dominates". This structure is reproduced throughout the society. It is a social structure where male dominance over female (both as an individual and as group) is seen in all spheres i of life. Patriarchal society manifests subordination of women by sexual division of labour. The patriarchy comprises of two elements ; its structure and ideology.

The structural aspect is manifested in the hierarchical organization of social institutions and social relation. It thus relegates power to certain individuals, groups or class and some form of subservience to others. The maintanance of this hierarchical structure and authority needs acceptance by many. The patriarchal ideology serves to reinforce this acceptance. It is a rationalization of the inequality and subordination, which is accepted by those who are i subordinate position. Quite often this is ligitimised through religion and formal legislations.

Family

Basic formations is based on marriage and blood relationship. Family has its own hierarchical structure, where eldest male is usually the head of the family. The relationship in the family culturely defined according to the positions in hierarchical structures (i.e. sex, age and birth order).

Constitution of India has declared equality of sex as a guiding principal but in reality the family emerges as a unit where subordination of women to men and junior to senior pervades. Family with its underlying basis of hierarchical structure and sexual division of labour is a unit where violence is used as a tool to maintain the structure of the family and to ensure the continuation of the assigned roles.

Violence inflicted on women in the internal life of the family, in so called 'privacy' of the home extends beyond it, and so it should be understood in its total context. Even in wider political context violence runs along the lines of power in class-caste-gender stratified society. The ideology of subordination is required by material structure of production also. This subordination in material sphere leads to dependency of women. This gender based disparity of our system (i.e. lower wages under reporting in labour force, discriminatory status of women in health and education) has been justified on the assumption that women's employment and existence is secondary to that of men. Practices which exclude women from inheritance of land are quite evident.

All of us know the inadequacies of inheritance law, and in most of the cases daughters waive their property - rights in favour of their brothers. An argument is often made that 'dowry' is a form of her share in the property but over that also she has no so control. Secondly, land is very rarely given as dowry. Family has recently emerged as apolitical issue in India. One side women's movement has raised the questions about, family structure and they have been questioning complex power relations in gender and violence : generation which underlies family.

On the other side government policies indicate towards planners belief that unmistakable way to improve women's status is to improve the condition of the family. It continues to be the basic unit of development. Under the pressure of women's organisations and scholars a chapter entitled' Women and Development' has been added in XIth five year plan. Thus at one side efforts are being made to involve women in developmental process but on the other side they are being thrown out from economical sphere, and violence inflicted upon them both within and outside the family seems to be increasing. This violence is seen in the form of rape, dowry deaths, domestic violence, amniocenthesis and female infanticide. The basic question asked by all women's groups and social scientists is that 'why so much of violence is perpetuated against women? Answer to this question which connates its wide spread nature has to be found in its structural nature and not individualistic explanations.

Most of the progressive thinkers and activists perceive the issue and cause in terms of unequal power relations, domestic violence as a tool used to maintain control and use of force and coarsion to maintain subordinate status. Socialisation and religious rituals play a major role in this dominative and submissive mentality. Apparently meaningless songs of 'Bhondala' also communicate the threat of violence by in- laws, an apathy of the parents.

Usually we can identify three trends in theories related to domestic violence:

— Psycho-analytical theories

— Social learning theories

— Socio-political critique

Psycho analytical theories—These focus upon stress, anxiety, anger and guilt instilled during child rearing. They frequently depict the abused women as masochistic or exhibiting 'learned helplessness'. The men who better, from this perspective, are fearful and hateful towards women because of the childrearing they have received. Men develop hypermasculanity to overcompensate for their emotional insecurities.

Social learning theories—They consider the abuse to be an out-growth of learned patterns of aggressive communication to which both husband and wife contribute, These theories consider family as "cradle of violence" where violent behaviour is inter-generational i.e. bitterer learns to be violent by watching or experiencing the violence of his parents. Similarly a battered child learns to be recipient of violence. Especially in Indian context most of the adults rule and behaviour learned where the aggressive and submissive behaviour by male and female respectively, has a social sanction.

Socio-political critique—These theories give emphasis on domestic violence as being manifestation of patriarchal and hierarchical (class+caste) social structure. It excludes women from political, business and religious leadership. Women are forced into subordinate position by two processes.

i) Discrimination that block women from being in influential position.

ii) Ideology of innate inferiority which is often enforced by religious values, and glorification of feminine virtues. The aggression and dominance as masculine virtues and sacrifice tolerance etc., as feminine virtues are emphasized right from childhood through plays, playmaterials, songs, sayings and idioms. In this process women start believing (and are forced to believe via domestic violence) that it is 'right for them to be subordinate.'

In Indian context it has another peculiar dimension. Even though wife beating is a universal phenomenon, in Indian families domestic violence is not only inflicted by husband alone but the entire husband's family participates in it. Especially the 'Mother-in law' emerges as dominating figure who inflicts violence or harasses the daughter-in-law. This also leads to most popular myth that women are women's enemies 'or' women only are responsible for the harassment which closes all the discussion of power relations. Women as agents of patriarcy are hardly vizualized. In India caste stratification and institution of family is very closely linked together. This was brought forward first in Maharashtra by Shri Ketkar and Dr. Babasaheb Ambedkar.

The ban on sexual relations was much rigidly followed in case of higher case women than higher caste men or lower caste women. Men from higher caste were allowed to have the sexual relations with of lower caste but not with the women of higher caste. At the same time the rigidity regarding sexual relations was not so much enforced as low caste women were 'to be available' for upper castes. This was basically to ensure that father of the child was from the family only. This indicates direct linkage with in heritance and property. Such prâctices along with others such as Sati and Marriage before puberty were proved to be beneficial for maintenance of 'Purity' of the caste.

All these links between patriarchy, caste and class should be more clearly seen to understand the complexity of subordination of women. Unless there is significant change in the hierarchical and dominating structure of the society and family, the extent of women' freedom from structural violence would be limited. Many social scientists and theorists are theorising on these issues such as subordination, its origin; and links between patriarchy, class and caste; but still there are lots of gaps in the academic work done.

Nari Samanta Manch is a Pune based organisation; active on the issue of domestic violence since 1983. The data base for this part of the paper is 90 cases handled by Nari Samanta. Manch during the last four years. Even though this number is very small to make generalization, especially compared to the extent of the problem, observations made cannot be totally ignored.

Significant observations

1. An exercise was done to find out the type of atrocities which women face before asking for help. This table shows the extent and nature of the domestic violence as reported by women herself.

While collecting this information, incidences of child abuse were looked for; as one explanation for the violence is given in terms of violence personality' or it being defence mechanism. Only in three cases the incidence of child abuse was reported, and that too when children interfered with 'just' act of violence against mother. In 46% of the cases in-laws (other than husband) were found to be physically aggressive towards women and in 6% cases father/brothers had beaten up woman to sen her back form 'Sasural'. Everybody in the family in-laws family assumed the right to punish If daughter-in-law deviates from her best behaviour which is being submissive, good cook, hardworking, obedient and demonstrating selflessness about her possessions.

Research was recently conducted in Pune on women who had applied for maintenance in the district court; which highlights the expectations about 'Best Behaviour' and punishment given for not being so. This requires no further comment.

For this research 6 district courts out of 11 in Pune district were selected, which have rural, slums and better residential area under their jurisdiction.

Alchoholism is a commonly state cause for violent behaviour of husband. Only 10 cases out of 90 (11.00) reported alchoholism being main cause, 3 cases (3.6%) complained about gambling while 11 women (13.4%) felt that extra-marital relations were mostly responsible factor. Another popular myth which needs to demystified is about 'Maher' (Maika). 'Maika' as concept is always glorified in terms of it being her house, where she is taken care of, which will be her support during crises, etc. But in reality workers found that parents are not always sportive or understanding as we except them to be. In 39% of the cases parents either didn't know that she was harassed or didn't take cognisance of it. In 31% of cases they supported her only for a short time but refused to support her later on (wanted her to go back to her husband) and in 31% of cases they extended her full support. Out of the 21 families which had sharable property, only 2 women got their share in ancestral property one had to fight in the court and other got it willingly from her brother. Data also shows that education or earning capacity has no direct relation with the incident of domestic violence but being trained and earning improves her chances of having different alternatives later on.

Even though higher officials of police department are supportive, the perspective or attitude of personnel atchowki/ station level hasn't changed. This results into not taking down complaint, humiliating treatment, siding with husband etc. On the other hand differential treatment given to women workers of activist group make women (victims) and their parents think that women's groups are powerful and can help them to take revenge.

One of the most frustrated experience, as expressed by workers is with the existing shelter homes, which are mainly destitute homes and are covered under various government schemes. The rigidity of rules, dependency on the government grants and lack of financial resources lead to poor management and poor living conditions. In addition to it, perspective (rather the lack of it) leads to humiliating and unsympathetic treatment towards women who have already gone through most humiliating and cruel experiences. Forced option between rescue homes (where age limitations and rigid rules exist) and working women's hostels (where employment in formal organisation is a necessity) exclude only those who are self employed, college students or those who are taking some training. Until violence continues in larger world as tool of oppression and maintenance of subordination, it would continue to be so in the family also. But certain policies and programmes will be of immense help to victims of domestic violence.

In those cases of domestic violence where proof of violence is available along with the incidence of alchoholism, wife could be given maintenance from the source itself. (This is possible only in formal sector). The understanding of the domestic violence issue should be reflected through various government policies such as housing, loan facilities, income generating schemes, jobs etc. Treating this group as a target group of economic development and welfare services can make rehabilitation an easier job.

Training programmes of police personnel should include issues like domestic violence which may help to change the perception. Change in the perception is not only required in police force but also in judicial system. Interactions with activist groups, social workers and psychiatris is may be of help to bring about desirable change.

Creche: Sufficient creche facilities are also required to increase the participation of women in employment force, as economic independence can lead to more strength and self esteem.

Strategies

Working with existing Mahila Manuals both in urban and rural areas: With the help of continuous dialogue and other programmes of these groups could be strengthened as they could provide support on the spot where it most often lacks.

Campaign against domestic violence to create more awareness and build up public opinion on this issue. Camps for young Adults (men and women) on the issue of domestic violence, man-women relationship and women's subordinate position may help to have better under- standing and sensitivity. Overall strategies could be both long term and short term; long term for addressing the entire social problems of domestic violence and short term for providing more effective help to the-victims of violence. While violence against teen-age girls and wives in the family makes headlines in the newspapers all over the world, there are very few, if any, references of violence to the females of the elder generation.

Violence to the elderly women, whether in our country or abroad, remains, nevertheless, a hard fact, which unfortunately, has eluded attention of social scientist all these days. Elderly women, after their reproductive and gainfully remunerative stage, become, to all intents and purposes, a drag on the family, forfeiting their "entitlement", whatsoever, to all that is comfy and cosy. Consequently there is dirth and paucity of studies and even information on the state of females of the elder generation. It will take time to collect indicator-based data concerning this very poignant question. The family is the basic kinship unit, in its form consisting of a husband, wife, and children. In its widest sense, it refers to all relatives living together or recognized as a social unit, including adopted persons.

The family is often called the basic social institution because of its important functions of procreation and socialization, and because it is found, in some form, in all societies. From the very definition, it appears that family is to be found, in some form or the other, in all societies, preliterate and civilized, ancient, medieval and modern. Indeed, so far human knowledge goes, this basic social institution has been with us from time immemorial. This is not to say, however, that the types and patterns have remained the same and unchanged throughout the long stretch of the march of human civilization. As such, even in the preliterate societies, a number of variations is to be found, let alone in developed and civilized societies. This has given sociologists and anthropologists some thought, for the classification and grouping of families in different societies at different stages of development.

Consequently, classifications are, really many more that we can think of, and this is based on different parameters like residence, pattern of inheritance, etc. When we have got a hang of this basic social institution, we shall have to go deep into it in the context of the present discussion. We shall deal with it both diachronically and synchronichally. The historical and developmental study of the institution of the family, again, is not uniform. While one group of social scientists will vaunt of the pristine glory of the family? Marxists take an altogether different view of the origin and development of this institution.

The marxist framework may fit-well with the subject —"Violence in Family". To Marxists, the bourgeois and the proletariat situations may be exchangeable with man and woman in family. As Engels amply put it "The husband is the bourgeois in the family, and wife, the prletariat. The relationship between man and woman is antagonistic and not non-antagonistic. Hence, as production is the outcome, violence is endemic in the institution of the family, and its nature and extent would depend upon the production relations available to the family in the wider context of a society.

The term 'Violence' has been used and also appropriated to situations from large scale annihalation of human beings in wars, in conditions of revolutions, in human interactions of various categories like violence by insurgents, violence by terrorists and also violence by robbers, bandits and dacoits. Then the term has also been used to denote situations like violation of human rights, rights of citizen, rights of individuals in groups and institutions, etc. There is, however, a fundamental difference between the corpus and the psyche-including personality-with which the human kind differs from the rest of the species, living in the planet. From time immemorial, definition and meaning of the term violence have been changing depending on the level of sensitization and socialization of the nations and societies in its two fold meanings.

The Appolonioan and Dionycian dishotomics of violent and nonviolent societies are too well known to social scientists to be discussed *de novo.* Nature has been depicted as 'red' in tooth and 'claws' where prediction is the natural rule. Earliest life close to nature transferred the biological metaphor of nature to the life in the human societies. *Homo Homini Lupus* idea might have given rise to Charles Darwins 'survival of the fittest'. An example may be had from the transference of animal norms over relationships with other lesser 'human beings'; like humans required to perform tasks which animals could do. Slavery, bonded labour etc. do reflect this paradigm. On the one hand, there was a lack of recognition of the corpus of an individual, on the other it was supposed that only the master or the slave-drover had mind/ psyche and the captive or the slave was a replica of any other member of the live-stock: There were families of the masters, families of the slaves, including men and women, obviously within the broad framework of socio-political existence.

A foster-mother's breast-feed could be bought for the master's infant at the cost of the natural feed for her own infant-in the transferred image of the bovine milkfeed for human infants. All the law givers the world over, from the earliest days of civilization, thought of the human body and its sancity. The Roman Law enunciated the provision of 'emancipatio', for providing mode of getting emancipation from the slavery after efficiently performing some specified 'tasks' enumerated legally.

The latest in the same series could be identified by laws declaring slavery and bonded labour illegal in countries at different levels of social, political and legal developments-dependent on the basic economy. Thus, there could be independent humans-so to say in slave Societies! Violence, therefore, (overt or/and covert) is both stucturally and functionally cast in societies in its different shades of acceptability. Families are not islands. Effecting and getting conditioned is the dialectics in which families could be comprehended while discussing the prevalence of violence over time and in scar with the variations so reckoned as to affect the different levels in which population tends to get divided, as also, to the depth of a 'persons' hurt, getting caused or perpetrated.

Although including male, female is a category of humanity equated with nature because of the natural, biological, procreative function. Having been afraid of the devastative potential of nature in terms of its furies in floods and fires, humans transferred the epithic to the female as well. Women were feared in early civilizations as witches, sorceresses. But, simultaneously, their image in benedictive terms as 'durga' and the 'mother-goddess' also got acceptability. The concept of female as a friend is also available, particularly from the Indian mythology in the form of 'shiva-parvati' however, the feudal concept of the female relationship with the male came to be visible in terms of 'vishnu-charan-sevila-lakshmi', the female at the level of this has been inconfirmity with human interrelationship with nature.

The processes in both these respect have started from fear to friendship and then exploitation. Both nature and female principles the world over have come into open self-assertion against this tide of waning stature and status. If fear had to be discared, which is generic to violence, exploitation/annihilation has to be totally banished test the clock should be taken back. That could be the most violent situation. One may call it ecosystem and feminist approach to human nature relationship. This is the definition of female which is being accepted for the present paper.

Female has not tobe equated with her reproductive role only. But her partnership in other productive processes has to be reckoned so that all the myths are done away with and reality is vindicated. This is wisdom derived from a diachronic understanding of the 'female'. For the synchrpnic comprehension of the question, a of the elder generation, therefore, have to be understood in the general background of the formulations about the perception of females-in general. There are two variations possible. Females of the age group starting from above 45 years could belong 10 the first category, female of an elder generation could also be a woman who got married at the age below 35 years. It between the true universally, for the basic reason of the differential concept of generation perse, 25 years to reckon a generation which has come to prevail all over is because of the model of marriages at the later age. This may be true in variation in the developed world. But the developing world has its problems regarding this concept of generation.

Population growth and sex ratio, a migration, literacy and working population are the important inicators provided, concerning females in families and situations whereby the social and working conditions can perpetrate violence against them. Since violence against females of the elder generation is not of the some variety and the same kind as that which is perpectrated to women of younger age, including teen-age girls, newly married brides, new mothers and son, the flashpoint of this chapter is that elderly women are subject to violence culminating into rejection by the family, by neighbourhood and by the society.

The term elderly differs in rural and urban perception. In the rural areas where the average age of marriage is below 18 years, elder generation may, in those cases, include a female of 36 years when she marries off her daughter, however, in urban areas above 45 years could be the age for coming to be reckoned in the elder generation. Simultaneously, physical, biological component of a female, sometimes, is also responsible for giving a particular female to belong to the elder generation on account of her self-perception and perception by other around her the menopause stage. So, these three categories of females of the elder generation, like any other set of categories, should find ramification in terms of population size, marital status, fertility, migration, literacy and as workers. Also, sociologically, they can be seen in terms of types of families they are in.

The quantum of work in terms of statistical data has to be tabulated for three categories, in six situations, each situation to be subdivided into the two types of families thc nuclear and the extended. Statistical data on categories in relation to the two types of families can only be derived from micro-studies, so as to design the matrix, accordingly. However, for the present paper, to illustrate from the macro-data. we have taken one situation in this paper. The situation of workers, we find, exciting enough for illustrating my point their other part of the work-the work they had been doing as women in the families/household. As an indicator, net years of active life for females has a high priority for planning purposes.

Also, mortality rates for females aged 50 and above

who die in inactivity has a fairly high priority inorder to plan for social security and pension schemes, but according to the expert, direct data is difficult; only estimations are possible. Even recognition of this difficulty would not do. As mentioned in the preceding paragraph women are workers in their dual role. Even if they are out of work in one role, their work at home continues and that has its impact on families and on their own personalities when attached/trempledwith/ guillotined/cut/or when it is forced on them inspite of their geriatric compassions.

The coping up mechanisms, so much talked about post-retirement adjustments, must be understood in this dual role context. The coping up mechanism for retiring from this field of work should necessarily determine their role perception by families, where this work takes place, as basic units of the societies changing very fast, and also their self- perception and evaluation.

The latter goes a long way in letting them become empowered women for the old age as also belonging to the elder generation in a changing family nexus. Perpetration of crimes is both the function of the preparation of crime is both the function of the perpetrator and the one who willily/nillyly accepts it succembs to it because of some difficulty, physical, social emotional or thought-organizational. Total population figures showth at 80 percent of the females are in the rural habitat, whereas urban habitat is occupied by only 20 percent of the females in the age groups, fifty to sixty years. Their break up in terms of main-workers, marginal workers and non-workers bring certain very important points for consideration of the systemic violence against females as reflected in the family set-up.

40-49 years age group of women has been considered separately, on purpose, as elaborated in the preceding pages. Out of 78% non-workers in the age group in India, 61% are rural based, Whereas about 18% are urban based. This is a group which requires attention of a different kind so as to minimise overt an covert violence against them. In the aggregate, 16% continue to be main workers. The break-up is 14% for the rural and only 2% for the urban areas.

The state of their well-being depends on the way they are being treated. Are they being forced to be main workers? Who is forcing them? For what rewards? What are the social security provisions governing their future when they are getting sapped of their energies.? Out of the 6% of marginal workers, almost all of them are rural-based, with very small, year from the futuristic trend-setter point of view, sizeable of 2% is in the urban areas. Future has to be guarded for them both in the interest of the future generation of city-dwellers. This is an imperative if we have any design to keep our urban population at least at the level of humanism that has been a gift to us from the past, and not become insensitive.

The type of crimes that are bring perpetrated against them could be indifferent sorts of inter-personal relationships.

— between the buyer of their services and their own selves;
— between the younger members of the families and these women; and above all,
— between their situation and the situation that is available to others in society at their age and at their level of economy.

These are some of the questions emerging. One has to be conscious of the fact that the levels of economy do get generated by skills and by opportunities made available to a group of population. That by far would be the worst crime when neither the opportunities were ever made available to them nor they could ever improve their skills and now, to top it all, family and society also ventilate themselves by different types of oppressions for them, certainly amounting to Violence, which may not be a violence against a younger group of females in similar situations. Work is a reward in itself, it could never uphold its dictum in face of deprivation of literacy and education and health services.

These twin indicators are set against almost all of them, with 75% females are literate in the rural areas, and when in some of the districts these rural women have been blessed with a literacy figure of 1% only, we can very well infer their state and plight! Hence the Structure is set against them. Maternal and child care services would have cared for them. But to what extent the injury already caused to them, in case they have been saved from maternal mortality rates, would make them or leave them capable of looking after their personal needs.

Since they have been used to being mothers to look after the needs of the members of the family, they would be left to fiend for themselves for much more extensively. In case of poor health, there would be terrible risks of violence; in case of better health, they might also add to the tensions in the families with the younger generation because without understanding the rapid change in mores and norms they may be able to adjust themselves. It is both ways necessary to look into this aspect. Planning for them at the rural level should be taken up as top-priority along with population education programme and 'for of god'—the old age-must also be added to other indicators set against early marriage and quick multiplication of offsptings. The aging population in urban areas needs attention because of the increasing trend on account of migration. It stends at 9.1% for the world, 12.4% for the more developed regions and 4.7 percent for the less developed regions. Logivity for females has also increased in our country and according to the Census of India, 1981 women can expect to live till 51 years of age.

Recent demographic analysis shows that with the progress of urbanisation and other correlated development more and more families and more older persons become committed to urban places of residence. It is, therefore, likely that the urban population may become more aged and more feminine. Trends from developed world show that very often the younger, more capable, emigrate from slums when they have an opportunity, leaving the aging in the decaying areas. This is a heinous violence. Studies also indicate that in the developing countries, the age "pyramids in squatter settlements and slums resemble those of the country as a whole.

However, the number of the aging appear to be increasing as urban growth and growth of slums and squatter the aging in accelerage. The social integration and participation urban areas and slums, their economic and social needs require appraisal, policies and programmes." Rejection by the son, the natural career of the old-mother, as highlighted by Kerala study, is no more there and that has been the worst of the violence against these. Just a theoretical exposition of asocial issue is, to my considered opinion, not enough. One should think in terms of some measures of alleviation of the misery and plight that go along with the elderly women both in rural and urban areas in our country.

The plight of the elderly women in the tribal areas is, again a multidimensional one, different from those in rural and urban areas. As has been observed there are indicators and there and there are variables too; but there have to be carved out many more of them and put to bench-mark surveys before we can reach scientific data for macro- mark surveys before we can reach scientific data for macro-planning, macro-intervention and macro all-eviation.

However, even before getting into the macro aspects, it would be necessary to have quick micro-studies conducted, just as has come out from kerala and has been reported, both for understanding the depth of causes and the remedical measures to control violence against this generation. Till then, hypothesis building can be resorted to from the oberservation of perceptive sociologists and family-life-counsellors. Unfortunately, the family court movement in India has not stretched its helping hand towards the elderly women in the family.

The family courts could also be something about them. As in socialist countries and industrially developed capitalist countries of the west, social security measures could be extended to the elderly women in our country as well. To understand the nature of the social grouping as well as the quality of interrelationship that exists among the members, it is essential to understand their demographic background. Young children are expected to behave differently as compared with adult population.

Similarly, age at marriage determines fertility span. Marital status is also linked with differential role performance and evaluation. Additionally, the presence or absence of children in the family gives rise to different types of role responsibilities to which the couples have to make adjustments. To find out the correlates of wife abuse, the demographic variables which have been considered for the present study are: Age at marriage; present age; number of children; sex of the children household composition. Age at marriage does not differentiate battered from non-battered wives yet younger age at marriage puts a lot of stress for adjustment which may be exhibited in violent behaviour pattern on the part of young batterers. It can thus be assumed that women who are married at a younger age are at higher risk of physical violence.

The women who got married at younger age were more victims of physical violence by their husbands in contrast to those who got married at later age. Further, it was noted that there was a progressive decrease in the percentages of victims of physical violence from lower age at marriage category to higher age group. Out of 60 respondents who got married below the age of 18 years, 45 per cent were the victims. In contrast to this who were married after the age of 21 years, only 24.71 per cent were the victims of physical violence. It is also interesting to note that median age at marriage of victims of physical violence was lower than those of non-victims. It can, thus, be concluded that those women who married at lower age were at high risk of physical violence in comparison with those who got married at later age in the Indian society although the age at marriage is increasing yet in the rural areas it still remains quite low that is, 17.81 years. Therefore, class and situational factors may play an important role in determining the age at marriage which in turn may be associated with violence because young couples are under lot of stress to adjust to new role responsibilities.

A few studies indicate that wives of younger age group are at higher risk of abuse as compared with those of older age group because older women are not prone to file assault charges either because of traditional attitudes or because of the possibility of divorce. The results of National Family Violence Survey conducted in America indicate that all forms of marital violence occur most frequently among those under 30 years of age. The rate of marital violence among those under 30 years of age was found to be more than double the rate for the age for 31 to 50 years. The data for the present study were tabulated to find out association between the age of the wife and her being victim of physical violence.

The respondents were distributed into four age categories. There was a progressive decrease in the percentages of victims of physical violence from lower age category to higher age category. Among the victims of physical violence 45.45 per cent were below the age of 30 years. In contrast to this those who were in the age group of 50 years above, only 18.18 per cent were the victims. Similarly, if the median age of the victims of physical violence is compared with non-victims, it was noticed that median age of victims was 35 years in contrast to 39.24 years median age of the non-victims. In short, an inverse relationship was found between the age of wives and their physical abuse.

In other words, physical violence against wives of younger age group was more frequent as against those of higher age groups. The data of the present study support the findings of studies cited above. Wife abuse can occur at any age but the data on age indicate that wives of younger age are at higher risk of being abused. It may be due to the fact that younger couples are still learning to make adjustment with each other and addition of children in the family puts enormous demands and stresses on the younger people. Presence or absence of children in the family is likely to affect the quality of relationship between husband and wife. Further, presence of more children in the family would create problem of management and proper training of the younger ones.

Researches on the impact of children on marriages consistently show that the level of marital satisfaction and marital adjustment goes down after the birth of the first child. An additional child would imply a decrease in time for parents to pursue, their own interests. Further, each additional child increases the work load and conflicts. In the traditional societies like India, child care still remains under the domain of mothers and for any deviance on the part of child it is the mother who is blamed. Further, more children put a lot of stress on the limited resources of the family.

Among the victims of physical violence it was found that the rate of violence against mothers who had five or more children or no child was more than double the rate for those who had one or two children. Keeping in view the number of children it was noted that there was a progressive increase in the percentages of victims of physical violence from one to two children category to women having five or more children or with no child. In short, it can be concluded that a large number of children in the family become a source of conflict resulting into violence against wife or mother.

The highest percentages of physical violence was found in those house- holds which had no child. It may be attributed to their younger age as well as wives' inability to have children because children are valued in the Indian society and those women who are unable to bear a child are ridiculed. In the patriarchal society like India, greater importance is given to the male child. The female child is not only considered a liability because of associated dowry problems but mothers who give birth to female children only do not get much respect in the family as compared with those who give birth to male children lately with the help of amniocentesis the couples would like to know the sex of the child. In case the foetus is of the female sex, they go for abortion.

The victims of physical violence were almost equally divided in the categories of those who had only male or female children of both the sexes. In the present study sex of the children in the family was not found to be associated with wife abuse. Wives living in extended and joint households are required to make adjustments with a large number of kin in contrast to those who are living in nuclear households. Further, patrilocal residence and patriarchal structure of the family places women into subservient position.

The men are more likely to act as sons rather than husbands. The parents-in- law and other kinsmen continue to have greater affiliation with the sons as compared with daughters-in-law. A number of cases have been reported where because of backbiting, the husbands have maltreated their wives. Hence presence of a large number of members in the family not only creates the problem of adjustment but they also act as instigators for wife abuse. Although there was no marked difference in the percentage of victims living in nuclear and extended households, yet among the victims a relatively higher percentage (36.67) were found to be living in joint and extended households in contrast to those living in nuclear households (32.94).

Social behaviour is a function of the life situations which may be physical, economic, social or cultural or an interplay of these elements. It is assumed that persons having differential life situations would react differently to the same stimuli. It is, therefore, essential to explicate the role of these social variables for understanding the quality of conjugal relationship.

The social variables considered for the present study are educational and occupational status of the respondents, their social class background, their caste and religious background, their attitudes regarding traditional gender roles in the family and their value orientation in favour of use of violence for the resolution of conflict. Formal education helps an individual to know what is happening outside one's immediate surroundings. It also facilitates him to develop rational outlook towards life.

Education widens the horizon and makes the individual more knowledgeable. Education also helps an individual to get jobs of high prestige and with high economic returns. Further, higher education enhances one's social prestige. Efforts have been made to find out association between the level of education one has and the quality of interpersonal relations. A few studies indicate that the less education a person has, the more likely he or she is to approve of and support violence. Some other studies, however, contradict their findings and on the other hand, they are of opinion that couples with the lowest educational levels are less prone to violence than those who had attained higher education. It is argued that low education level does not cause violence but it aggravates the frustration.

The reason for more violence among those who have higher education, may be that women with high education may not endorse the traditional role relationship and this may be considered as threat to the dominant position by their husbands. However, education can provide people with alternatives for resolving family disagreements. It is, therefore, expected that with the help of education individual learns different mechanisms to resolve the conflict in the conjugal relationships. The educational background of the victim wives indicates that those who have low educational attainment or higher educational attainment had over representation as compared with those who had moderate level of education. There is a progressive decrease in the percentage of the victims from illiterate educational category up to graduation with the exception of those who had higher education. This curvilinear distribution of victims of violence indicates that women who have no education or have higher educational attainment are more prone to physical violence by their husbands.

The women with low education designate their complete dependency because with low educational background they will not be able to have economic independence or would be engaged in occupations with low economic returns and low prestige. In the case of those who have higher education they may be in better position to gain economic independence and with the higher education they may start questioning the dominant position of their husbands. Such a threat is not tolerated by the husbands and they use physical violence as their ultimate resource to maintain their dominant position in the family.

Occupation is an important indicator of a person's position in society. It is believed that the higher the education one has, the higher the occupation one holds and the higher the prestige he gets in society. Conversely, the lower the occupation, the lower will be the economic returns and as a consequence thereof, there are likely to be higher frustrations and greater marital conflicts. Many studies indicate that persons engaged in occupations of lower prestige are more likely to resort to physical violence against their wives to give vent to their economic stresses. It is also argued that women who stay at home and are not engaged in paid work outside their homes are at somewhat greater risk of being physically abused than those engaged in paid work. This is probably because housewives are perceived to contribute less to family subsistence and are consequently valued less than women who are engaged in paid work outside the home.

Wife beating is far less common in societies in which

women have independent economic and social resources, perhaps because these resources are valuable enough to make a husband think twice before acting in ways that might force his wife to terminate the marriage. In the sample there are only 65 women respondents who were found to be engaged in paid work. Out of these 47.69 per cent were victims of physical violence of their husbands. On the other hand, out of those not engaged in paid work outside their homes, only 26.67 per cent were physically abused by their husbands. The results of the present study support the findings of Homung *et al.* who, in one representative sample, found housewives had a lower risk of violence than working wives.

The reason housewives are abused less than working wives is because keeping in view their economic dependency they may have "Learned helplessness" with the result they have developed tolerance of such violence and do not share with outsiders that they are being abused or they would endorse the traditional gender roles and would not question the authority of their husbands. Hence, they do not provoke their husbands to use physical violence to maintain their dominant position in the conjugal relationship.

On the other hand, the working wives may not accept the dominant position of the husband in family decision making and raise questions about asymmetrical conjugal relations. Such a situation may prompt the husband to use physical force to retain his dominant position. The general contention that working gives economic Independence to women, hence, they would be relatively free dependence to be correct in the present from abuse is also not found to study on the other hand, it is the working women who are than the non-working women. The association abused more, status and her physical abuse will between wives' working which these become more clear if the type of occupation in which women are engaged in, is taken into consideration. As the number of respondents under the working category were limited to 65 cases only, their occupations were grouped under three categories, i.e., occupations with low prestige, medium prestige and high prestige.

The data reveal that the percentage of the victims goes on decreasing from low occupational prestige category to higher prestige category. In short, there was inverse relationship between occupational prestige and physical violence, i.e., the lower the prestige of paid work, the greater was the violence against wives. The results indicate that it is not the working status per se which provides women freedom from physical violence of their husbands but it is the nature of the occupation and associated prestige and economic returns which facilitate women to be free from physical abuse.

One salient feature of different definitions is that members of a class group have common style of living and value orientation. Similarly, a number of scholars have tried to find out association between class background and family violence. One set of studies maintains a positive association between lower class and wife battering. Whereas some researchers do not endorse their findings and they have contended that wife battering transgresses the boundaries of class. An attempt has been made to find out association between class background and wife beating.

The class background of the respondents has been worked out based on education, occupation and income of the husbands of the respondents because a majority of the women respondents were not found to be working and hence, had no independent income of their own. While selecting the sample their living arrangement was taken into consideration and 50 cases from each house type were included in the sample, which were redistributed into different social classes.

The class background of the respondent was also divided into lower, working, middle and high for the purpose of finding out differential behaviour pattern, i.e., wife abuse in different classes. The data indicate that in contrast to 19.23 per cent victims of physical violence in the upper class, there were 51.85 per cent victims in the lower class. There is a progressive decrease in the percentages of victims of physical violence from the lower through the middle to the upper class. Similarly, among the non-victims the higher per cent (80.77) belong to the upper class. In short, women belonging to the lower class were at a higher risk of being physically abused by their husbands.

The results of the study indicate inverse relationship between class background and wife battering. These findings support the contention of those researchers who found that women belonging to the lower class were at a higher risk of physical violence which was attributed to their way of life. The use and approval of physical violence in the lower class has been attributed to what Lewis calls, the culture of poverty.

The concept implies that the poor people have a distinct subculture. Due to common experiences they have developed certain attitudes and behaviour pattern which have been transmitted from parents to children. These include the casual resort to physical violence, an inability to plan for the future, seeking of immediate gratification, weak impulse control and fatalistic attitude towards the future. Davis while describing the class linked, violence contends that physical violence in the lower class families is normal, socially approved and socially, in-culcated type of behaviour.

Similarly, Whitehurst while making a distinction between the middle and the lower class families with regard to control over violence, maintained that violence-responses were much more built into lower class subculture as a means to achieve some goals to assert independence and masculinity. The members of the lower class are subject to a lot of economic pressures and strains and they cannot show their resentment and frustration, against those who are highly placed and hence they give vent to their frustrations at the slightest provocation by beating their wives on whom they can exert their power.

On the other hand, members of the middle and upper classes have more resources and can keep their violence private and additionally, because of the sensitivity of the issue and embarrassment, the victims are not likely to admit its existence in their conjugal relationship. Individual's social status is determined by his ascriptive and acquired attributes. In the Indian society ascriptive attributes, like caste, determine not only his social milieu as castes are hierarchically placed but also his opportunities to acquire new attributes.

Although an individual is now theoretically permitted to achieve any position and support any ideology yet caste plays an important role in influencing his behaviour pattern. Keeping in view the importance of caste in the Indian society, it will be worthwhile to find out an association between caste and wife battering. The distribution of the victims of physical violence according to their caste background indicates that respondents belonging to the lower castes group and those who have not specified their caste were more victims in contrast to the respondents belonging to the higher castes.

Among the twice-born, the respondents belonging to trading castes were at a higher risk in contrast to Khatris and Aroras. Similarly, among the non-victims the higher percentages of respondents were found among the twice-born. The higher frequency of physical violence present among the members of the lower castes may be attributed to their lower class background. Similarly, among those cases who have not specified their caste, most of them belonged to Muslim and Christian religion and these respondents were having lower socio-economic status.

The association between caste background and physical violence would remain incomplete unless their economic status is also considered. Preceding analysis has indicated that members belonging to the lower class were more likely to resort to physical violence for the resolution of conjugal conflicts. Religion is an important institution which instills a particular philosophy of life in an individual. His outlook towards himself and others as well as his behaviour pattern are likely to be influenced by his religious belief system.

The results of the present study do not establish any association between religion and wife battering. The family as a social institution lays down norms and values to regulate the behaviour of the members of the social group. Family as a social group is structured in such a manner that one member, usually the husband, assumes the dominant position and the other members take up subordinate positions. In the patriarchal traditional societies, like India, sex role expectations favour male dominance in the family. Traditional ideology promotes and serves to justify male dominance as well as helps in cultivating a belief system among the husbands and wives as to how they should behave in the marital relationship. Motivated by traditional ideology, division of labour in the family was worked out into a male provider and a female to focus more narrowly on the domestic realm. Such a task specialization and differential evaluation helped men not only to have greater control over economic resources but also a greater access to power in the family.

The power structure in the family is maintained through the actions of the members involved in the relationships. Those at the top of the power structure behave in dominant ways and they do not hesitate to use coercive methods to retain their dominant position. Attempts have been made to find out association between traditionality and wife abuse.

A number of studies have concluded that men who were more traditional in their attitudes towards women were more likely to become wife abusers. Some importance is also given to sex role orientation of the victims. Walker is of opinion that non-traditional wives if paired with traditional husbands are at higher risk of being abused. An attempt has been made in the present study to find out correlation between wives' traditional orientation and their being victims of abuse. Traditional sex role orientation of the respondents was worked out based on the responses to eight statements.

The level of traditionality was further divided into three: High, Medium and Low, to find out association between level of traditionality and wife battering. It is assumed that respondents who have low level of traditional role orientation are at higher risk of physical violence than those at high level of traditionality because wives with low level of traditional orientation are more likely to question asymmetrical power relations in the family.

Data on traditionality and wife abuse reveal that there is a progressive decrease in the percentage of victims from low level of traditionality to high level of traditionality. In contrast to 22.86 per cent of the wives showing high level of traditional sex role orientation, 40.32 per cent wives indicating low level of traditionality were the victims of physical violence by their husbands. Similarly, among the non-victims, their percentages go on increasing from low level of traditionality to high level of traditionality. In short, it can be concluded that wives with non-traditional sex role orientation are at higher risk of being physically abused.

The reason for wives showing less traditional sex role orientation being victims of physical violence may be attributed to their attempt in questioning the traditional power structure in the family. The husbands in such situation are likely to use physical force as the last resort to maintain their dominant position. The norms and values relating to intra-family violence indicate cultural contradiction. On the one hand, there is a myth of family non-violence which reflects cultural norms for the family as a group characterised by love and harmony.

The legitimation of violence in the family is explicit and mandatory—as in the case of rights and obligations of the parent to use a necessary and appropriate level of physical force to adequately train and control a child. Violent wives as well as violent husbands express more approval of violence than do non-violent husbands and wives. Levinson in his cross cultural study on family violence came to the conclusion that wife beating was more common and frequent in societies in which adults solved conflicts by resorting to physical violence, indicating attitude in favour of violence. The cultural norms and values permitting and sometimes encouraging husband to beat wife actually reflect hierarchical and male dominant type of society like India.

The right to use force exists, to provide the ultimate support for the existing power structure of the family in which the wife assumes a subordinate position. Respondents' values in favour or against use of violence in the family were obtained from their reactions to 12 statements. Their scores were divided into three categories depicting low, medium and high scores. This exercise was done with an assumption that the respondents with high score on values in favour of violence in the family would be at a higher risk of being victims than those with low score. The data did not depict any clear-cut association.

On the other hand, it was noted that those respondents who had medium score on values favouring use of violence to resolve family conflict were more victims in contrast to those who had high or low score. The reason for lack of association may be attributed to the fact that there is a lot of gap between values and actual behaviour pattern. Secondly, the values were taken of the wives rather than the husbands who were the perpetrators of physical violence against their wives.

The respondents might be holding values against the use of violence but had no control over the values and behaviour pattern of their husbands. The above discussion on social variables highlights certain salient features which contribute to husbands' physical violence against wives. Lower caste background, low and high educational attainment, lower working status, lower social class background and low level of traditionality were found to be contributing factors for husbands' physical violence against wives. However, no association was found between religious background and value system of the respondents and their being victims and non-victims of physical violence. Dependency is a state, both physical and mental, depicting assistance from a person or persons for continuing living in the community. The human child has to depend upon his parents for his growth, development and social recognition.

The Indian society has placed women in a state of dependency as a daughter on her father, as a sister on her brother, as a wife on her husband and lastly as a mother on her son. Further, sexual division of labour and gender roles accentuate these differences. Additionally, patriarchal social norms not only grant control of family resources and property to men but also provide dominant position to them. To maintain their dominant position, the husbands are likely to use coercive methods including physical violence against their wives.

Dependency is also treated as a cause of physical violence in the conjugal relationships. Researches have utilized this explanation in two ways. In case, a wife is completely dependent, both physically and socially, her husband exploits her dependency and uses violence at whim to reinforce his dominant position in the conjugal relationship. A few scholars are also of opinion that when a husband is dependent upon his wife he resorts to physical violence as a last resort against his wife as he is afraid of losing his spouse or a person on whom he can exert his dominant position.

Hence, dependency of husband over his wife is also treated as a cause of wife abuse. As the present study is limited to wife abuse, the analysis is limited to wife's perception regarding the conditions which make her dependent upon her husband and how this state of dependency results into her being abused. To find out association between wife's dependency and her abuse, dependency has been divided into objective and subjective. It does not, however, mean that we can draw watertight compartments between the two.

In certain cases objective dependency may lead to subjective dependency, whereas in other cases even though there is no objective dependency yet the individual remains subjectively dependent upon her spouse. It can, however, be assumed that a wife who experiences both objective and subjective dependency is at higher risk of being abused in contrast to those who have only objective or only subjective dependency. For the purpose of analysis wife's objective dependency stands for conditions like not working, i.e., being economically dependent upon husband; not having any property in her name; not receiving any financial assistance from her family of orientation; inability to live alone; inability to do shopping alone, and inability to go outside the city alone. Further, level of objective dependency may vary from case to case hence, objective dependency was further divided into three levels: low, medium and high.

The wives who are objectively dependent upon their husbands are at higher risk of being abused because it would be difficult for these women to come out of the abusive relationship as they do not have the resources to live alone. Their objective dependency is also known to their spouses who may fully exploit the situation knowing fully well that their wives would not be able to leave them. It is further envisaged that wives who have high level of objective dependency are at greater risk of being abused. Wives with high level of objective dependency are physically abused more in contrast to those who have low level of objective dependency. This is evident in the percentages of the victims at different levels of dependency. Similarly, the percentage of non-victims goes on decreasing to high level. There were 33 respondents who had high level of objective dependency, out of which 60.61 per cent were not the victims of physical violence. The results of the study support the contention of a few scholars who are of opinion that high level of women's marital dependency is not associated with wife abuse because husbands of dependent wives can maintain their dominant positions without resorting to violence as their wives are in no position to question their dominance.

Although no cause and effect relationship can be established between dependency and wife abuse yet the data show an indicative trend that wives who have high level of objective dependency are abused more as compared to those who have low level of objective dependency. A few scholars contend that objective dependency of the wife per se does not result into her abuse but is mediated by her tolerance. One may, however, raise the question why she develops this tolerance to abuse? One reason may be that she remains subjectively dependent upon her husband because her social reality has not been constructed outside the marital relationship. In Indian society marriage is a must for every woman, unless she adopts a life of celibacy. Remaining unmarried or living a life of a divorcee is looked down upon.

Hence, whether a wife is objectively dependent upon her husband or not she remains subjectively dependent. It is not, however, true in the case of husbands. Remarriage after divorce or separation is easily available to a man than a woman. Such a discriminatory practice perpetuate subjective dependency in the wives. Subjective dependency in the present study stands for, not leaving the husband even under adverse circumstances; divorce not considered good; perception that married women even if abused enjoy higher status than divorced; lack of support from kin; greater commitment and more devotion to marital relationship. It is also expected that wives are likely to have different levels of subjective dependency.

Physical violence

Marital status is also linked with differential role performance and evaluation. Additionally, the presence or absence of children in the family gives rise to different types of role responsibilities to which the couples have to make adjustments. To find out the correlates of wife abuse, the demographic variables which have been considered for the present study are: Age at marriage; present age; number of children; sex of the children household composition. Age at marriage does not differentiate battered from non-battered wives yet younger age at marriage puts a lot of stress for adjustment which may be exhibited in violent behaviour pattern on the part of young batterers. It can thus be assumed that women who are married at a younger age are at higher risk of physical violence.

The women who got married at younger age were more victims of physical violence by their husbands in contrast to those who got married at later age. Further, it was noted that there was a progressive decrease in the percentages of victims of physical violence from lower age at marriage category to higher age group. Out of 60 respondents who got married below the age of 18 years, 45 per cent were the victims. In contrast to this who were married after the age of 21 years, only 24.71 per cent were the victims of physical violence. It is also interesting to note that median age at marriage of victims of physical violence was lower than those of non-victims. It can, thus, be concluded that those women who married at lower age were at high risk of physical violence in comparison with those who got married at later age in the Indian society although the age at marriage is increasing yet in the rural areas it still remains quite low that is, 17.81 years.

Therefore, class and situational factors may play an important role in determining the age at marriage which in turn may be associated with violence because young couples are under lot of stress to adjust to new role responsibilities. A few studies indicate that wives of younger age group are at higher risk of abuse as compared with those of older age group because older women are not prone to file assault charges either because of traditional attitudes or because of the possibility of divorce.

The results of National Family Violence Survey conducted in America indicate that all forms of marital violence occur most frequently among those under 30 years of age. The rate of marital violence among those under 30 years of age was found to be more than double the rate for the age for 31 to 50 years. The data for the present study were tabulated to find out association between the age of the wife and her being victim of physical violence.

The respondents were distributed into four age categories. There was a progressive decrease in the percentages of victims of physical violence from lower age category to higher age category. Among the victims of physical violence 45.45 per cent were below the age of 30 years. In contrast to this those who were in the age group of 50 years above, only 18.18 per cent were the victims. Similarly, if the median age of the victims of physical violence is compared with non-victims, it was noticed that median age of victims was 35 years in contrast to 39.24 years median age of the non-victims. In short, an inverse relationship was found between the age of wives and their physical abuse.

In other words, physical violence against wives of younger age group was more frequent as against those of higher age groups. The data of the present study support the findings of studies cited above. Wife abuse can occur at any age but the data on age indicate that wives of younger age are at higher risk of being abused. It may be due to the fact that younger couples are still learning to make adjustment with each other and addition of children in the family puts enormous demands and stresses on the younger people. Presence or absence of children in the family is likely to affect the quality of relationship between husband and wife. Further, presence of more children in the family would create problem of management and proper training of the younger ones.

Researches on the impact of children on marriages consistently show that the level of marital satisfaction and marital adjustment goes down after the birth of the first child. An additional child would imply a decrease in time for parents to pursue, their own interests. Further, each additional child increases the work load and conflicts. In the traditional societies like India, child care still remains under the domain of mothers and for any deviance on the part of child it is the mother who is blamed. Further, more children put a lot of stress on the limited resources of the family. Among the victims of physical violence it was found that the rate of violence against mothers who had five or more children or no child was more than double the rate for those who had one or two children. Keeping in view the number of children it was noted that there was a progressive increase in the percentages of victims of physical violence from one to two children category to women having five or more children or with no child. In short, it can be concluded that a large number of children in the family become a source of conflict resulting into violence against wife or mother.

The highest percentages of physical violence was found in those house-holds which had no child. It may be attributed to their younger age as well as wives' inability to have children because children are valued in the Indian society and those women who are unable to bear a child are ridiculed. In the patriarchal society like India, greater importance is given to the male child. The female child is not only considered a liability because of associated dowry problems but mothers who give birth to female children only do not get much respect in the family as compared with those who give birth to male children lately with the help of amniocentesis the couples would like to know the sex of the child. In case the foetus is of the female sex, they go for abortion. A study of 8000 cases of abortion showed that 7999 of them involved a female foetus.

The high female foeticide reinforces the sex preferences prevalent in our society. The victims of physical violence were almost equally divided in the categories of those who had only male or female children of both the sexes. In the present study sex of the children in the family was not found to be associated with wife abuse. Wives living in extended and joint households are required to make adjustments with a large number of kin in contrast to those who are living in nuclear households. Further, patrilocal residence and patriarchal structure of the family places women into subservient position. The men are more likely to act as sons rather than husbands. The parents-in- law and other kinsmen continue to have greater affiliation with the sons as compared with daughters-in-law.

A number of cases have been reported where because of backbiting, the husbands have maltreated their wives. Hence presence of a large number of members in the family not only creates the problem of adjustment but they also act as instigators for wife abuse. Although there was no marked difference in the percentage of victims living in nuclear and extended households, yet among the victims a relatively higher percentage (36.67) were found to be living in joint and extended households in contrast to those living in nuclear households (32.94).

Similarly, among the non-victims no marked difference Was found with regard to their pattern of living arrangement. Hence, the composition of household was not found to be associated with wife abuse. From the foregoing discussion on the demographic correlates of wife abuse, it was found that the younger age at marriage, young wives and those having no child or a large number of children were at higher risk of being victims of physical violence.

However, no association was found between the sex of the children as well as living arrangement and wife abuse. Based on the results of this exploratory research the following hypotheses can be formulated for verification in future researches.

1. The younger the age at marriage of the women, the greater is the possibility of their being battered.
2. The younger the age of wife, the greater are the chances of her being victim of physical violence.
3. The greater the number of children, a woman has the greater is the possibility of her being victim of physical violence of her husband.
4. The absence of child is likely to result in wife battering.

An individual's social milieu not only influences his social position, network of relationships and contents of learning but also his social behaviour pattern. Social behaviour is a function of the life situations which may be physical, economic, social or cultural or an interplay of these elements. It is assumed that persons having differential life situations would react differently to the same stimuli. It is, therefore, essential to explicate the role of these social variables for understanding the quality of conjugal relationship.

The social variables considered for the present study are educational and occupational status of the respondents, their social class background, their caste and religious background, their attitudes regarding traditional gender roles in the family and their value orientation in favour of use of violence for the resolution of conflict. Formal education helps an individual to know what is happening outside one's immediate surroundings. It also facilitates him to develop rational outlook towards life. Education widens the horizon and makes the individual more knowledgeable.

Education also helps an individual to get jobs of high prestige and with high economic returns. Further, higher education enhances one's social prestige. Efforts have been made to find out association between the level of education one has and the quality of interpersonal relations.

A few studies indicate that the less education a person has, the more likely he or she is to approve of and support violence. Some other studies, however, contradict their findings and on the other hand, they are of opinion that couples with the lowest educational levels are less prone to violence than those who had attained higher education. It is argued that low education level does not cause violence but it aggravates the frustration.

The reason for more violence among those who have higher education, may be that women with high education may not endorse the traditional role relationship and this may be considered as threat to the dominant position by their husbands. However, education can provide people with alternatives for resolving family disagreements. It is, therefore, expected that with the help of education individual learns different mechanisms to resolve the conflict in the conjugal relationships.

The educational background of the victim wives indicates that those who have low educational attainment or higher educational attainment had over representation as compared with those who had moderate level of education. There is a progressive decrease in the percentage of the victims from illiterate educational category up to graduation with the exception of those who had higher education. This curvilinear distribution of victims of violence indicates that women who have no education or have higher educational attainment are more prone to physical violence by their husbands.

The women with low education designate their complete dependency because with low educational background they will not be able to have economic independence or would be engaged in occupations with low economic returns and low prestige. In the case of those who have higher education they may be in better position to gain economic independence and with the higher education they may start questioning the dominant position of their husbands. Such a threat is not tolerated by the husbands and they use physical violence as their ultimate resource to maintain their dominant position in the family. Occupation is an important indicator of a person's position in society. It is believed that the higher the education one has, the higher the occupation one holds and the higher the prestige he gets in society. Conversely, the lower the occupation, the lower will be the economic returns and as a consequence thereof, there are likely to be higher frustrations and greater marital conflicts.

Many studies indicate that persons engaged in occupations of lower prestige are more likely to resort to physical violence against their wives to give vent to their economic stresses. It is also argued that women who stay at home and are not engaged in paid work outside their homes are at somewhat greater risk of being physically abused than those engaged in paid work. This is probably because housewives are perceived to contribute less to family subsistence and are consequently valued less than women who are engaged in paid work outside the home.

Wife beating is far less common in societies in which women have independent economic and social resources, perhaps because these resources are valuable enough to make a husband think twice before acting in ways that might force his wife to terminate the marriage. In the sample there are only 65 women respondents who were found to be engaged in paid work. Out of these 47.69 per cent were victims of physical violence of their husbands. On the other hand, out of those not engaged in paid work outside their homes, only 26.67 per cent were physically abused by their husbands.

The results of the present study support the findings of Homung *et al.* who, in one representative sample, found housewives had a lower risk of violence than working wives. The reason housewives are abused less than working wives is because keeping in view their economic dependency they may have "Learned helplessness" with the result they have developed tolerance of such violence and do not share with outsiders that they are being abused or they would endorse the traditional gender roles and would not question the authority of their husbands. Hence, they do not provoke their husbands to use physical violence to maintain their dominant position in the conjugal relationship.

On the other hand, the working wives may not accept the dominant position of the husband in family decision making and raise questions about asymmetrical conjugal relations. Such a situation may prompt the husband to use physical force to retain his dominant position. The general contention that working gives economic Independence to women, hence, they would be relatively free dependence to be correct in the present from abuse is also not found to study on the other hand, it is the working women who are than the non-working women.

The association abused more, status and her physical abuse will between wives' working which these become more clear if the type of occupation in which women are engaged in, is taken into consideration. As the number of respondents under the working category were limited to 65 cases only, their occupations were grouped under three categories, i.e., occupations with low prestige, medium prestige and high prestige.

The data reveal that the percentage of the victims goes on decreasing from low occupational prestige category to higher prestige category. In short, there was inverse relationship between occupational prestige and physical violence, i.e., the lower the prestige of paid work, the greater was the violence against wives. The results indicate that it is not the working status per se which provides women freedom from physical violence of their husbands but it is the nature of the occupation and associated prestige and economic returns which facilitate women to be free from physical abuse.

Social class

One salient feature of different definitions is that members of a class group have common style of living and value orientation. Wolfgang and Ferracuti in their study of subculture of violence have even divided a class into subclasses depending upon value orientation of the members. Similarly, a number of scholars have tried to find out association between class background and family violence.

One set of studies maintains a positive association between lower class and wife battering. Whereas some researchers do not endorse their findings and they have contended that wife battering transgresses the boundaries of class. An attempt has been made to find out association between class background and wife beating. The class background of the respondents has been worked out based on education, occupation and income of the husbands of the respondents because a majority of the women respondents were not found to be working and hence, had no independent income of their own. While selecting the sample their living arrangement was taken into consideration and 50 cases from each house type were included in the sample, which were redistributed into different social classes.

The class background of the respondent was also divided into lower, working, middle and high for the purpose of finding out differential behaviour pattern, i.e., wife abuse in different classes. The data indicate that in contrast to 19.23 per cent victims of physical violence in the upper class, there were 51.85 per cent victims in the lower class. There is a progressive decrease in the percentages of victims of physical violence from the lower through the middle to the upper class. Similarly, among the non-victims the higher per cent (80.77) belong to the upper class. In short, women belonging to the lower class were at a higher risk of being physically abused by their husbands.

The results of the study indicate inverse relationship between class background and wife battering. These findings support the contention of those researchers who found that women belonging to the lower class were at a higher risk of physical violence which was attributed to their way of life. The use and approval of physical violence in the lower class has been attributed to what Lewis calls, the culture of poverty. The concept implies that the poor people have a distinct subculture. Due to common experiences they have developed certain attitudes and behaviour pattern which have been transmitted from parents to children. These include the casual resort to physical violence, an inability to plan for the future, seeking of immediate gratification, weak impulse control and fatalistic attitude towards the future.

Davis while describing the class linked, violence contends that physical violence in the lower class families is normal, socially approved and socially, in-culcated type of behaviour. Similarly, Whitehurst while making a distinction between the middle and the lower class families with regard to control over violence, maintained that violence-responses were much more built into lower class subculture as a means to achieve some goals to assert independence and masculinity. The members of the lower class are subject to a lot of economic pressures and strains and they cannot show their resentment and frustration, against those who are highly placed and hence they give vent to their frustrations at the slightest provocation by beating their wives on whom they can exert their power.

On the other hand, members of the middle and upper classes have more resources and can keep their violence private and additionally, because of the sensitivity of the issue and embarrassment, the victims are not likely to admit its existence in their conjugal relationship. Individual's social status is determined by his ascriptive and acquired attributes. In the Indian society ascriptive attributes, like caste, determine not only his social milieu as castes are hierarchically placed but also his opportunities to acquire new attributes.

Although an individual is now theoretically permitted to achieve any position and support any ideology yet caste plays an important role in influencing his behaviour pattern. Keeping in view the importance of caste in the Indian society, it will be worthwhile to find out an association between caste and wife battering. The distribution of the victims of physical violence according to their caste background indicates that respondents belonging to the lower castes group and those who have not specified their caste were more victims in contrast to the respondents belonging to the higher castes. Among the twice-born, the respondents belonging to trading castes were at a higher risk in contrast to Khatris and Aroras. Similarly, among the non-victims the higher percentages of respondents were found among the twice-born.

The higher frequency of physical violence present among the members of the lower castes may be attributed to their lower class background. Similarly, among those cases who have not specified their caste, most of them belonged to Muslim and Christian religion and these respondents were having lower socio-economic status.

The association between caste background and physical violence would remain incomplete unless their economic status is also considered. Preceding analysis has indicated that members belonging to the lower class were more likely to resort to physical violence for the resolution of conjugal conflicts. Religion is an important institution which instills a particular philosophy of life in an individual. His outlook towards himself and others as well as his behaviour pattern are likely to be influenced by his religious belief system. Is wife abuse a characteristic of a particular religious group? To find out an answer to the question religious background of the respondents was considered. No clear-cut association was found between religious background and physical violence against wives. Among the two main religious groups present in Chandigarh, there was no marked difference in the percentage of victims.

In case of Muslims and Christians 50 per cent of the respondents belonging to these religious groups were the victims of husband's violence. This again may be attributed to the low economic status of the respondents. The results of the present study do not establish any association between religion and wife battering. The family as a social institution lays down norms and values to regulate the behaviour of the members of the social group. Family as a social group is structured in such a manner that one member, usually the husband, assumes the dominant position and the other members take up subordinate positions.

The family provides a so cial setting where husband and wife play complementary roles. One of the conditions which maximises the cooperative elements in the family is the similarity of social values and ideologies which promotes not only cohesiveness and harmony but also helps in the proper functioning of the group.

In the patriarchal traditional societies, like India, sex role expectations favour male dominance in the family. Traditional ideology promotes and serves to justify male dominance as well as helps in cultivating a belief system among the husbands and wives as to how they should behave in the marital relationship. Motivated by traditional ideology, division of labour in the family was worked out into a male provider and a female to focus more narrowly on the domestic realm. Such a task specialization and differential evaluation helped men not only to have greater control over economic resources but also a greater access to power in the family.

The power structure in the family is maintained through the actions of the members involved in the relationships. Those at the top of the power structure behave in dominant ways and they do not hesitate to use coercive methods to retain their dominant position.

Attempts have been made to find out association between traditionality and wife abuse. A number of studies have concluded that men who were more traditional in their attitudes towards women were more likely to become wife abusers.

Some importance is also given to sex role orientation of the victims. Walker is of opinion that non-traditional wives if paired with traditional husbands are at higher risk of being abused. An attempt has been made in the present study to find out correlation between wives' traditional orientation and their being victims of abuse. Traditional sex role orientation of the respondents was worked out based on the responses to eight statements. The level of traditionality was further divided into three: High, Medium and Low, to find out association between level of traditionality and wife battering. It is assumed that respondents who have low level of traditional role orientation are at higher risk of physical violence than those at high level of traditionality because wives with low level of traditional orientation are more likely to question asymmetrical power relations in the family. Data on traditionality and wife abuse reveal that there is a progressive decrease in the percentage of victims from low level of traditionality to high level of traditionality. In contrast to 22.86 per cent of the wives showing high level of traditional sex role orientation, 40.32 per cent wives indicating low level of traditionality were the victims of physical violence by their husbands.

Similarly, among the non-victims, their percentages go on increasing from low level of traditionality to high level of traditionality. In short, it can be concluded that wives with non-traditional sex role orientation are at higher risk of being physically abused. The reason for wives showing less traditional sex role orientation being victims of physical violence may be attributed to their attempt in questioning the traditional power structure in the family.

The husbands in such situation are likely to use physical force as the last resort to maintain their dominant position. The norms and values relating to intra-family violence indicate cultural contradiction. On the one hand, there is a myth of family non-violence which reflects cultural norms for the family as a group characterised by love and harmony. On the other hand, there seems to be social norms which imply right of the family members to strike each other.

The legitimation of violence in the family is explicit and mandatory—as in the case of rights and obligations of the parent to use a necessary and appropriate level of physical force to adequately train and control a child. Violent wives as well as violent husbands express more approval of violence than do non-violent husbands and wives. Levinson in his cross cultural study on family violence came to the conclusion that wife beating was more common and frequent in societies in which adults solved conflicts by resorting to physical violence, indicating attitude in favour of violence. The cultural norms and values permitting and sometimes encouraging husband to beat wife actually reflect hierarchical and male dominant type of society like India.

The right to use force exists, to provide the ultimate support for the existing power structure of the family in which the wife assumes a subordinate position. Respondents' values in favour or against use of violence in the family were obtained from their reactions to 12 statements. Their scores were divided into three categories depicting low, medium and high scores. This exercise was done with an assumption that the respondents with high score on values in favour of violence in the family would be at a higher risk of being victims than those with low score. The data did not depict any clear-cut association.

On the other hand, it was noted that those respondents who had medium score on values favouring use of violence to resolve family conflict were more victims in contrast to those who had high or low score. The reason for lack of association may be attributed to the fact that there is a lot of gap between values and actual behaviour pattern. Secondly, the values were taken of the wives rather than the husbands who were the perpetrators of physical violence against their wives.

The respondents might be holding values against the use of violence but had no control over the values and behaviour pattern of their husbands. The above discussion on social variables highlights certain salient features which contribute to husbands' physical violence against wives. Lower caste background, low and high educational attainment, lower working status, lower social class background and low level of traditionality were found to be contributing factors for husbands' physical violence against wives.

However, no association was found between religious background and value system of the respondents and their being victims and non-victims of physical violence. Dependency is a state, both physical and mental, depicting assistance from a person or persons for continuing living in the community. The human child has to depend upon his parents for his growth, development and social recognition.

The Indian society has placed women in a state of dependency as a daughter on her father, as a sister on her brother, as a wife on her husband and lastly as a mother on her son. Further, sexual division of labour and gender roles accentuate these differences. Additionally, patriarchal social norms not only grant control of family resources and property to men but also provide dominant position to them. To maintain their dominant position, the husbands are likely to use coercive methods including physical violence against their wives.

Sometimes physical violence is used as a means to an end and at other times as an end in itself. Dependency is also treated as a cause of physical violence in the conjugal relationships. Researches have utilized this explanation in two ways. In case, a wife is completely dependent, both physically and socially, her husband exploits her dependency and uses violence at whim to reinforce his dominant position in the conjugal relationship. A few scholars are also of opinion that when a husband is dependent upon his wife he resorts to physical violence as a last resort against his wife as he is afraid of losing his spouse or a person on whom he can exert his dominant position.

Hence, dependency of husband over his wife is also treated as a cause of wife abuse. As the present study is limited to wife abuse, the analysis is limited to wife's perception regarding the conditions which make her dependent upon her husband and how this state of dependency results into her being abused. To find out association between wife's dependency and her abuse, dependency has been divided into objective and subjective. It does not, however, mean that we can draw watertight compartments between the two. In certain cases objective dependency may lead to subjective dependency, whereas in other cases even though there is no objective dependency yet the individual remains subjectively dependent upon her spouse. It can, however, be assumed that a wife who experiences both objective and subjective dependency is at higher risk of being abused in contrast to those who have only objective or only subjective dependency.

For the purpose of analysis wife's objective dependency stands for conditions like not working, i.e., being economically dependent upon husband; not having any property in her name; not receiving any financial assistance from her family of orientation; inability to live alone; inability to do shopping alone, and inability to go outside the city alone. Further, level of objective dependency may vary from case to case hence, objective dependency was further divided into three levels: low, medium and high.

The wives who are objectively dependent upon their husbands are at higher risk of being abused because it would be difficult for these women to come out of the abusive relationship as they do not have the resources to live alone. Their objective dependency is also known to their spouses who may fully exploit the situation knowing fully well that their wives would not be able to leave them. It is further envisaged that wives who have high level of objective dependency are at greater risk of being abused. Wives with high level of objective dependency are physically abused more in contrast to those who have low level of objective dependency. This is evident in the percentages of the victims at different levels of dependency.

Similarly, the percentage of non-victims goes on decreasing to high level. There were 33 respondents who had high level of objective dependency, out of which 60.61 per cent were not the victims of physical violence. The results of the study support the contention of a few scholars who are of opinion that high level of women's marital dependency is not associated with wife abuse because husbands of dependent wives can maintain their dominant positions without resorting to violence as their wives are in no position to question their dominance.

Although no cause and effect relationship can be

established between dependency and wife abuse yet the data show an indicative trend that wives who have high level of objective dependency are abused more as compared to those who have low level of objective dependency. A few scholars contend that objective dependency of the wife per se does not result into her abuse but is mediated by her tolerance.

One may, however, raise the question why she develops this tolerance to abuse? One reason may be that she remains subjectively dependent upon her husband because her social reality has not been constructed outside the marital relationship. In Indian society marriage is a must for every woman, unless she adopts a life of celibacy. Remaining unmarried or living a life of a divorcee is looked down upon.

Hence, whether a wife is objectively dependent upon her husband or not she remains subjectively dependent. It is not, however, true in the case of husbands. Remarriage after divorce or separation is easily available to a man than a woman. Such a discriminatory practice perpetuate subjective dependency in the wives. Subjective dependency in the present study stands for, not leaving the husband even under adverse circumstances; divorce not considered good; perception that married women even if abused enjoy higher status than divorced; lack of support from kin; greater commitment and more devotion to marital relationship. It is also expected that wives are likely to have different levels of subjective dependency.

Depending upon their scores they are divided into three categories: low, medium and high. It is expected that wives having higher level of subjective dependency will be at higher risk of being physically abused in contrast to those having lower level of subjective dependency. In contrast to 23-94 per cent wives having low subjective dependency more than 42 percent of the wives with high level of dependency are the victims of physical violence of their husbands. There was a steady increase in the percentage of abused wives from low level of subjective dependency through medium level to high level of subjective dependency. Taking into account 38 cases having high level of subjective dependency it was noted that more than 42 per cent were the victims of husbands' physical violence and approximately 58 per cent were free from being physically abused.

Although, no positive correlation could be established between subjective dependency of wife and her being victim of physical abuse yet the high percentage of victims having high level of subjective dependency designate a partial association between subjective dependency and her being battered.

The reason for high percentage of such victims can be attributed to wife's commitment to marriage and her inability to use alternative mechanisms to get out of the abusive relationships. Such a situation forces her to cultivate tolerance and continue living in the abusive relationship. Similarly, the husband uses coercive methods to assert his dominant position in the familial network of relationship because he is confident that his violent behaviour would not be challenged and he can attain the desired goal, that is, subduing his wife.

The results of the present study on subjective dependency and wife abuse partially support the findings of other researchers. Subjective dependency in certain cases may be treated as a consequence of objective dependency. In other cases subjective dependency may not be the outcome of objective dependency. It was for this reason that these two facets of dependency were treated separately, however, to find out the impact of dependency on wife abuse both objective and subjective dependencies have to be combined. In other words, to find out the validity of dependency framework to explicate wife abuse, both the facets of dependency are combined to find out their combined effect on physical violence.

The total dependency scores of the respondents have been arranged into three categories—low, medium and high. The data indicate that wives with higher level of dependency are at higher risk of being abused in contrast to those with lower level of dependency. In contrast to 27.42 per cent of wives with low level of dependency more were the victims of husbands' physical violence. The percentage of non-victims goes on decreasing from lower level of dependency to higher level. Under these circumstances, though no clear cut correlations could be found between dependency and wife abuse yet it was found that with the increase in the level of dependency there was an increase in the percentage of victims.

6

Custodial Justice to Women

Accordingly, custodial justice to women has been one of the thrust areas of the activities of the Commission since its inception. The Chairperson as well as Members of the Commission visited individually or jointly, a number of jails in various states of India to have a first hand knowledge of the period under report visits were undertaken to the following jails:

1. Assam	District Jails a Guwahati, Jorhata and Nowgaon. Nari Sadan, Barpeta (a jail exclusively for women)
2. Gujarat	Sabarmati central jail, Ahmedabad.
3. Maharashtra	Central jail, Bombay.
4. Madhya Pradesh	District jails at Jabalpur and Dantewada.
5. Manipur	Central jail, Sagiva,
6. Meghalaya	District jails at Shilong and Moulai
7. Karnataka	Central jail, Bangalore.
8. West Bengal	Central Jail, Calcutta
9. Delhi	Tihar Jail

The visits to these jails revealed extremely unsatisfactory conditions under which women prisoners live. While the visiting members conveyed to the concerned authorities their general observations about the living condition of women and made specific suggestions about certain hard cases, it was felt that a study should be undertaken to assess the existing conditions in the jails throughout the country.

Observations and Suggestions made by Members Inspecting the Jails

(i) Adequate arrangements for vocational training should be made for women inmates in jail and a programme prepared for rehabilitation of released prisoners. To take an example the visiting Members came across the case of life convict in Assam who was to be released shortly but was very apprehensive of her future since the thought that her husband and society might not accept her. She wanted to acquire some professional skill to be economically independent. She had aptitude for nursing. At the suggestion of the Member she was given training in mid-wifery and was ultimately able to make her by into the profession.

(ii) Courts should ensure that female prisoners are handed over to *bona fide* guardians after release so that they may not fall into the hands of imposter guardians who may force them into immoral trafficking as hand come to light in many cases.

(iii) Mentally ill women should be kept separate from the other women prisoners.

(iv) Certain women prisoners had been kept in custody on the ground of being lunatic despite the fact that they were not actually lunatics. There should therefore, bean objective medical examination of such cases.

(v) The women's wing of Tihar jail was found to be overcrowded by more than four times its capacity. Construction of additional accommodation was suggested to ameliorate the condition of women inmates. It was noted that the women inmates were encouraged to engage themselves in the training of various vocations. Also, a de-addition centre had been set up by the jail authorities. However revamping of the training programme was suggested so that the inmates were enabled to produce marketable goods and make an earning for themselves for future security.

(vi) In the Jail, Delhi there was a case of a smart girl who had secured the job of a police A.S.I. by impersonation but she was a Karate expert. It was suggested to the Jail authorities to engage her in some fruitful activity like imparting physical training to other come prisoners. A similar approach is necessary in alike cases.

(vii) In certain prisons, some women inmates were found to suffer from T.B. It was suggested that they should be suggested that they should be segregated from the others and also given proper medical treatment.

(viii) In the Central Jail at Bombay the Tata Institute of Social Science was conducting some useful services for the jail inmates in collaboration with the Bombay Police such as literacy classes, creches for children vocational training counselling, legal guidance, placement on release, etc. This was considered as a good example to be followed.

(ix) The authorities at Sabarmati Central Jail, Ahmedabad expressed the view that the vocational training facilities for male prisoners could not be extended to female inmates as their number was too small. It was suggested that in such cases women inmates could be congregated in one or two suitable jails for making such facilities available or, alternatively provided with such other work as gardening cooking, etc. and wages paid for the same.

(x) In several jails, regular visits by doctors are not made but they are called only when needed. Also no facilities for lady doctors or nurses exist for women prisoners. It was suggested to the concerned jail authorities that it is desirable that women prisoners are treated only by women doctors, unless the prisoners opt otherwise. However, medical examination should be provided as a matter of routine.

(xi) In the jails visited in Madhya Pradesh, it was found that most of the prisoners were tribals and had their own cultural traditions. The crimes committed by them were not pre-planned and had altogether different background. Therefore, instead of convicting them straightaway under the provisions of Criminal Procedure Code, a lenient view should be taken in the context of their socio-economic environment. It was as suggested that suitable training should be given to Adivasi women prisoners in bidi making sericultre and other related industries to which they are traditionally accustomed.

(xii) Women prisoners convicted under TADA were generally found to be young school and college going girls. It was suggested that they should be provided with facilities to continue their studies and persistently motivated to return to the mainstream of life.

Assessment of Existing Conditions in Jails

The personal visits of Members to the jails convinced the

Commission that there was a serious shortfall in the delivery of services to women who are in custody in jails. The Commission therefore decided to issue a Questionnaire to all the States and Union Territories calling for data/information in respect of facilities available to women inmates with regard to diet accommodation medical aid sanitation education vocational training legal aid, recreational opportunities provisions for children accompanying prisoners, visitorial facilities ventilation of grievances, etc. The information received from all over the country is being processed in the Commission and an analysis thereof will be presented before the Export Committee with a view to formulating recommendations bearing on the conditions of women in custody and norms therefor.

Recommendations made to the Government

The commission also thought it fit that some immediate suggestions should be preferred it the Ministry of Home affairs, Government of India, for adoption in order to secure custodial justice for women behind the bars. While drawing up these suggestions consideration was given also to the aspect of gender justice in the relam of criminal law a administration after taking a stock of the recommendations made by various Commissions and Committees on the subject, notable among which is the Report of the National Expert Committee on Women prisoners headed by justice Krishna Iyer as well as that of All India Committee for Jail Reforms and also various findings of the Supreme Court of India on the subject. The suggestions were want for immediate implementation as these are supposed not to entail any substantial strain on the governmental exchequer and are implementable as a short term measure. These are given below.

Arrest of Women, Search, Bail, etc.

(1) Women shall not be arrested between sun-set and

sun-rise and shall not be arrested expect in the presence of women. This will necessitate amendment of section 46 Cr. P.C. 1973.

(2) In all cases of bailable offences bail on her bond shall be granted forthwith by the police themselves. As far as possible in non-bailable cases also, bail should be granted unless special circumstances warrant a different course, in which case, the arrested woman shall be remanded to judicial custody with utmost expedition.

(3) On arrest the police should immediately obtain from the arrestee the name a relative or friend to whom the intimation of her arrest should be promptly given.

(4) If consideration of arrestee's own safety and freedom from ensnarement by anti-social elements demand detention in public institutions bail shall be refused to the women in her own interest unless she is specifically states her willingness to be thus released even after being altered to the above consideration.

(5) The person of a women shall not be searched except by a women authorised by law, and in a manner strictly in accordance with the requirement of decency. Whether in custody or in transit, the arrested woman must always be guarded by a women police or female surrogate. Wile resorting a relative may be permitted to accompany the female arrestee.

(6) Whenever a women is to be examined by the police or other investigative agency as a witness it should be done only at her residence; nor should she be summoned to the police or investigative station unless she expresses her preference to be examined at the station.

(7) No female prisoner shall be subjected to any form of corporal punishment or use of handcuffs fetters or isolation as a form of disciplining.

(8) When women are examined in court as accused or as witnesses, sue courtesy and decency shall be shown. If circumstances so demand in the interest of modesty and privacy of a women the trial may be held in camera or the women may be examined on commission through women advocates.

Exclusive Custody for Women

(1) There should be police stations exclusive for women and exclusive lockups under the control of women police. This will necessitate amendment of prison Act and police Act. Separated space for female arrestees in every police lockup and complete segregation of women prisoners in jail and other custody should be maintained.

(2) Where such facility is not available, a female arrestee may be lodged in a special home or institution designated under any law for the time being in force to receive women. At no time shall a women arrestee be left unguarded by a women guard or surrogate. In all places of police custody, basic amenities such as living space, water, toilet, food medical examination and care, and provisions to meet the special needs of women shall be provided.

(3) As far as possible each state should have at least one or more separate jail for women.

(4) There should be separate custodial facilities for convicts and undertrial women. Separate institutions or reception centres where undertrial and remanded women may be kept, should be set up in larger cities district headquarters, and in female-crime-endemic areas. Where convicts and undertrials are currently

housed in one institution they must kept apart in separate wings until independent facilities are set up.

Visitorial Provision in Custody

(1) Additional provision should be made in the existing legislation conferring visitorial rights on recognised institutions or individuals institutional and individual accountability for lapses and exesses should also be provided for.

(2) Information on women in custody should be made available to recognised social organisations and individuals on request. Persons and institutions accredited as visitors should be allowed as of right free access to police stations and records.

(3) Visiting Committees to jails should be constituted in consultation with professional bodies and university department of laws, criminologists, social workers and social scientists from the neighbouring area. Visitors should be nominated on the bases of merit public spiritedness activist record and actual time likely to be made available to the visitorial function.

Women DIG

A women DIG should be appointed at state headquarters preferably from the prison service to specifically look after the work relating to women prisoners and women prison staff.

Autonomous Prisons for Women

Women superintendents of separate prisons for women (currently six in number) should be made fully autonomous in functioning.

Prisoners Councils

Prisoners Councils or Bandi Sabhas should be set up in

all prisons to help airing prisoners grievances and difficulties.

Socio-legal Counselling

(1) Socio-legal counselling cells should be set up in every prison for women inmates.

(2) In exceptional circumstances when a women arrestee is taken to a police lock-up the police should immediately give intimation to the nearest Legal Aid Committee or recognized legal service or body which must render all necessary legal services at State expense.

(3) Magistrates shall inform women when first produced of their right to legal aid at state expense and direct the provision of necessary services. They shall also explain the nature and scope of the proceedings against her and her rights in it.

(4) Legal aid and counselling through professional bodies assisted by para-legal and social workers should be institutionalised in respect of every prison and custodial institution. Law schools and schools of social work should be encouraged and permitted to render socio-legal counselling service to the inmates.

(5) In the disposition of women offenders courts should mandatory call for and give due regard to the probation officers report and to the report of medical/psychiatric examination. Where probation officers are not available probation investigation should be entrusted to recognized and accredited institutions and individuals.

Released Prisoners Aid Society

(1) Released Prisoners Aid Societies should operate in every district to provide a single-window assistance towards rehabilitation and mainstreaming of the released women prisoners.

(2) Before a female prisoner is released her relatives should be informed and where no relative exists or shows up the released prisoner should be sent to her destination with a female escort.

(3) Appropriate assistance should be rendered to every female prisoner on release whether during or after completion of sentence. For this purpose a centre for assisting released prisoners should be set up to service a cluster of prisons and custodial institutions on an area-wise basis. Even without the centre the prison authorities should take necessary steps to arrange the rehabilitation of the released prisoner either through the family the relief centre or a voluntary organisation.

(4) Aftercare and short-stay homes for women prisoners may be established in every state to serve those prisoners who are homeless or rejected by their families.

Children Accompanying Women in Police Custody/Jail Custody

(1) When arresting a women, proper arrangements for the protection and care of her accompanying children should be the responsibility of the state. Children who need to be custodialized jointly with their mothers should enjoy rights justly needed, while in custody in terms of food, living space, health, clothing and visitation.

(2) In the disposition of women to custody or otherwise, the magistrate must enquire and direct that suitable for the welfare of their children be made in a manner that protects the rights of children. While sentencing women to imprisonment or any form of custodialisation suitable orders should be made for the custody and welfare of their children.

(3) Expectant mothers in custody should be shown Special consideration by way of medical and

nutritional care, education in child rearing and mother craft.

Women's Assistance Police Unit

(1) Women's Assistance Police Unit contacting cadre of men and women police with specific task of crime prevention work and assistance to women should be set up in each district.

(2) In endemic female crime areas, or wherever otherwise desirable exclusive police station or booths and counters within police stations, shall be set up to deal with women needing protection of or coming in conflict with law. Such booths and police stations should be managed by an integrated cadre of men and women police specially trained and sensitized to deal with women.

Conference of Inspectors General of Prisons

On 3rd February, 1993, the Commission organised in New Delhi a conference of Inspectors General of Prisons from all over the country with a view to obtaining their views on the diverse issues relating to custodial justice as well as gender justice in the realm of criminal law administration.

The Conference discussed at length a host of issues arising out of the topic of custodial justice to women as well as gender justice in the realm of criminal law administration. It was felt that the issues deserve a more thorough probe in the light of desirability as well as implement ability of the various suggestions emerging out of the Conference. Moreover, the suggestions were also desired to be screened and reviewed by the Expert Committee on Custodial justice in order that light may be shed from all angles of views and a consensus arrived at. Accordingly a sub-committee of eight persons out of the participants of the Conference was appointed to inter-act with the Expert Committee on Custodial justice to women on all the significant suggestions and in particular about the suggested amendments to the laws in force in the realm. This culminated in formulation of recommendations by the Commission for amendment of the code of Criminal Procedure.

Training Programme for Custodial Staff

It was unanimously voiced in the Conference of Inspectors General of prisons that it is the custodial staff who constitute the key element in any attempt to bring about custodial reforms rather than allocation of extra funds. It was strongly advocated that the Superintendents of Jails, remand homes borstals, etc. should constitute the first target group to be motivated to re-orient their approach towards women in custody and this process of sensitization should spread down below to all levels of functionaries in custodial institutions. Accordingly, it was decided to organise suitable training programmes for superintendents of Jails/Remand homes/Borstals etc. under the ages of the National Commission for women at regular intervals in different zones of the country which should gradually encompass all levels of custodial functionaries in the country.

7
Women and Development

In a world of continuing brutality, impunity and abuse of human dignity and freedoms, the United Nations' Universal Declaration of Human Rights (UDHR) has been the centrepiece of an ambitious project to promote universal respect and protection of basic human rights worldwide.

According to some third world activists, in celebrating 50 Years of UDHR we are actually violating the human rights of the non-west, non-developed countries because that is how we are subscribing to that notion of human rights which has been framed and dictated by the postwar imperialist power represented by the US-West Europe Bloc. There is no escape from this, as the UN list of human rights were initially formulated not to protect and guarantee universal human rights, but with the primary and sole purpose of containing communism or the Soviet bloc, which was growing in both power or influence and geographical expanse. The idea was to protect the rights of the capitalist world *vis a vis* the economic justice to the real producers, which the newly established socialist governments were claiming to ensure. It could also have been actually ensured to a not too insignificance extent. In the new democracies of the newly independent countries the elected leaders were taking the place of the colonial rulers. Rights were defined and granted by these rulers; people did not get them as a matter of their right.

In a true democracy, on the other hand, people are born naturally with rights and the people only grant power to their governments, instead of the small powerful group called government granting power as charity, as if. This is so because human rights are as old as human beings; human rights were born the moment human beings were born.

In 1947 the United Nations Human Rights Commission had its first meeting under the chairmanship of Eleanor Roosevelt to create an international bill of rights. Eleanor was a powerful human rights campaigner no doubt, but she was also the wife of the American President. Therefore, she naturally used American State ideals as the template. J.P. Hendricks, then a senior US official and advisor to Ms. Roosevelt, had admitted that the US policy was to make UDHR a carbon copy of the American Declaration of Independence and the American Bill of Rights. Originally, there was a three member Drafting Committee, consisting of Ms. Roosevelt, P.C. Chang of China and Charles Malik of Lebanon. To accommodate a hostile Soviet Union, threatening to stay out of the human rights project, she recast this Committee with representatives from Australia, Chile, France, U.K. and the Soviet Union, in addition to the existing members.

Inspite of these additions, the Committee was starkly unrepresentative. It did not represent any African or Islamic nation among the total membership of 58. That is why when the UDHR draft came to be debated by the member nations in 1948, 168 resolutions proposing amendments were bled during the 81 meetings. These countries felt that it was a western model applicable in a very different social and cultural context only. It draws primarily from the western conceptions of individual rights, ignoring the ancient religious values, philosophic traditions and the sociocultural practices in the third world societies. Finally 48 States supported and 8 abstained. But this i.e. overlooking regional/national cultural peculiarity/speciality, perhaps is the real value behind the Human Rights Document. It discounts the social context in favour of an absolute human being, unlike the understanding of the nature of the individual within the society, as characterized i most authoritarian religions. What is remarkable about UDHR therefore, is that it does not invoke God, Nature, morality, etc. It talks of a social and international order in which the right and freedoms set forth in the Declaration can be fully realized, or of the duties to the community in which alone the free and full development of his personality is possible.

In the western natural rights construct it had transpired that certain rights were inherent in the individual who must be protected against the arbitrary use of State power. Doctrines such as the rule of law, the separation of powers and other theories restraining social and political structures and promoting respect for human dignity seeped into the 18th century dialogues. They, in turn, influenced Declarations like the American in 1776 and the French in 1789. Ms. Roosevelt comforted the nations in power by assuring them that the Declaration is not, and does not, purport to be a statement of law or legal obligation. It was merely a common standard of achievement. Eight years later, the UN summoned the first international conference on human rights which proclaimed, on December 19, 1968, that the UNDHR constitutes an obligation for the members of the international community.

Today the human rights issues are more difficult and complex and even richer than what they were 50 years ago. Human Rights are a powerful tool for development provided, of course, the political rights are firmly secured through a democratic process. Otherwise, the ideology of development can be used to suppress human rights and freedoms.

True democracy, which instils the right kind of motivation and confidence in the people, can also insulate the State and the people from the opportunistic use of human rights issues by outside powers, who may take advantage of the discontent and dissensions born out of the development models evolved and exported by the US imperialist-led west. The pervasiveness of poverty thus gets compounded by the problems of displacement as a result of anti-indigenous people policies, the prime most of which is environmental degradation.

In the volatile situation of high community sensitivity and the struggle for resources, which get scarcer to scarcer, communalism raises its head as a highly disruptive influence. In such circumstances, the ideology of development is made to have greater appeal than human rights because human rights allow no space to any authority or dictum or dictat.

Planned and programmed development, as opposed to natural development cannot be effected without authority and authoritarianism. Indigenous and tribal peoples usually live in less developed, hinterland areas of the states. Their lands are often the sites of programmes or projects designed to serve the interests of others. History abounds in such instances whereby indigenous or aboriginal peoples lost their land, resources, culture, tradition and even their history and identity.

The most glaring example in the case of India is the dispossession of the original inhabitants by the Aryans —a warring tribe from the barren lands of Central Asia —who invaded India in search of water and agricultural land and then settled down permanently. They had to create and institutionalize division between the conquered and the conqueror, the ruled and the ruler, in order to enforce and stabilize their usurped power.

Thus, the original inhabitants not only lost their property and resources, but were forced into compulsory labour little different from slavery. They were also subjected to alien systems of law, administration and culture. They were discriminated in the eyes of law in an obvious manner and sometimes, even exterminated. The international community has been slow in acknowledging this injustice.

In 1957, for the first time, the Indigenous and Tribal People's Convention has been convened. But that was to stabilize the status quo. The Recommendations sponsored by the International Labour Organization hinted that the remedy lay in their assimilation into the culture and way of life of the communities that ruled over them. In other words, the path prescribed was not of individualism of the western liberal thoughts. This approach was however, abandoned in 1989 when the Convention on the Indigenous and Tribal Peoples in Independent Countries recognized the values of their culture, ecology and their dignity as a people. There can be no destruction of natural environment and no displaced person or refugees if what is put on paper is honoured as pragmatic and beneficial for the entire humanity. According to Pundit Jawaharlal Nehru:

> People should develop along the lines of their own genius and we should avoid imposing anything on them. We should try to encourage in every way

> their traditional art and culture. Tribal rights in land and forests should be respected. We should try to train and build up a team of their own people to do the work of administration and development. Some technical person from outside will, no doubt, be needed, especially in the beginning. But we should avoid introducing too many outsiders into tribal territory. We should not over administer these areas nor over administer these areas nor overwhelm them with a multiplicity of schemes. We should rather work through, and not in rivalry to, their own social and cultural institutions. We should judge results, not by statistics or the amount of money spent, but by the quality of human character that is evolved.

This advice or director from the politically most powerful person of newly, developing India is a commendable thought, considering that ii comes out from a leader of the mainstream. It appears to be in line with the spirit and the Articles of the Constitution—perfectly democratic and socialistic. But we must not miss the word try to; it is the key word and portrays the bad faith with which both our Constitution makers and the political leaders went about.

The special section of the Directive Principles was carefully charted out with the hidden consensus of democratic socialism without meaning it. In the so long years of swaraj, eradication of poverty, illiteracy, untouchability and gender—inequality—everything have remained at the level of trying and noble words only. Intentions trudged always on the opposite path. That is why our leader and the mainstream group talk of privatisation and people's good, secularism and uniformity in the same breath and love for one's own culture, which does not subscribe to that of the mainstream, is branded as anti-national or unpatriotic.

On the other hand, the continuous disasters in

man's history are mainly due to his excessive capacity and urge to become identified with a tribe, nation, church or a cause, and to espouse its credo uncritically and unenthusiastically, even if its tenets are contrary to reason, devoid of self-interest and detrimental to the claims of self-preservation. It is for reasons such as these that we have created refugees: people who have a well-founded fear of being persecuted for reasons of race, religion, nationality, membership of a particular social group or political opinion.

All the adivasis, dalits and some of the religious minorities, who are poor, and women, of all socioeconomic categories, are refugees in their own lands, they are refugees even if they do not have to migrate. They are permanent victims of planned neglect and economic underdevelopment, so that they can remain marginalised permanently. Declaration of the Principles of Indigenous Rights, adopted by the World Council of Indigenous Peoples in 1984, says the traditions and custom of the indigenous people must be respected by the states and recognized as fundamental sources of law.

Convention on Indigenous and Tribal Peoples in Independent Countries, in its Article 3 says, indigenous and tribal peoples shall enjoy the full measure of human rights and fundamental freedoms without hindrance or discrimination. The provisions of the Convention shall be applied without discrimination to male and female members of these peoples.

In Article 29 of Constitution of India it is written that any section of the citizens having a distinct language, script or culture of its own shall have the right to conserve the same. Article 46 says, the State shall promote with special care the educational and economic interests of the weaker sections of the people, and, in particular, of the Scheduled Castes and the Scheduled Tribes, and shall protect them from social injustice and all forms of exploitation. We must specially take note of the fact that there is no mention or intention of developing these distinct cultures, nor the mode or methods are prescribed. Secondly, the notion of weaker sections is rather vague. It implies, in a very subtle way, that, further one is from the mainstream cultural pattern weaker that individual or the community is.

Declaration of the United Nations Conference on the Human Environment says in Principle 1 that man has the fundamental right to freedom, equality and adequate conditions of life, in an environment of a quality that permits a life of dignity and wellbeing. Universal Declaration of Human Rights says in Article 3 that everyone has the right to life, thereby making it clear that right to life has no meaning without the adequate right to environment.

After all, before industries and technologies, as a weapon in the hands of the capitalists cum imperialists, started having its sway, human beings were basically and primarily. Nature's children. UN General Assembly Resolution on the World Charter for Nature demanded in its General Principle 1 that nature shall be respected and its essential processes shall not be impaired. It is not clear from this noble statement whether this concern from the First World-directed UN General Assembly was for those who are totally dependent on nature not only for their livelihood but also for their very living and life-pattern.

Considering the history of the moral/peace positions the UNO takes and has generally taken a true human rights fighter tends to believe that this principle was actually to conserve the Natural environment for their own needs. The Treaty of Rome (Article 130r) and the Constitution of India (Article 48A) sings the same tune. The former proclaims that the action by the community relating to the environment shall have the following objectives: to preserve, protect and improve the quality of the environment and the latter endorses that the state shall endeavour to protect and improve the environment and to safeguard the forests and wild life of the country. The mere protection or even improvement of environment does not necessarily protect and improve the life of those who are completely dependent on it. The protection and improvement can be cleverly tailored and located for the benefit of the vested interests like the timber merchants, pharmaceutical companies and industries seeking raw materials, etc.

The Namibian constitution states that the state shall actively promote and maintain the welfare of the people by adopting inter alia policies aimed at the following :

(1) The maintenance of ecosystems, essential ecological processes and biological diversity of Namibia;

(2) Utilization of living natural resources on a sustainable basis for the benefit of all Namibians, both present and future.

Most of the socialist countries even make statements on environmental protection either as aspiration or as purporting to represent what the state does, and not what the state should do or is bound to do. On the whole, the constitutional statements in this field are at the highest level of generality. At best, the constitutions impose duties upon the state, rather than granting rights to the citizens.

India has among the finest bodies of environmental legislation in the world. Most provisions of those laws have either remained on paper or have been mauled completely out of shape during their implementation. Kenya has 50 enactments relevant to environmental protection, but very little of it is applied. Hong Kong has had a substantial body of legislation which has only recently begun to be seriously enforced. Some countries lack the law, some the resources, but all lack the elusive quality of political will to enforce the implications of introducing human rights into development are far reaching.

Once human rights are accepted as human, that is universal, human rights obligations reach far beyond national borders. Wide disparities in the opportunities to enjoy human rights thereby become one of the principal challenges in human rights, and the principal challenge in development. There is a connection, if by no means a rigid one, between inequality and environmental degradation.

Ethnic minorities, the old and the very young, women and the poorest sections of society, often suffer disproportionately. While the cities often the most affluent sectors of developing nations—stiffer from air and noise pollutions and water shortages, it is in rural areas that the worst effects tire felt—indigenous people arc deprived of their forest homes in Malaysia, for example; tribal people lose their land to dams and reservoirs in India; villages in Bangladesh arc flooded; and women, all over, have to walk miles for water and firewood.

These dispossessed and displaced suffer the worst environment, or levels of pollution, when they migrate to the cities. Those who dispossess them and vitiate the environment enjoy relatively less pollutions, as they live in less congested localities with the best available civic amenities. They travel in air-conditioned cars, insulated from air pollution, thus generating pollution for those whom poverty forces to commute by bicycles or scooters or even on foot.

Therefore, strengthening and strict and sincere enforcing of all other human rights, particularly those related to health, livelihood and identity, are absolutely imperative for the conservation of environment and sustainable growth. Repressive and discriminating practices lead to pervasiveness of ethnic conflict, the humiliations heaped daily on the lower caste communities and on the members of the indigenous and minority peoples They live in constant fears about their lives; civilized life or dignity become impossible. Neither the government nor the dissident forces respect the rights of the civilians, thus disregarding the principles and the rules of humanitarian law. Many are driven to seek refuge abroad. Others live in such abject poverty or deprivation that even the discourse on human rights sounds obscene. Needless to remind, women and children are the most prominent among the victims of social and environmental discrimination and deprivation. The women and children of the outcastes and the tribals happen to be the worse among the worst. Women tend to be less educated, less nourished and work harder for smaller returns even in developed and rich economics.

Eighty percent of refugees are women and children fleeing from persecuting and serious amount of deprivation, they are in general, compelled to live in degrading conditions and without adequate legal safeguards in the land of their asylum also. They manage to get employed in the unorganized sector only thus Setting further exploited. There are over 15,000,000 refugees in the world today. Women in Australia constitute 75% of the total number of people living in poverty Like always, men take the decision to migrate and they continue to take all other decisions thereafter, even though the burden of managing with meagre income, changed and new livelihood and the strange demands of the new society is invariably much more on the women. The host government and the society, which usually is not favourable or friendly, tends to be more exploitative to the refugee women because they are exploited by their own men also.

Ironically, it is the women who are more capable of providing the best insights into the problems which affect the needs, security and the future of their family and their society. This is a well researched, well-recognized fact, observable in both tribal and mainstream societies.

Ratifications of and reporting on various/sundry human rights declarations only deals with symptoms. At the heart of discriminations against women lie deep-rooted cultural traditions in both developed and developing countries. In many ways the issues of women's rights have accentuated the constant tension between tradition and modernity. Women have been classically recognized as bearers of tradition from one generation to another.

Therefore, the transformation of their role in society, as a result of human rights, is seen as an erosion of the foundations of traditional cultures. Women of all ages suffer avoidable premature death, avoidable sickness and avoidable disadvantages in education and economic and social opportunities. Article 2 of the Universal Declaration of Human Rights says, everybody is entitled to all the rights and freedoms set forth in the Declaration, without distinction of any kind, such as race, colour, sex, language, religion, political or other status.

International Covenant on Civil and Political Rights declares in its Article 3 that the state parties to the present Covenant undertake to ensure the equal right of men and women to the enjoyment of all economic, social and cultural rights set forth in the present Covenant. International Covenant on Economic, Social and Cultural

Rights of January, 1976, declares exactly the same thing.

The famous International Convention on the Elimination of all forms of Discrimination Against Women (CEDAW) of 1979, prohibits, in Article 1, any distinction, exclusion or restriction made on the basis of sex which has the effect of purpose of impairing or nullifying the recognition, enjoyment or exercise by women, irrespective of their marital status, on the basis of equality of men and women, of human rights and fundamental freedoms in the political, economic, social, civil or other field.

It is important for all women—refugee, mainstream of tribal to know that as a result of the Communique of Commonwealth Ministers Responsible for Women's Affairs, the Ministers recognized that economic equality between women and men is an important dimension of gender equality and economic advancement of women as well as a basic premise for all human rights and national economic development. National and international policies and programmes arc formulated without regard for gender issues and any number of such declarations and resolutions have no effect and no validity.

While the United Nations Declaration of Human Rights does not explicitly exclude women, it does not elaborate on how the rights set out in this declaration relate to women. It does not talk of the private sphere, the area in which most violations of women's human rights occur. This separation of women's rights from human rights rendered most violations of women's rights invisible.

Bunch wrote in 1995 that the west-educated, propertied men feared the violations of their civil and political rights in the private sphere because that would affect their property and privileged position; they were not concerned with the violations in the private sphere of their home as they were the masters of that territory. He further opines that private-public distinction is a dichotomy largely used to justify female subordination and to exclude human rights abuses at home from public scrutiny.

In addition, the exclusion of sexual and other violences against women from the human rights agenda stems from the failure to view the oppression of women as political. Bunch, thus rightly remarks, female subordination runs so deep that it is still viewed as inevitable or natural. It is actually politically construed reality maintained by patriaichal interest, ideology and institutions. The physical territory of this political struggle is women's bodies. The United Nations Decade For Women was seen as a watershed in placing women's concerns on the international agenda and for facilitating women's cooperation. Women participated in the NGO Forums, etc. where women from different countries were able to exchange strategies and develop ongoing working relationships.

The CEDAW was one of the most outstanding outcomes of the decade and has subsequently become the international standard for the protection and promotion of women's human rights. It sets out the duties that the States are required to promote in all areas of a woman's life, living and livelihood. The signatories to this human rights charter are required to take all the necessary legislative, judicial, administrative or other appropriate measures to guarantee women the exercise and enjoyment of human rights and fundamental freedoms on the basis of equality with men.

The bad faith of the framers of CEDAW—supposed to be the most comprehensive document for women's human rights—is shamelessly expressed in the provision that the signatory countries are allowed to make reservations. There are countries like Thailand who have demanded so many reservations that the noble rights have remained noble only on paper. The usefulness of CEDAW or any such document, with regard to which the signatories are allowed to have reservations, is definitely in doubt. But, at the same time, the prolonged discussions and deliberations definitely make violations a little more difficult. The victims can possibly see a light at the end of a long, dark tunnel.

Before the UDHR and before the democratic, socialist, secular Constitution of India it was the dead end or the pit of a very deep well. The fate of women, refugees and the indigenous people was like that of the Sikh women jumping into a well to avoid communal violence during the partition frenzy.

Human rights instruments and mechanisms provide avenues for challenging the systematic abuse of women, and governments can be made to take gender-based violations more seriously by being held accountable for the implementation of laws against them. Mayer identifies two important positions taken with regard to human rights that have an important bearing on women's human rights issues, viz.: the universalist and cultural relativist positions. The former position holds that all members of the human family share the same inalienable rights. The cultural relativist position, on the other hand, demands the universal acceptance of different traditions and cross-cultural standards. The danger in this position, as Rao argues, is in the probability of placing community rights above, or holier than, individual human rights. Abuses justified by this position is most blatantly in case of women's human rights.

All the gender-exploitative religious laws are

accepted and protected by the Indian governments with the humane intention of protecting the rights of a minority community as if the women of that oppressed community are not oppressed by the patriarchs in that community itself. Power relations may appear so secure and well-established that both subordinate and dominant groups" tend to be unaware of their oppressive implications or are incapable of imagining alternative ways of being and doing.

The latest report of the International Food Policy Research Institute says that the important but problematic aspects of the human rights agenda relating to women's rights to socioeconomic development. In rural Africa it is women's access to productive resources, viz: land, credit, cattle and technical knowledge rather than income, that provides the relevant measures of social status. Women's access to land has diminished as its value as a marketable commodity has increased. Even the Land Reform Laws have discriminated against women needless to remind that such law-based discriminations are is blatant in our country and against the letter and spirit of CEDAW.

Women experience countless barriers to achieving their full potential as producers and providers of food. The greatest barrier is the absence/denial of this significant recognition. They do everything in the field except the actual act of ploughing because that is an was prohibited for them by religious dictum. Recently a women was tied to the plough, dragged along like a plough and beaten up mercilessly because she dared plough her husband's field. She had to defy religion cum patriarchy because her husband was a drunkard, He was not ploughing the field and her children were starving. As a mother she had to opt for human rights as opposed to tier religious duties. A woman always is the food provider for their family even if she is not allowed to earn or have access to any source of income by her own right.

Women are the best protectors of the environment not only as food providers, but also because they are much more concerned about the future of their future generation. Thus, no development can be sustainable unless nature and women are allowed complete freedom—unless environment is conserved and women have major roles in the formulations of policies and implementations of plannings related to development. Extension and research programmes rarely acknowledge or take into account women's indigenous knowledge regarding environment and agriculture.

Achieving gender equity, particularly in the countryside, will have an important bearing on the ability of the third world countries to meet their future food needs and sustainable development. The kinds of actions to be taken on behalf of women touch at the cornerstones of agrarian reform laws, family laws, rural employment strategy and a deeply embedded patriarchal mentality. Hence, it is imperative that women find mechanisms for addressing such issues as a whole, through self-reliant, participatory collective initiatives, in which these issues are addressed as fundamental to women's human rights. As a result of globalisation of capital and capitalism and the consequent capitalism-oriented development, women and other have nots are getting more and more deprived and therefore, marginalised. As an inevitable consequence, landlessness and poverty, have forced increasing number of women into casual labour or work in the low-paid unorganized sector, where the work and living conditions are shamelessly violative of all human rights, including the laws of the land. Men only are preferred in the organized and industrial sectors; women get less paid for the same work.

On the contrary, most of the time women have to work longer on die pretext that women are physically weak, not skilled and therefore, less productive. And, when it comes to promotion, women are hardly considered. On the other hand, women are invariably preferred in all labour-intensive jobs. The arguments offered are that they have greater dexterity, speed and endurance. More "exploitative" than this is the argument that women and children are disciplined, docile, not inclined to industrial action and quiet about accepting low wages.

More often than not pregnant women are retrenched, even if retained, they get no maternity benefits. A majority of the industries make it a point to appoint not more than 14 women workers because otherwise they will have to open a creche for their children. In almost all the underdeveloped economies the twin brothers, capitalism and patriarchy, have a good hold. Thus violations of human rights are double with regard to women. The men of the deprived-marginalised sections, however exploited, do not obviously, become the victims of this kind of oppression. Woman in the unorganized sector not only work 16 hours on an average for a meagre income to support her family, but also in her household, viz: to cook, clean, wash and take care of the children and the old.

The magnitude of the problems facing women workers is indicated by the fact that despite their overwhelming responsibility for household and the reproduction of the tabour force, they are not classified as economically active population. The measurement standard is (i) anti-nature, (ii) procapitalist and (iii) patriarchy guided. Production, national income of contribution to economy is calculated purely by money; that is why, most of women's work is considered unproductive and is not calculated in the national income. That is why again, women are not allowed/ encouraged in the sectors where minimum wages are enforceable by law.

Domestic work is unpaid and therefore, not regarded as an economic activity. The day is still far off when working women will everywhere be equal partners with men in the efforts to achieve economic and social progress (ILO). The latest ILO survey shows that women constituted more than one-third of the worldwide work-force. The great majority of them live in the developing countries and about two-thirds of them are in the agricultural sector. Despite this, their access to or control over land is minimal, especially in South Asian and sub-Saharan African countries.

If UNDHR of 1948 could generate any seriousness in the minds of the framers and the signatories, so many declarations and statements every now and then would not have been necessary. Ironically, "human rights" were formulated and endorsed by those members who were on the top of the list of the violators. They had to appear noble, but had also to create loopholes so that noble words remain words only and cannot get translated into action.

The following are a few excerpts, referring to women's human rights, from the Vienna Declaration and Programme of Action of 1993.

> Recognizing and affirming that all human rights derive from the dirty and worth inherent in the human person, and that the human Person is the central subject of human rights and fundamental freedoms.

The Vienna Declaration recalls the Preamble to the Charter of the United Nations, in particular the determination to reaffirm faith in fundamental human rights and in the equal rights of men and women and of nations large and small. The group was deeply concerned by various forms of discriminations and violence, to which women continued to be exposed all over the world. It also recognized that the activities of the United Nations in the field of human rights should be rationalised and enhanced to further the objectives of universal respect for the observance of international human rights standards.

The excerpts above are from the Preamble to the Vienna Declaration. The following are from Part II of this document.

> The World Conference on Human Rights reaffirms the sole commitment of all States to fulfil their obligations to promote universal respect for, and observance and protection of all human rights and fundamental freedoms. Democracy, development and respect for human rights and fundamental freedoms are interdependent and mutually reinforcing. The World Conference reaffirms the right to development and the human person is the central subject of development. But in reality, particularly under a capitalist structure and system, the human persons become the ingredients like fodders in the canon Natural human rights or the rights to conserve Nature get completely eroded in, the process and Human, Rights Conferences and Charters, thus become necessary a futile attempt to cover up the misdeeds and anti-human rights programmes.

The human rights of women and the girl children are an inalienable, integral and indivisible part of universal human rights. The full and equal participation of women in the political, civil, economic, social and cultural life at the national, regional and international levels and the eradication of all forms of discrimination on the grounds of sex are priority objectives of the international community, because gender based violence and all forms of sexual harassment, and exploitation, including those resulting from cultural prejudices and worth of human trafficking are incompatible with the dignity and worth of the human person, and therefore, must be eliminated. This can be achieved by legal measures and through national action and international cooperation. But the framers of this Body of Rights are the leaders of the violators; these are the political powers who constantly dig the soil from under the foundation of international cooperation. This, i.e. gender based violence and discrimination, is the primary reason why, the need for special human rights charter for women was so anxiously felt. Ironically but, there has been a rise, in geometrical proportions in all kinds of inhumanity against women and girl children ever since the UNDHR and CEDAW were declared and ratified.

When capitalism holds the spectre of imperialism all over the world, how can any space be left for socialism, egalitarianism and human rights? More the repressions, more the cover up by noble ideas just as religion, which is supposed to be the epitome of humanitarianism, is actually the birthplace and perpetrator of all kinds of inhuman divisions between man & man and man & woman.

In Part III, the World Conference coming out with the Vienna Declaration, recognizes the importance of enjoyment by women of the highest standard of physical and mental health throughout their life-span. In the context of the three World Conferences on Women and the Convention on the Elimination of all forms of Discrimination against Women, a woman's right to accessible and adequate health-care and the widest range of family planning services, as well as equal access to education at all levels is recognized.

Interestingly, and disturbingly enough for women,

family planning services are recommended for women, but not family planning choices, which means full reproductive choices and complete, uninterferred control over her reproductive system. Even the Cairo Conference on Population overlooks the vital factor that it is the woman's body which is the sole owner of the reproductive system and therefore, women and women only should be sole decision makers. The erring governments lately, are paying more attention to the Nobel Laureate Amartya Sen than they ever paid to women screaming loud and hoarse. This Conference had also urged the governments and the regional and international organizations to facilitate the access of women in decision making posts and their greater participation in the decision making process. But, when, if ever at all, will the parliaments and other decision taking bodies in the various democracies of the world represent fifty percent of the population proportionately? Right to decision making is the mother of all other basic human rights. Till that is acquired and exercised, all other rights will remain piecemeal and inconsequential. Once that happens, the discourse on rights will be meaningless or totally unnecessary, because people will enjoy rights automatically like a birth right.

8
Advancement of Women Rights

1. The Charter of the United Nations is the first international instrument to mention equal rights of men and women in specific terms. In its Preamble, the Charter proclaims the determination of the peoples of the United Nations "to reaffirm faith in fundamental human rights, in the dignity and worth of the human person, in the equal rights of men and women" and "to employ international machinery for the promotion of the economic and social advancement of all peoples". One of the purposes of the United Nations, as set out in Article 1, is "to achieve international cooperation in solving international problems of an economic, social, cultural, or humanitarian character, and in promoting and encouraging respect for human rights and fundamental freedoms for all without distinction as to race, sex, language or religion". Article 8 states that "The United Nations shall place no restrictions on the eligibility of men and women to participate in any capacity and under conditions of equality in its principal and subsidiary organs". Articles 13, 55 and 76 call for the realization of human rights and fundamental freedoms "for all without distinction as to race, sex, language or religion". Under

Article 56, Member States have pledged themselves to take joint and separate action, in cooperation with the United Nations, to achieve such aims.

2. This basic principle is elaborated in the Universal Declaration of Human Rights, which proclaims that "all human beings are born free and equal in dignity, and rights" (article 1), and that "everyone is entitled to all the rights and freedoms set forth [therein] without distinction of any kind", including distinction based on sex (article 2).

3. The principle of equality of men and women and the prohibition of discrimination against women are clearly set out in both International Covenants on Human Rights. They are also at the heart of many United Nations instruments which deal with particular rights of women, such as the Convention on the Political Rights of Women, the Convention on the Nationality of Married Women, the Convention and the Recommendation on Consent to Marriage, Minimum Age for Marriage and Registration of Marriages; and, in so far as they concern the status of women, the Supplementary Convention on the Abolition of Slavery, the Slave Trade, and Institutions and Practices Similar to Slavery and the Convention for the Suppression of the Traffic in Persons and of the Exploitation of the Prostitution of Others. In addition, these principles inspired a number of instruments adopted by the International

Labour Conference, including the Underground Work (Women) Convention, 1935 (No. 45); the Night Work (Women) Convention (revised), 1949 (No. 89); the Equal Remuneration Convention for Men and Women Workers for Work of Equal Value of 1951 (No. 100); the Discrimination (Employment and Occupation) Convention of 1958 (No. 111); and the Workers with

Family Responsibilities Convention, 1981 (No. 156); as well as the Convention against Discrimination in Education, adopted by the General Conference of the United Nations Educational, Scientific and Cultural Organization in 1960.

4. For more than forty years competent organs of the United Nations have worked energetically to improve the status of women in various fields and to eliminate discrimination against women. Within the established United Nations system, most of the measures designed to attain these goals originated in the Commission on the Status of Women, a functional commission of the Economic and Social Council. In recent years, the Committee on the Elimination of Discrimination against Women, a treaty-based body established in accordance with the Convention on the Elimination of All Forms of Discrimination against Women, has assumed the task of monitoring measures taken by Governments to put an end to discrimination on the basis of sex.

5. In the early years of its existence, the Commission on the Status of Women concentrated on improving the status of women in law, particularly private law, and in broadening women's enjoyment of their rights to education, to employment and to health care. It submitted comments and made suggestions on matters of particular interest to women to the Commission on Human Rights and the Economic and Social Council relating to the Universal Declaration of Human Rights and both International Covenants on Human Rights as they were being drafted.

6. In addition, the Commission undertook studies and made recommendations on many other questions of interest to women, such as access to education at all levels, economic rights and opportunities for women, including equal pay for equal work, and various aspects

of family law and property rights. It based its consideration these questions on information contained in reports prepared by the Secretary-General of the United Nations and the Directors-General of the specialized agencies competent in the subject. The Commission's work resulted in the adoption of many resolutions addressing recommen-dations to Governments aimed at improving the status of women and establishing the principle of equality of rights for men and women.

7. In 1949 the Commission decided to prepare an international convention as a further means of promoting equal political rights for men and women. On the basis of a draft prepared in the Commission, the Convention on the Political Rights of Women was adopted and opened for signature and ratification or accession by the General Assembly on 20 December 1952. Three additional Conventions, one Declaration and one Recommendation have since been concluded under the auspices of the United Nations as a direct result of the work of the Commission. The first is the Convention on the Nationality of Married Women, adopted by the General Assembly in 1957. The second is the Convention on Consent to Marriage, Minimum Age for Marriage and Registration of Marriages, adopted by the General Assembly in 1962; this Convention was followed by a Recommendation on the same subject, adopted by the General Assembly in 1965.

9. The Declaration on the Elimination of Discrimination against Women, drafted by the Commission, was adopted and proclaimed by the General Assembly in 1967. It was followed by the Convention on the Elimination of all Forms of Discrimination against Women, adopted and opened for signature, ratification or accession by the General Assembly in 1979.

10. With the completion of the drafting of the Convention, which provided for the establishment of the Committee on the Elimination of Discrimination against Women, the Commission on the Status of Women assumed a new role: first it served as the preparatory body for two major international observances: of the International Women's Year (1975) and of the United Nations Decade for Women (1976-1985); then it served as the preparatory body for three worldwide conferences, held at Mexico City, Copenhagen and Nairobi respectively, in connection with the activities of the Decade.

11. The Commission's mandate was revised recently "to include the functions of promoting the objectives of equality, development and peace, monitoring the implementation of measures for the advancement of women, and reviewing and appraising the progress made at the national, subregional, regional, sectoral and global levels".

12. A brief overview of the broad historical background underlying action by the United Nations for the advancement of women, as seen by participants in the 1985 World Conference to Review and Appraise the Achievements of the United Nations Decade for Women: Equality, Development and Peace appears in the Introduction to the Forward-looking Strategies for the Advancement of Women which the Conference adopted by consensus; as follows:

> The founding of the United Nations after the victory in the Second World War and the emergence of independent States following decolonization were some of the important events in the political, economic and social liberation of women. The International Women's Year, the World Conferences held at Mexico City in 1975 and Copenhagen in 1980, and the United Nations Decade for Women:

Equality, Development and Peace contributed greatly to the process of eliminating obstacles to the improvement of the status of women at the national, regional and international levels. In the early 1970s, efforts to end discrimination against women and to ensure their equal participation in society provided the impetus for most initiatives taken at all of those levels. Those efforts were also inspired by the awareness that women's reproductive and productive roles were closely linked to the political, economic, social, cultural, legal, educational and religious conditions that constrained the advancement of women and that factors intensifying the economic exploitation, marginalization and oppression of women stemmed from chronic inequalities, injustices and exploitative conditions at the family, community, national, subregional, regional and international levels.

In 1972, the General Assembly, in resolution 3010 (XXVII), proclaimed 1975 International Women's Year, to be devoted to intensified action to promote equality between men and women, to ensure the full integration of women in the total development effort and to increase women's contribution to the strengthening of world peace. The World Plan of Action for the Implementation of the Objectives of the International Women's Year adopted by the World Conference of the International Women's Year at Mexico City in 1975, was endorsed by the General Assembly in its resolution 3520 (XXX). The General Assembly, in that resolution, proclaimed 1976-1985 the United Nations Decade for Women: Equality, Development and Peace. In its resolution 33/185, the General Assembly decided upon the sub-theme "Employment, Health and Education" for the World Conference of the United Nations Decade for Women: Equality, Development and Peace, to be held at Copenhagen to review and evaluate the progress made in the first half of the Decade.

In 1980, at the midpoint of the Decade, the

Copenhagen World Conference adopted the Programme of Action for the Second Half of the United Nations Decade for Women: Equality, Development and Peace which further elaborated on the existing obstacles and on the existing international consensus on measures to be taken for the advancement of women. The Programme of Action was endorsed by the General Assembly that year in its resolution 35/136.

Also in 1980, the General Assembly, in resolution 35/36, adopted the International Development Strategy for the Third United Nations Development Decade and reaffirmed the recommendations of the Copenhagen World Conference (General Assembly resolution 35/56, annex, para. 51). In the Strategy, the importance of the participation of women in the development process, as both agents and beneficiaries, was stressed. Also, the Strategy called for appropriate measures to be taken in order to bring about profound social and economic changes and to eliminate the structural imbalances that compounded and perpetuated women's disadvantages in society.

The strategies contained in the World Plan of Action and in the Programme of Action were important contributions towards enlarging the prospect for the future of women. In most areas, however, further action is required. In this connection the General Assembly confirmed the goals and objectives of the Decade—equality, development and peace—stressed their validity for the future and indicated the need for concrete measures to overcome the obstacles to their achievement during the period 1986-2000.

13. Important international initiatives designed to further the advancement of women include the following:

— Adoption of the Declaration on the Elimination of Discrimination against Women by the General Assembly of the United Nations (1967); adoption and opening for signature, ratification and accession of the Convention on the Elimination of All Forms of Discrimination against Women by the General Assembly (1979), and commencement of the work of the Committee on the Elimination of Discrimination against Women (1982);

— Observance of International Women's Year (1975), convening of the World Conference of the International Women's Year, and adoption by the Conference of the Declaration of Mexico on the Equality of Women and their Contribution to Development and Peace;

— Establishment of the United Nations Development Fund for Women (1974) and of the International Research and Training Institute for the Advancement of Women (1976);

— Observance of the United Nations Decade for Women: Equality, Development and Peace (1976-1985), convening of the World Conference of the United Nations Decade for Women (1980), and adoption by the Conference of the Programme of Action for the second half of the United Nations Decade for Women;

— Convening of the World Conference to Review and Appraise the Achievements of the United Nations Decade for Women (1985), and adoption by the Conference of the Nairobi Forward-Looking Strategies for the Advancement of Women.

14. These major initiatives, and many of the activities which preceded or developed out of them, are described below.

Equality

Meaning of equality and obstacles to its achievement

15. As recognized in the Forward-looking Strategies,

equality is both a goal and a means whereby individuals are accorded equal treatment under the law and equal opportunities to enjoy their rights and to develop their potential talents and skills so that they can participate in national, political, economic, social and cultural development and can benefit from its results. For women in particular, equality means the realization of rights that they have been denied as a result of cultural, institutional, behavioural or attitudinal discrimination. Equality is important for development and peace because national and global inequities perpetuate themselves and increase tensions of all types.

16. The Nairobi Conference examined many obstacles to the achievement of a major international objective: the full observance of the equal rights of women and the elimination of *de jure* and *de facto* discrimination on the basis of sex. Its analysis of these obstacles included the following observations:

> On of the fundamental obstacles to women's equality is that *de facto* discrimination and inequality in the status of women and men derive from larger social, economic, political and cultural factors that have been justified on the basis of physiological differences. Although there is no physiological basis for regarding the household and family as essentially the domain of women, or the devaluation of domestic work and for regarding the capacities of women as inferior to those of men, the belief that such a basis exists perpetuates inequality and inhibits the structural and attitudinal changes necessary to eliminate such inequality.
>
> Women, by virtue of their gender, experience discrimination in terms of denial of equal access to the power structure that controls society and determines development issues and peace initiatives. Additional differences, such as race, colour and ethnicity, may have even more serious

implications in some countries, since such factors can be used as justification for compound discrimination.

Fundamental resistance creates obstacles, which have wide-ranging implications for the objectives of the Decade. Discrimination promotes an uneconomic use of women's talents and wastes the valuable human resources necessary for development and for the strengthening of peace. Ultimately society is the loser if the talents of women are under-utilized as a result of discrimination.

The sharp contrasts between legislative changes and effective implementation of these changes are a major obstacle to the full participation of women in society. *De facto* and indirect discrimination, particularly by reference to marital or family status, between persists despite legislative action. The law as a recourse does not automatically benefit all women equally, owing to the socioeconomic inequalities determining women's knowledge of and access to the law, as well as their ability to exercise their full legal rights without fear of recrimination or intimidation. The lack or inadequacy of the dissemination of information on women's rights and the available recourse to justice has hampered, in many instances, the achievement of expected results.

Some legislative changes are made without a thorough understanding of the relationship between existing legal systems. In practice, however, certain aspects of the law—for instance, customary provisions—may be in operation in societies with multiple and conflicting legal systems. Emerging and potential obstacles resulting from possible contradictions should be anticipated so that preventive measures can be taken. When passing new legislation, whatever its subject matter, all possible care should be taken to ensure that it implies no direct or indirect discrimination so that women's right to equality is fully respected in law. In some countries, discriminatory legislative provisions in the social, economic and political spheres still exist, including civil, penal and commercial codes and certain administrative rules and regulations. Civil codes in some instances have not vet been adequately studied to determine action for repealing those laws that still discriminate against women and for determining, on the basis of equality, the legal capacity and status of women, married women in particular, in terms of nationality, inheritance, ownership and control of property, freedom of movement and the custody and nationality of children. Above all, there is still a deeply rooted resistance on the part of conservative elements in society to the change in attitude necessary for a total ban on discriminatory practices against women at the family, local, national and international levels.

Declaration on the elimination of discrimination against women

17. The Declaration on the Elimination of Discrimination against Women was adopted unanimously by the General Assembly in resolution 2263 (XXII) on 7 November 1967, after four years of debate and detailed drafting in the Commission on the Status of Women and in the Assembly. The need for this Declaration is stated in the preamble, which expresses concern that despite the Charter, the Universal Declaration of Human Rights, the International Covenants on Human Rights and other instruments, and despite the progress made, "there continues to exist considerable discrimination against women."

18. The Declaration represents a general pronouncement of United Nations policy in regard to equality of rights of men and women and the elimination of

discrimination based on sex. It restates and consolidates a series of principles, many of which were embodied in earlier international instruments emanating from the Unites Nations and the specialized agencies. It also sets forth a series of important principles not contained in earlier treaties and recommendations.

19. The Declaration contains 11 articles. Those of a general nature are:

— *Article 1,* which states that "discrimination against women, denying or limiting as it does their equality of rights with men, is fundamentally unjust and constitutes an offence against human dignity";

— *Article 2,* which calls for the abolition of existing laws, customs, regulations and practices which are discriminatory against women, and the establishment of adequate legal protection for equal rights of men and women; and which also calls for the ratification of, or accession to the international instruments of the United Nations and the specialized agencies relating to the elimination of discrimination against women, and their full implementation, as soon as possible;

— *Article 3,* which, describes discrimination against women as "customary and all other practices which are based on the idea of the inferiority of women", and which contains the first reference, in an instrument of international law, to the need to educate public opinion and to direct national aspirations towards the eradication of prejudice and the abolition of discrimination against women. This article is of paramount importance because it touches upon a field in which the United Nations can make a substantial contribution for the advancement of women: the changing of attitudes towards the actual realization of the equal dignity and worth of all women and men and the different roles that women and men can play in society.

20. Other articles deal with specific rights or groups of rights: that is, political rights (article 4); the right to a nationality (article 5); rights under civil law (article 6); discriminatory provisions under penal law (article 7); traffic in women (article 8); educational rights (article 9); and economic and social rights (article 10).

21. By providing that all appropriate measures shall be taken to ensure to women, on equal terms with men and without any discrimination, the right to vote in all elections and be eligible for election to all publicly elected bodies, and the right to hold public office and to exercise all public functions, the Declaration restates the principal provisions of the 1952 Convention on the Political Rights of Women; however, it also includes a specific reference to the right to vote in all public referenda, which is not mentioned in the Convention.

22. In proclaiming the principle that women shall have the same rights as men to acquire, change or retain their nationality, and in providing that marriage to an alien shall not automatically affect the nationality of the wife, the Declaration restates the provisions of the Convention on the Nationality of Married Women of 1957, although in other provisions the Declaration is less far-reaching than the Convention.

23. In providing that "all appropriate measures, particularly legislative measures, shall be taken to ensure to women, married or unmarried, equal rights with men in the field of civil law", the Declaration lists a number of fields in which this equality shall apply. It thus consolidates a series of solemn statements by the General Assembly and the Economic and Social Council, adopted over the years on the initiative of the Commission on the Status of Women. Article 6 of the Declaration also

restates provisions of earlier instruments such as the Convention on Consent to Marriage, Minimum Age for Marriage and Registration of Marriages of 1962 and its Recommendation of 1965. The Declaration also calls, in article 7, for the abolition of all provisions in penal codes which constitute discrimination against women.

24. In providing that "All appropriate measures shall be taken to ensure to girls and women... equal rights with men in education at all levels", the Declaration incorporates the principle on which the UNESCO Convention against Discrimination in Education of 1960 is based. In proclaiming that "All appropriate measures shall be taken to ensure to women... equal rights with men in the field of economic and social life", the Declaration incorporates principles set out in a number of International Labour Conventions, such as the Equal Remuneration Convention, 1951 (No. 100) and the Discrimination (Employment and Occupation) Convention, 1958 (No. 111).

25. The Declaration, in its categorical injunction that "all appropriate measures... shall be taken to combat all forms of traffic in women and exploitation of prostitution of women", reaffirms provisions of several earlier international instruments, including the Convention for the Suppression of the Traffic in Persons and of the Exploitation of the Prostitution of Others of 1949.

26. The Economic and Social Council, in resolution 1325 (XLIV) of 31 May 1968, adopted on the recommendation of the Commission on the Status of Women, initiated a reporting system on the implementation of the Declaration. Member States, the specialized agencies and the non-governmental organizations concerned were requested to inform the Secretary-General of publicity given to the Declaration, and of action taken by them in compliance with its

principles. The Secretary-General was requested to submit reports on the information received for consideration by the Commission.

27. The Committee on the Elimination of Discrimination against Women has responsibility for monitoring implementation of provisions of the Convention on the Elimination of All Forms of Discrimination against Women on the basis of reports which States parties submit to the Committee at regular intervals.

28. All other issues relating to the advancement of women and the elimination of discrimination based on sex are monitored by the Commission on the Status of Women.

Committee on the elimination of discrimination against women

29. Members of the Committee on the Elimination of Discrimination against Women, established in accordance with the Convention on the Elimination of All Forms of Discrimination against Women, were elected by representatives of States parties to the Convention at their first meeting, on 16 April 1982. The first session of the Committee was held at the United Nations Office at Vienna from 18 to 22 October 1982. The Committee elected a Chairman, three Vice-Chairmen and a Rapporteur, adopted its agenda, and considered a number of organizational questions. In accordance with article 17, paragraphs 5 and 6, of the Convention, the Chairman selected by lot the 11 experts of the Committee whose terms would expire in 1984. The Committee then examined and adopted its rules of procedure, and considered its programme of future work. In addition, it examined briefly the question of guidelines for reports by States parties to the Convention.

30. Up to the end of 1987 the Committee had held six sessions, had adopted its rules of procedure and had formulated general guidelines on the form and contents of reports received from States parties under article 18 of the Convention. It had also made a contribution to the World Conference at Nairobi, Kenya, in 1985 by submitting a report on the achievements of and obstacles encountered by States parties in the implementation of the Convention and decided on guidelines for the preparation of second periodic reports.

31. It had considered the initial reports of 34 States parties: Austria, Bangladesh, Bulgaria, Byelorussian Soviet Socialist Republic, Canada, China, Colombia, Cuba, Czechoslovakia, Denmark, Ecuador, Egypt, El Salvador, France, German Democratic Republic, Greece, Hungary, Mexico, Mongolia, Norway, Panama, Philippines, Poland, Portugal, Rwanda, Republic of Korea, Spain, Sri Lanka, Sweden, Ukrainian Soviet Socialist Republic, Union of Soviet Socialist Republics, Venezuela, Viet Nam and Yugoslavia.

32. It had also discussed at several sessions, ways and means of implementing article 21 of the Convention, which provides that the Committee may make suggestions and general recommendations based on nation of reports. At the sixth session, the Committee repeated in general recommendation No. 2, a recommendation already adopted at its fifth session, namely that States parties, in preparing their reports, should follow the general guidelines, that initial reports should cover the situation up to the date of submission and, thereafter, reports should be submitted at least every four years after the due date of the first report and should cover obstacles encountered in the implementation of the Convention and measures adopted to overcome them. In general recommendation No. 3 the Committee urged all States parties effectively to adopt

education and public information programmes, which should help eliminate prejudices and current practices that hindered the full operation of the principle of the social equality of women. By general recommendation No. 4 the Committee suggested to all States parties concerned to reconsider reservations made with a view to withdrawing them.

33. In resolution 42/60 of 30 November 1987, the General Assembly took note of the report of the Committee on the work of its sixth session and expressed concern about the Committee's account of the constraints under which it had operated with respect to the backlog of reports awaiting examination. It encouraged the Committee to intensify its discussion on ways and means of dealing with this problem, and welcomed its efforts to rationalize its procedures and to expedite the consideration of reports from States parties. It also requested the Secretary-General to provide, facilitate and encourage public information activities relating to the Committee and the Convention, giving priority to the dissemination of the Convention in the official languages of the United Nations.

International Women's Year (1975)

34. By resolution 3010 (XXVII) of 18 December 1972, the General Assembly proclaimed the year 1975 International Women's Year and decided to devote the year to intensified action.

(a) To promote equality between men and women;

(b) To ensure the full integration of men in the total development effort, especially by emphasizing women's responsibility and important role in economic, social and cultural development at the national, regional and international levels, particularly during the Second United Nations Development Decade;

(c) To recognize the importance of women's increasing contribution to the development of friendly relations and cooperation among States and to the strengthening of world peace.

The Assembly invited

> all Member States and all interested organizations to take steps to ensure the full realization of the rights of women and their advancement on the basis of the Declaration on the Elimination of Discrimination against Women,

and requested the Secretary-General to prepare, in consultation with Member States, specialized agencies and interested non-governmental organizations, a draft programme for the International Women's Year.

35. The Economic and Social Council, in resolution 1851 (LVI-) of 16 May 1974, requested the Secretary-General to convene an international conference during the International Women's Year to examine to what extent the organizations of the United Nations system had implemented the recommendations for the elimination of discrimination against women made by the Commission on the Status of Women since its establishment, and to launch an international action programme including short-term and long-term measures aimed at achieving the integration of women as full and equal partners with men in the total development effort and eliminating discrimination on grounds of sex and at achieving the widest involvement of women in strengthening international peace and eliminating racism and racial discrimination.

(a) World Conference of the International Women's Year

36. The focal point of the international celebration of the International Women's Year was the World Conference of the International Women's Year held in Mexico City from 19 June to 2 July 1975.9 The Conference was

attended by 133 States represented by more than 1,000 delegates, about 70 per cent of whom were women. Three Governments were represented by observers. Nine offices of the Secretariat, seven United Nations bodies, seven specialized agencies and IAEA were also represented. In accordance with General Assembly resolution 3276 (XXIX) of 10 December 1974, seven national liberation movements sent observers. The Commission on Human Rights and eight intergovernmental organizations were also represented by observers, as well as 114 non-governmental organizations in consultative status with the Economic and Social Council following Economic and Social Council decision 73 (LVIII) of 28 April 1975.

37. The Conference adopted the Declaration of Mexico on the Equality of Women and Their Contribution to Development and Peace, 1975; the World Plan of Action for the Implementation of the Objectives of the International Women's Year; regional plans of action; 35 resolutions; and a decision recommending the convening of a second world conference in 1980.

38. The Declaration promulgates 30 principles. These deal among other things with: equality between women and men; equal rights and responsibilities of women and men in the family and society; equal access to education and training; the right to work and to equal pay for work of equal value; the right of couples and individuals to determine the number and spacing of children; the right of every woman to decide freely whether to marry; the right to participate in and contribute to the development effort; the full participation of women in the economic, social and cultural sectors; the role of women in the promotion of international cooperation and peace; the role of women in promoting human rights of all peoples; and the need to eliminate violations of human rights committed against women and girls.

39. The Declaration urges Governments, the United Nations system, regional and international intergovernmental organizations, and the international community to dedicate themselves to the creation of a just society where women, men and children can live in dignity, freedom, justice and prosperity.

40. The World Plan of Action for the Implementation of the Objectives of the International Women's Year was adopted to strengthen the implementation of the instruments and programmes which had been adopted concerning the status of women, and to broaden and place them in a more timely context. Its purpose was mainly to stimulate national and international action to solve the problems of underdevelopment and of the socioeconomic structure which placed women in an inferior position, in order to achieve the goals of the International Women's Year. In order to promote equality between women and men, the Plan recommended that Governments ensure for both women and men equality before the law, the provision of facilities for equality of educational opportunities and training, equality in conditions of employment, including remuneration and adequate social security. The Plan drew attention to nine specific areas for national action and made several recommendations for international and regional action.

41. The General Assembly, at its thirtieth session, overwhelmingly endorsed the action proposals of the Conference by adopting ten resolutions and one decision outlining action for the future.

(b) United Nations Development Fund for Women

42. The Economic and Social Council, in resolution 1850 (LVI) of 16 May 1974, welcomed voluntary contributions from Member States, intergovernmental and non-governmental organizations, private foundations

and interested individuals, to supplement the resources available to implement the programme for the International Women's Year; and called upon the Secretary-General to accept such voluntary contributions.

43. At its 2441st plenary meeting, on 15 December 1975, the General Assembly decided that the voluntary fund for the International Women's Year should be extended to cover the period of the United Nations Decade for Women. At its thirty-first session, after considering the report of the Secretary-General on the Voluntary Fund for the Decade," the Assembly adopted, in resolution 31/133 of 16 December 1976, criteria for the management of the Voluntary Fund for the United Nations Decade for Women; requested the Secretary-General to report annually there on; and requested the President of the General Assembly to select five Member States, each of which should appoint a representative to serve, for a three-year period, on the Consultative Committee to advise the Secretary-General on the application of the criteria to the use of the Fund.

44. In resolution 31/133 of 16 December 1976, the Assembly set out a series of criteria for the use of the Fund, requested the Secretary-General to report annually there on, and requested its President to select five Member States, each of which should appoint a representative to serve, for a three-year period, on a Consultative Committee to advise the Secretary-General on the use of the Fund.

45. In resolution 31/137 of the same date, the General Assembly requested the Secretary-General to convene during its thirty-second session a pledging conference for contributions to be made to the Voluntary Fund for the United Nations Decade for Women and to the International Research and Training Institute for the Advancement of Women. The first Pledging Conference

for the United Nations Decade for Women was accordingly held at United Nations Headquarters on 8 November 1977. Noting the results of that Conference with satisfaction, the General Assembly, in resolution 32/139 of 16 December 1977, called for a second pledging conference to be convened during its thirty-third session. Similar pledging conferences have been convened annually since then. At its thirty-fourth session the General Assembly, after considering the report of the Secretary-General on the Fund, adopted resolution 34/156 of 17 December 1979 in which it noted with satisfaction the decisions of the Consultative Committee, expressed its desire to see the activities developed by the Fund continued beyond the United Nations Decade for Women, and requested the Secretary-General and the Committee to study that question.

46. The General Assembly continued its examination of various aspects of the operation of the Voluntary Fund on an annual basis up to 1985 (resolutions 32/141, 33/188, 34/156, 35/137, 36/129, 37/62, 38/106, 39/125 and 40/104); thereafter it considered the item biennially.

47. In resolution 39/125 of 14 December 1984, the Assembly decided that the activities of the Voluntary Fund should be continued through establishment of a separate and identifiable entity, in autonomous association with the United Nations Development Programme, which would play an innovative and catalytic role in relation to the United Nations system of development cooperation. Accordingly it endorsed arrangements for the future management of the Fund, annexed to solution, and requested the Consultative Committee monitor their implementation.

48. The establishment of the United Nations Development Fund for Women, in autonomous association with the UNDP, was effected on 1 July, 1985;

and the UNDP Administrator has since submitted to the General Assembly, through the Secretary-General, reports on its activities.

49. The report submitted to the Assembly at the forty-second session indicated that UNDP and the United Nations Development Fund for Women (UNIFEM) were preparing a set of guidelines to regulate their functional relationship and facilitate and deepen the close cooperation between the Fund and UNDP, and pointed out that the Governing Council of UNDP, in its decision 87/41 of 18 June 1987, commended the Fund's new operational directions, with special reference to its programming approach, urged the Fund to intensify its approaches to secure mainstream consideration of women, and noted the collaboration between the Fund and the UNDP Division for Women in Development.

50. In resolution 42/63 of 30 November 1987, the General Assembly took note of the note by the Secretary-General 14 containing the report of the Administrator of the United Nations Development Programme and the report of the Consultative Committee on the United Nations Development Fund for Women at its twenty-first session, and welcomed the constructive cooperation between the Programme and the Fund. It expressed its appreciation for the financial contributions to the Fund made by Governments, intergovernmental organizations, national committees and individuals; and invited States to continue and, where possible, to increase their contributions in order to enable the Fund to give greater support to deserving project requests received for technical assistance.

(c) International Research and Training Institute for the Advancement of Women

51. In resolution 26, the World Conference of the International Women's Year decided "to recommend the

establishment, under the auspices of the United Nations, of an International Training and Research Institute for the Advancement of Women, financed through voluntary contributions, which in collaboration with appropriate national, regional and Inter-regional economic and social research institutes and the specialized agencies", would

(a) Undertake research and the collection and dissemination of information as the basis for the formulation of programmes and policies for the effective participation of women;

(b) Assist in the design of research for the monitoring of changes in the situation of women and the impact on their lives of economic, social and technological changes;

(e) Develop, adapt and provide training programmes for women, in particular those of the developing countries, which would enable them to undertake national research, to assume leadership roles within their own societies and to increase their earning possibilities.

The Secretary-General was invited to appoint a group of experts to assist him in the establishment f his Institute and to draw up its terms of reference.

52. The General Assembly, in resolution 3520 (XXX) of 15 December 1975, decided in principle to establish such an Institute, and requested the Secretary-General to report to the Economic and Social Council on the basis of the recommendations of the Group of Experts.

53. The 11-member Group of Experts on the Establishment of an International Research and Training Institute for the Advancement of Women met at United Nations Headquarters from 17 to 23 February 1976. On the basis of its recommendations the Secretary-General submitted a report" to the Economic and Social Council

at its sixtieth session in which he expressed agreement that the Institute should be established, subject to the availability of extrabudgetary funds that would be needed to ensure its opera on for an initial period of at least three years, and to the Institute's scope and objectives, terms of reference and priorities.

54. The Council, in resolution 1998 (LX) of 12 May 1976, decided to establish the Institute not later than 1977, provided the necessary financial provisions were made, as an autonomous body under the auspices of the United Nations, funded by voluntary contributions. As guidelines, the Council decided that the Institute should work in close collaboration with all relevant organizations within the United Nations system, and national and regional centres and institutes which have similar objectives; that it should take the activities of those organizations fully into account and coordinate its work with theirs; that it should direct its activities with special attention to the needs of women in developing countries and their integration in the development process; and that it should maintain close contact with the Commission on the Status of Women.

55. Later the Council, in resolution 1979/11 of 9 May 1979, recommended that the Institute should be located in the Dominican Republic. The Assembly endorsed this decision in resolution 34/157 of 17 December 1979, and accepted with appreciation the offer of the Government of the Dominican Republic to act as host for the Institute. In resolution 1981/13 of 6 May 1981, the Council expressed its satisfaction at the conclusion of the agreement between the Government of the Dominican Republic and the United Nations concerning the installation of the Institute at Santo Domingo, welcomed the appointment of the Director of the Institute, and expressed the hope that the Institute would start functioning shortly.

56. At its thirty-fifth Ad thirty-sixth sessions, the General Assembly invited Governments to contribute to the United Nations Trust Fund for the Institute. At its thirty-seventh session it endorsed the network concept to be developed in stages with the organizations of the United Nations system, and regional and national organizations, as a mode of operation for the execution of its programme.

57. In 1983, the Assembly examined the report of the Institute on its programme activities In resolution 38/104 of 16 December 1983, it expressed its satisfaction at the official inauguration of the Institute at its permanent headquarters at Santo Domingo and requested it to continue activities that contribute to the full integration of women in the mainstream of development.

58. By decision 1984/124 of 24 May 1984, the Economic and Social Council approved the Statute of the Institute. Welcoming this development, the General Assembly in resolution 39/122 of 14 December 1984 took note with satisfaction of the Institute's programme, requested it to bear in mind trends in research and training relevant to women and development; and again invited contributions to the Institute's Trust Fund.

59. Further reports on the activities of the Institute were examined and noted with satisfaction by the General Assembly at its 1985 and 1987 sessions. 17 In resolution 42/65 of 30 November 1987, the Assembly expressed its satisfaction at the significance and scope of the activities of the Institute, particularly as they relate to statistics and indicators on women and training for the formulation of policy analysis, planning and programming relevant to an increased participation and the integration of women in development. The Institute was requested to continue and strengthen its research, training, information and communication activities,

particularly the developing of innovative training methodologies on women and socioeconomic issues related to development, networking as far as possible with other relevant research and training activities. It was also requested to promote general awareness and training on the pragmatic approach to the integration of women into policy designs, including the elaboration of special methodologies for monitoring and evaluation purposes, with particular reference to the implementation of the Nairobi Forward-looking Strategies for the Advancement of Women and the feedback of results into the operational system.

UN's Decade for women

60. The General Assembly, in resolution 3520 (XXX) of 15 December 1975, after taking note of the report of the World Conference of the International Women's Year" and endorsing the action proposals emanating from that Conference, proclaimed the period from 1976 to 1985 United Nations Decade for Women: Equality, Development and Peace, and called for it to be devoted to effective and sustained national, regional and international action to implement the resolutions of the Conference.

61. Also, pursuant to the decision of the Conference to recommend the convening of a second world conference in 1980, the Assembly, in the same resolution, decided to convene in 1980, at the midterm of the Decade, a world conference to review and evaluate the progress made in implementing the objectives of the International Women's Year. The Assembly also called upon Governments, as a matter of urgency, to examine the recommendations of the Conference.

(a) World Conference of the United Nations Decade for Women: Equality, Development and Peace, 1980

62. The World Conference of the United Nations

Decade for Women: Equality, Development and Peace, was held at Copenhagen from 14 to 30 July 1980 in conformity with General Assembly resolution 33/191 of 29 January 1979.

63. The Conference was attended by 145 States represented by more than 2,000 delegates. Nine offices of the United Nations, 13 United Nations bodies and programmes and five specialized agencies were also represented. The United Nations Council for Namibia and the Special Committee Against *Aparthied* were represented, as well as 10 intergovernmental organisations attended as observers. A large number of non-governmental organizations in consultative status with the Economic and Social Council, or on the Roster, attended the Conference.

64. At the midpoint of the United Nations Decade for Women, the Conference formulated a Programme of Action for the Second Half of the Decade, 10 1980-1985. The Programme was designed to promote the attainment of the three objectives of equality, development and peace, with special emphasis on the sub themes namely, employment, health and education-as significant components of development, taking into account that human resources cannot achieve their full potential without integrated socioeconomic development. It aimed at strengthening comprehensive and effective strategies to remove obstacles and constraints on women's full and equal participation in development, including actions to solve the problems of underdevelopment and of the socioeconomic structure which places women in an inferior position and to increase their contribution to the strengthening of world peace.

65. In addition to preparing the Programme of Action for the Second Half of the Decade, the Conference reviewed and evaluated the progress made and obstacles

encountered in attaining the objectives of the Decade at the national, regional and international levels from 1975 to 1980, and considered the effects of *aparthied* on women in southern Africa as well as the effects of Israeli occupation on Palestinian women inside and outside the occupied territories. It adopted 48 resolutions and suggested that, since all the objectives of the World Plan of Action could not be achieved within a short span of time, the possibility of a second Decade could be envisaged for the period 1985-1995.

66. The General Assembly took note with satisfaction of the report of the Conference in resolution 35/136 of 11 December 1980, and endorsed the Programme of Action for the Second Half of the Decade. It recognized that the Conference had made an important and constructive contribution by appraising the progress achieved and the obstacles encountered in the implementation of the objectives of the Decade and by preparing and adopting a programme for the coming five years, and affirmed that the implementation of the Programme of Action should result in the complete integration of women into the development process and the elimination of all forms of inequality between men/ and women and would guarantee broad participation by women in efforts to strengthen peace and security throughout the world. The Assembly, further, urged Governments to take appropriate measures to implement the Programme of Action and other relevant resolutions and decisions of the Conference at the national, regional and international levels; and urged all organizations of the United Nations system to take the necessary measures to ensure a concerted and sustained effort for the implementation of the Programme and of other relevant resolutions and decisions of the Conference in the course of the second half of the Decade.

(b) World Conference to Review and Appraise the Achievements of the United Nations Decade for Women, 1985

67. The General Assembly decided, in resolution 35/136 of 11 December 1980, to convene a World Conference to Review and Appraise the Achievements of the United Nations Decade for Women. In resolution 36/126 of 14 December 1981 it requested the Commission on the Status of Women to give priority to preparations for the Conference.

68. The Commission prepared its recommendations on the question at its twenty-ninth session, in 1982, on the basis of a report by the Secretary-General. 21 The Economic and Social Council considered these recommendations at its first regular session of 1982.

69. In resolution 1982/26 of 4 May 1982, the Council decided that the Commission should be the preparatory body for the World Conference, operating on the basis of consensus The Council invited the widest possible participation 46 the preparatory body, and encouraged them to consider establishing national committees to assist, for example, national-level preparations for the Conference. The Council also invited the regional commissions, the specialized agencies, and non-governmental organizations having consultative status with the Council, to contribute to the preparatory work. Further, the Council recommended that the Commission should meet at Vienna in extraordinary session in 1983 and again in 1985 with conference preparations as the sole item of the agenda, and that its thirtieth regular session, in 1984, should be extended to allow additional time for conference preparations. It proposed that the Advancement of Women Branch of the Centre for Social Development and Humanitarian Affairs should serve as the secretariat of the preparatory body as

well as of the Conference. It also recommended that, with a view to the achievement of the goals of the Decade, a Forward-looking draft perspective on the status of women to the year 2000 should be prepared by the preparatory body for consideration by the Conference.

70. The General Assembly, in resolution 37/60 of 3 December 1982, endorsed the Council's decisions, and noted that the first session of the Commission as the preparatory body of the Conference would be held at Vienna from 23 February to 4 March 1983. In the same resolution the Assembly took note with appreciation of the report of the Secretary-General on the progress made in the preparation of a world survey on the role of women in development '22 and recommended that the survey should be submitted to the Conference.

71. The World Conference to Review and Appraise the Achievements of the United Nations Decade for Women: Equality, Development and Peace was held at Nairobi, Kenya, from 15 to 26 July 1985. The Conference was attended by 157 States. The United Nations Council for Namibia and the Special Committee against *Aparthied* were represented at the Conference. The Palestine Liberation Organization and the South West Africa People's Organization attended in the capacity of observers. Two national liberation movements, the African National Congress (South Africa) and the Pan Africanist Congress of Azania, were represented by observers. Five offices of the Secretariat, 18 United Nations bodies, eight specialized agencies, 17 intergovernmental organizations and 163 non-governmental organizations in consultative status with the Economic and Social Council were also represented. Miss Margaret Kenyatta, the head of the delegation of Kenya, was elected as President of the Conference.

72. The Conference considered two substantive agenda items: (1) Critical review and appraisal of progress achieved and obstacles encountered in attaining the goals and objectives of the United Nations Decade for Women: Equality, Development and Peace, and the sub-theme: Employment, Health and Education, bearing in mind the guidelines laid down at the World Conference of the International Women's Year held at Mexico City, and the World Conference of the United Nations Decade for Women: Equality, Development and Peace, held at Copenhagen; and (2) Forward-looking Strategies of implementation for the advancement of women for the period up to the year 2000, and concrete measures to overcome obstacles to the achievement of the goals and objectives of the United Nations Decade for Women: Equality, Development and Peace, and the sub-theme: Employment, Health and Education, bearing in mind the International Development Strategy for the Third United Nations Development Decade and the establishment of a new international economic order.

73. Two main committees were established to consider a large number of draft resolutions and a draft Declaration. Owing to lack of time, the Conference was unable to take action on any of them; they were appended to the Conference report and it was understood that they would be brought to the attention of the General Assembly for consideration and action as appropriate.

74. Both main committees were however able to recommend to the Conference for adoption the text of paragraphs to be incorporated in the chapters of the Forward-looking Strategies, and the Conference considered these paragraphs, and others on which it had not been possible to reach agreement in the Committee concerned. At its twentieth plenary meeting, on 26 July

1985, the Conference adopted the text of the Forward-looking Strategies as a whole by consensus.

(c) Implementation of the Nairobi Forward-looking Strategies for the Advancement of Women

75. The General Assembly considered the report of the World Conference to Review and Appraise the Achievements of the United Nations Decade for Women: Equality, Development and Peace, at its fortieth session. In resolution 40/108 of 13 December 1985, the Assembly took note of the report with satisfaction, endorsed the Nairobi Forward-looking Strategies for the Advancement of Women, and affirmed that the implementation of the Strategies should result in the elimination of all forms of inequality between women and men and in the complete integration of women into the development process-a development that would guarantee broad participation by women in efforts to strengthen peace and security in the world. The Assembly, further, called upon Governments to allocate adequate resources and to take effective appropriate measures to implement the Forward-looking Strategies as a matter of high priority, including the establishment or reinforcement, as appropriate, of national machineries to promote the advancement of women, and to monitor the implementation of these Strategies with a view to ensuring the full integration of women in the political, economic, social and cultural life of their countries.

76. At its forty-first session, in resolution 41/111 of 4 December 1986, the General Assembly took note of two reports of the Secretary-General concerning the implementation of the Forward-looking Strategies; 24 reaffirmed the need to translate those Strategies immediately into concrete action by Governments, as determined by overall national priorities, as well as by the organizations of the United Nations system, the

specialized agencies, and intergovernmental and non-governmental organizations; and called upon all Member States to establish specific targets at each level in order to increase the participation of women in professional and decision-making positions in their countries.

77. The Economic and Social Council, at its first regular session of 1987, considered the suggestions for monitoring and review and appraisal of the Nairobi Forward-looking Strategies set out in Chapter V, section C of the Strategies, together with the recommendations of the Commission on the Status of Women there on and the recommendation in General Assembly resolution 40/108 of 13 December 1985 which called for the further development of the established integrated reporting system. In this connection the Council received and noted the report of the Secretary-General on the existing system which identified its problems and suggested remedial measures. 25

78. In resolution 1987/18 of 26 May 1987, the Council set out a series of guidelines to be taken into account by the Secretary-General in further developing and implementing the reporting system. It invited the Secretary-General, the executive secretaries of the regional commissions, and the executive heads of the specialized agencies and other organizations of the United Nations system, to develop and implement, as an integral part of their programmes, a simple, concise and direct form of reporting to the Commission on the impact of their programmes and activities on women and the effectiveness of those programmes and activities in bringing the interests and needs of women into the mainstream of their organizations. Further, it authorized the Commission on the Status of Women, in consultation with the Statistical Commission, the Board of Trustees of the International Research and Training Institute for the Advancement of Women and other appropriate bodies,

to establish formal arrangements for the collection and distribution of the information required for the Commission to carry out its monitoring and review and appraisal functions.

79. In other resolutions adopted at the same session on the recommendation of the Commission on the Status of Women, the Economic and Social Council:

Called for further improvement of the status of women in the United Nations, and in particular for the Secretary-General to take the necessary measures, as requested in General Assembly resolution 41/206 D of 11 December 1986, to increase the number of women in posts subject to geographical distribution with a view to achieving, to the extent possible, an overall participation rate of 30 percent of total by 1990 without prejudice to the principle of equitable geographical distribution.

Recommended that world conferences to review and appraise the progress achieved in the implementation of the Forward-looking Strategies be held during the decade of the 1990s, at a date to be determined by the General Assembly not later than 1990, and in 2000 (Economic and Social Council resolution 1987/20 of 26 May 1987);

Decided that, commencing with its thirty-second session, the Commission on the Status of Women shall meet annually until the year 2000, and recommended that the officers elected to the Commission's bureau should serve for a term of office of two yea (Economic and Social Council resolution 1987/21 of 26 May 1987);

Decided to expand the terms of reference of the Commission on the Status of Women to include the functions of promoting the objectives of equality, development and peace, monitoring the implementation of measures for the advancement of women, and reviewing and appraising progress made at the national, subregional, regional, sectoral and global levels; and further decided to structure the agenda for the future sessions of the Commission around its functions, namely programming, coordination, monitoring and policy development (Economic and Social Council resolution 1987/22 of 26 May 1987);

Accepted in principle the need for an increase in the membership of the Commission, but referred the matter to the Commission with a request that it sumit appropriate proposals (Economic and Social Council resolution 1987/23 of 26 May 1987);

Endorsed priority themes for the thirty-second to thirty-seventh sessions of the Commission on the Status of Women, and decided that the work of the Commission in relation to the priority themes should be closely related to the relevant provisions of the Forward-looking Strategies and of other policy documents, the programmes elaborated in the system-wide midterm plan for women and development, and the relevant chapters of the World Survey on the Role of Women in Development, with a view to ensuring the effective implementation of the Forward-looking strategies and lasting improvement in the situation of women.

Recommended observance of the tenth anniversary of the operational activities of the United Nations Development Fund for Women by the General Assembly and by non-governmental organizations, including national committees; and urged Member States to pledge contributions to the Fund (Economic and Social Council resolution 1987/26 of 26 May 1987).

Taking the relevant resolutions and decisions of the Commission on the Status of Women and of the Economic and Social Council into account, specifically endorsing Council resolutions 1987/21 and 1987/24, and taking note of the Secretary-General's 1987 reports concerning the implementation of the Nairobi Forward-looking Strategies, the General Assembly in resolution 42/62 of 30 November 1987 reaffirmed a number of decisions which it had taken at its 1985 and 1986 sessions, among them:

The need for the Forward-looking Strategies to be immediately translated into concrete action by Governments, as determined by overall national priorities, as well as by the organizations of the United Nations system, the specialized agencies and intergovernmental and non-governmental organizations;

The central role of the Commission on the Status of Women in matters related to the advancement of the status of women. In this connection the Assembly called upon the Commission to promote the implementation of the Forward-looking Strategies and urged all organizations of the United Nations system to cooperate with the Commission in this task;

The role of the Centre for Social Development and Humanitarian Affairs of the United Nations Office at Vienna, in particular the Branch for the Advancement of Women, in the implementation of the Forward-looking Strategies, as the substantive secretariat of the Commission on the Status of Women and as a focal point for matters relating to women;

The catalysing role of the United Nations Development Fund for Women and the role of the United Nations International Research and Training Institute for the Advancement of Women in the promotion of the role of women in the context of the participation of women in development;

The need for the United Nations to develop an integrated reporting system with the Commission on the

Status of Women at its centre and, building upon existing information and resources, to monitor the review and appraisal of progress in the advancement of women, which are based on clear and relevant statistical and other measurable indicators and which will assist Member States in identifying problems and in developing remedial measures, at the national, regional and international levels.

81. The Assembly once again called upon the Secretary-General and the executive heads of the specialized agencies and other United Nations bodies to establish five-year targets at each level for the percentage of women in professional and decision-making positions, in accordance with the criteria established by the Assembly, in order that a definite upward trend in the application of Assembly resolution 41/206 D of 11 December 1986 be registered in the number of professional and decision-making positions held by women by 1990 and to set additional targets every five years. It requested the Secretary-General to extend the term of the women's Coordinator for a satisfactory period to ensure that the action programme-in which *inter alia* it is recommended that the situation of women in the United Nations Secretariat should be improved -will continue to be implemented. Further, it requested the Secretary-General to invite Governments, organizations of the United Nations system including the regional commissions and the specialized agencies, and intergovernmental and non-governmental organizations, to report periodically through the Commission on the Status of Women to the Economic and Social Council on the activities undertaken at all levels to implement the Forward-looking Strategies; and to report there on to the General Assembly.

6. Measure to ensure equality of man and women in the enjoyment of particular rights and freedom

82. Improvement of the legal status of women has been a concern of the Commission on the Status of Women since its first session, in 1947. On the recommendation of the Commission, the Economic and Social Council, in resolution 11 (11) of 21 June 1946, requested the Secretary-General "to make arrangements for a complete and detailed study of the legislation concerning the status of women and the practical application of such legislation".

83. Accordingly, the Secretary-General prepared a questionnaire on the legal status and treatment of women and circulated it to Governments. On the basis of the replies received, a number of reports were prepared and submitted to the Commission. Having examined these reports, the Commission made a series of recommendations to Governments through the Economic and Social Council.

(a) Political rights and participation of women

84. In one of its earliest decisions, resolution 56 (1) of 11 December 1946, the General Assembly, noting that certain Member States had not granted to women political rights equal to those of men, recommended that all Member States which had not done so should adopt the necessary measures to fulfil the aims of the Charter in that respect by granting women the same political rights as men. The Secretary-General was invited to communicate this recommendation to the Governments of all Member States.

85. The question of the political rights of women has since been dealt with, on the international level, in the Convention on the Political Rights of Women, adopted by the General Assembly on 20 December 1952, which entered into force on 7 July 1954; the Declaration on the Elimination of Discrimination against Women, proclaimed by the General Assembly on 7 November

1967; and the Convention on the Elimination of All Forms of Discrimination against Women, adopted by the General Assembly on 18 December 1979, which formally granted women the same political rights a entered into force on 3 September 1981.

86. The Convention on the Political Rights of Women contains the following provisions:

Article 1

Women shall be entitled to vote in all elections on equal terms with men, without any discrimination.

Article 2

Women shall be eligible for election to all publicly elected bodies, established by national law, on equal terms with men, without any discrimination.

Article 3

Women shall be entitled to hold public office and to exercise all public functions, established by national law, on equal terms with men, without any discrimination.

87. The Declaration on the Elimination of Discrimination against Women contains the following provision/

Article 4

All appropriate measures shall be taken to ensure to women on equal terms with men, without any discrimination:

(a) The right to vote in all elections and be eligible for election to all publicly elected bodies;

(b) The right to vote in all public referenda;

(c) The right to hold public office and to exercise all public functions.

Such rights shall be guaranteed by legislation.

88. The Convention on the Elimination of All Forms of Discrimination against Women contains the following provisions:

Article 7

States Parties shall take all appropriate measures to eliminate discrimination against women in the political and public life of the country and, in particular, shall ensure, on equal terms with men, the right:

(a) To vote in all elections and public referenda and to be eligible for election to all publicly elected bodies;

(b) To participate in the formulation of government policy and the implementation thereof and to hold public office and perform all public functions at all levels of government;

(c) To participate in non-governmental organizations and associations concerned with the public and political life of the country.

Article 8

States Parties shall take all appropriate measures to ensure to women, on equal terms with men, and without any discrimination the opportunity to represent their Governments at the international level and to participate in the work of international organizations.

89. Implementation of the provisions of the Convention on the Elimination of All Forms of Discrimination against Women is monitored by the Committee on the Elimination of Discrimination against Women,

90. In addition to preparing drafts of each of these instruments for consideration by its parent bodies-the General Assembly and the Economic and Social Council-the Commission on the Status of Women, with the cooperation of the ILO, UNESCO, and other international organizations, carried on continuing

programmes to encourage the civic and political education of women in public life, and encouraged Governments to do likewise. As early as 12 July 1963 the Economic and Social Council was able to note, in resolution 961 B (XXXVI), "that the great majority of States have formally granted women the same political rights as men.

91. The Commission has also initiated measures to improve the status of women in the Secretariat of the United Nations in accordance with Article 8 of the Charter, which provides that the United Nations "shall place no restrictions on the eligibility of men and women to participate in any capacity and under conditions of equality in its principal and subsidiary organs". On its recommendation the General Assembly, in resolution 2715 (XXV) of 15 December 1970, expressed the hope that the United Nations, including its special bodies and all intergovernmental agencies in the United Nations system of organizations, would set an example with regard to opportunities for the employment of women at senior and other professional levels. It urged the United Nations and the other bodies concerned to take or continue to take appropriate measures to ensure equal opportunities for the employment of qualified women in senior and other professional positions. It requested the Secretary-General to include in his report on the composition of the Secretariat data relevant to this questions.

92. Reports of the Secretary-General on the composition of the Secretariat presented to the General Assembly at its twentysixth and twentyeighth sessions included information on the employment of women in senior and other professional positions in the secretariats of organizations within the United Nations system. In resolution 3352 (XXIX) of 18 December 1974, the Assembly noted that these reports, and a report of the

United Nations Training and Research Institute entitled The Situation of Women in the United Nations revealed an unsatisfactory situation which called for specific measures and programmes in order to achieve an equitable balance between the number of men and women, particularly in senior and policy-making positions, including those of Under-Secretary-General and Assistant Secretary-General.

93. More recent reports of the Secretary-General indicated that he had appointed a Steering Committee for the Improvement of the Status of Women in the Secretariat and had accepted a number of measures recommended by that Committee to overcome earlier constraints. In resolution 41/206 of 11 December 1986 the Assembly requested the Secretary-General to take the necessary measures to increase the number of women in posts subject to geographical distribution with a view to achieving, to the extent possible, an overall participation rate of 30 per cent of the total by 1990, without prejudice to the principle of equitable geographical distribution of posts.

94. At its forty-second session the General Assembly received and took note, in resolution 42/220 C of 21 December 1987, of a report by the Secretary-General on his continuing efforts to improve the status of women in the Secretariat, 30 and requested him to continue those efforts and to consider the introduction of additional measures, if necessary, in order to increase the number of women in posts subject to geographical distribution with a view to achieving, to the extent possible, an overall participation rate of 30 per cent of the total by 1990. In this connection it urged the Secretary-General to increase his efforts to ensure an equitable representation of women from developing countries in posts subject to geographical distribution, and particularly in posts at senior and policy-formulating levels; and reiterated its

request to Member States to nominate more women candidates for such posts.

95. The Forward-looking Strategies for the Advancement of Women to the Year 2000,31 adopted by the World Conference to Review and Appraise the Achievements of the United Nations Decade for Women: Equality, Development and Peace, held at Nairobi from 15 to 26 July 1985, include the following paragraphs relating to equality in political participation and decision-making:

Governments and political parties should intensify efforts to stimulate and ensure equality of participation by women in all national and local legislative bodies and to achieve equity in the appointment, election and promotion of women to high posts in executive, legislative and judiciary branches in these bodies. At the local level, strategies to ensure equality of women in political participation should be pragmatic, should bear a close relationship to issues of concern to women in the locality and should take into account the suitability of the proposed measures to local needs and values.

Governments and other employers should devote special attention to broader and more equitable access and inclusion of women in management in various forms of popular participation, which is a significant factor in the development and realization of all human rights.

Governments should effectively secure participation of women in the decision-making processes at national, state and local levels through legislative and administrative measures. It is desirable that governmental departments establish a special office in each of them, headed preferably by a women, to monitor periodically and accelerate the process of equitable representation of women. Special activities should be undertaken to increase the recruitment, nomination and promotion of women, especially to decision-making and policy-making positions, by publicizing posts more widely, increasing upward mobility and so on, until equitable representation of women is achieved. Reports should be compiled periodically on the numbers of women in public service and on their levels of responsibility in their areas of work.

With respect to the increase in the number of couples in which both partner Y, are employed in the public service, especially the foreign service, Governments are urged to consider their special needs, in particular the couple's desire to be assigned to the same duty station, with a view to reconciling family and professional duties.

Awareness of women's political rights should be promoted through many channels, including formal and informal education, political education, non-governmental organizations, trade unions, the media and business organizations. Women should be encouraged and motivated and should help each other to exercise their right to vote and to be elected and to participate in the political process at all levels on equal terms with men.

Political parties and other organizations such as trade unions should make a deliberate effort to increase and improve women's participation within their ranks. They should institute measures to activate women's constitutional and legal guarantees of the right to be elected and appointed by selecting candidates. Equal access to the political machinery of the organizations and to resources and tools for developing skills in the art and tactics of practical politics, as well as effective leadership capabilities, should be given to women. Women in leadership positions also have a special responsibility to assist in this field.

Governments that have not already done so should establish institutional arrangements and procedures whereby individual women, as well as representatives of all types of women's interest groups, including those from the most vulnerable, least privileged and most oppressed groups, may participate actively in all aspects of the formulation, monitoring, review and appraisal of national and local policies, issues and activities.

96. With regard to participation in international affairs, the Strategies include the following paragraph:

Governments should take all appropriate measures to ensure to women, on equal terms with men and without discrimination, the opportunity to represent their Government at all levels on delegations to subregional, regional and international meetings. More women should be appointed as diplomats and to decision-making posts within the United Nations system, including posts in fields relating to peace and development activities. Support services, such as educational facilities and day care, for families of diplomats and other civil servants stationed abroad, of United Nations officials, as well as employment of spouses at the duty station, wherever possible, should be strongly encouraged.

Nationality of married women

97. The problem of the nationality of married women has been the concern of the United Nations since the Commission on the Status of Women decided to study this question in 1948. At its second session, held in January of that year, the Commission noted the many and varied discriminations against women that resulted from conflicts in nationality laws, and recalled The Hague Convention on Certain Questions relating to the Conflict of Nationality Laws (1930), the Montevideo Convention on the Nationality of Women (1933), and the

studies in the field which had been undertaken by the League of Nations. At its request the Economic and Social Council at its seventh session in 1948 requested the Secretary- General to prepare a report based on replies received to the Questionnaire on the Legal Status and Treatment of Women and a report on existing treaties and conventions in the field of nationality.

98. The Convention on the Nationality of Married Women was adopted by the General Assembly and opened for signature and ratification in resolution 1040 (XI) of 29 January 1957.

99. The Convention represented an important step in a development which had been foreshadowed in The Hague Convention on Certain Questions relating to the Conflict of Nationality Laws of 193032 and which tended to replace the traditional principle of the unity of the family with the principle of the independence of the nationality of the wife from that of her husband.

100. The Convention on the Nationality of Married Women contains the following provisions:

Article 1

Each contracting state agrees that neither the celebration nor the dissolution of a marriage between one of its nationals and an alien, nor the change of nationality by the husband during marriage, shall automatically affect the nationality of the wife.

Article 2

Each Contracting State agrees that neither the voluntary acquisition of the nationality of another State nor the renunciation of its nationality by one of its nationals shall prevent the retention of its nationality by the wife of such national.

Article 3

1. Each Contracting State agrees that the alien wife of one of its nationals may, at her request, acquire the nationality of her husband through specially privileged naturalization procedures; the grant of such nationality may be subject to such limitations as may be imposed in the interests of national security or public policy.

2. Each Contracting State agrees that the present Convention shall not be construed as affecting any legislation or judicial practice by which the alien wife of one of its nationals may, at her request, acquire her husband's nationality as a matter of right.

101. The Declaration on the Elimination of Discrimination against Women contains the following provision:

Article 5

Women shall have the same rights as men to acquire, change or retain their nationality. Marriage to an alien shall not automatically affect the nationality of the wife either by rendering her stateless or by forcing upon her the nationality of her husband.

102. The Convention on the Elimination of All Forms of Discrimination against Women contains the following provision:

Article 9

1. States Parties shall grant women equal rights with men to acquire, change or retain their nationality. They shall ensure in particular that neither marriage to an alien nor change of nationality by the husband during marriage shall automatically change the nationality of the wife, render her stateless or force upon her the nationality of the husband.

2. States Parties shall grant women equal rights with men with respect to the nationality of their children.

103. Implementation of the Convention is monitored by the Committee on the Elimination of Discrimination against Women.

Property rights of married women

104. Property relations between husband and wife are, in most countries, governed by a special body of regulations, usually set forth by law, or by special contracts envisaged by the law. These sets of rules are often termed "matrimonial regimes they control ownership and administration of property and the division of property when the marriage is dissolved. In cases where marriage is ended by the husband's death, laws on inheritance also must be taken into consideration.

105. The most common types of matrimonial regimes are those of community property and separation of property. Under the former, the property of the spouses is usually owned jointly, administered by the husband

Right of married women to engage in independent work

107. The Commission on the Status of Women also studied, at its eighth session in 1954, the right of a married woman to engage in a business, profession or other occupation, and noted that under some legal systems the husband had the power to prevent his wife from engaging in independent work and that under others he had control over her earnings. On its recommendation the Economic and Social Council, in resolution 547 I (XVIII) of 12 July 1954, recommended that Governments take all necessary measures to ensure the right of a married woman to undertake independent work, to carry it on and to administer and dispose of her

earnings without the necessity of securing her husband's authorization.

Parental rights and duties, including guardianship

108. In resolution 587 D (XX) of 3 August 1955 the Economic and Social Council, endorsing the recommendations of the Commission on the Status of women, noted that in some legal systems parental authority belonged exclusively or primarily to the father; that in some countries in the event of loss of such authority it did not automatically pass to the mother; and in some instances on dissolution of marriage the custody of the children was awarded to the father, regardless of the merits of the case. The Council was of the opinion that these limitations were incompatible with the principle of equality of rights of the spouses during marriage and at its dissolution and accordingly recommended that States Members of the United Nations take steps to ensure equality between parents in the exercise of rights and duties with respect to their children.

109. At its fifteenth session (1961), the Commission on the Status of Women decided to study this question further. It asked the Secretary-General to prepare a preliminary report on parental rights and duties, including guardianship, based on information available to him, including the documentation of the seminars on the status of women in family law.

110. A report on this subject was presented to the Commission at its twentieth session, in 1967. After considering this report the Commission recommended -and the Economic and Social Council adopted-resolution 1207 (XLII) of 29 May 1967, in which it welcomed the generally discernible trend in many legal systems towards a sharing of parental authority on a basis of equality. The Council recommended that Governments of

Member States take all possible measures to ensure equality between men and women in the exercise of parental rights and duties. It further recommended the following principles for ensuring such equality, taking account of the special characteristics of legislation in different countries and bearing in mind that in all cases the interest of the children should be paramount:

(a) Women shall have equal rights and duties with men in respect to guardianship of their minor children and the exercise of parental authority over them, including care, custody, education and maintenance;

(b) Both spouses shall have equal rights and duties with regard to the administration of the property of their minor children, with the legal limitations necessary to ensure as far as possible that it is administered in the interest of the children;

(c) The interest of the children shall be the paramount consideration in proceedings regarding custody of children in the event of divorce, annulment of marriage or judicial separation;

(d) No discrimination shall be made between men and women with regard to decisions regarding custody of children and guardianship or other parental rights in the event of divorce, annulment of marriage or judicial separation.

(f) Domicile of married women

In resolution 587 D (XX) of 3 August 1955 the Economic and Social Council, accepting the proposals of the Commission relating to the domicile of married women, noted that in the legal systems of many countries the domicile of the wife follows that of her husband; in these countries the wife, upon marriage, loses her original domicile and acquires the domicile of her husband, which she retains until the dissolution of the marriage, even if residing separately. The Council expressed the belief that such legal systems are incompatible with the principle of equality of spouses during the marriage, proclaimed in the Universal Declaration of Human Rights, and noted that their application resulted in particular hardships for married women in countries where domicile determined the jurisdiction of courts in matrimonial matters and where the law in the place of domicile governs a person's status. The Council recommended that Governments take all necessary measures to ensure the right of a married woman to an independent domicile.

Inheritance laws as they affect women

112. On the recommendation of the Commission on the Status of Women, the Economic and Social Council, in resolution 884 D (XXXIV) of 16 July 1962, recommended a number of measures designed to ensure equality of inheritance rights of men and women.

113. In the resolution, the Council noted that in the legal systems of many countries inheritance rights of women, in intestate as well as in testamentary succession, were not equal to those of men. In some systems, the law deprives women of all inheritance rights, while in other systems the share of a woman is a fraction of the share of a male heir in the same degree of relationship. In some systems, the male heir is always preferred to the female in the order of succession, and in some others, the interest of the widow in the estate is either smaller than that of the widower, or is affected by special restrictions. Moreover, in some countries the inheritance rights and the capacity of women to make a will, to accept or refuse an inheritance or to be administrators or executors of estates, are affected by marriage in a manner incompatible with the principle of equality of rights of the spouses.

114. The Council recommended that Governments

take all possible measures to ensure equality of inheritance rights of men and women by providing that men and women, in the same degree of relationship to the deceased, shall be entitled to equal shares in the estate and shall have an equal rank in the order of succession; and by providing further that the inheritance rights and the capacity of women to make a will, to accept or refuse an inheritance or to be administrators or executors of estates shall not be affected by marriage, and that the interest of the widow in the estate shall be equal to that of the widower.

Improvement of the status of the unmarried mother

115. In 1962, the Sub-Commission on Prevention of Discrimination and Protection of Minorities decided, in resolution 5 (XIV) of 2 February 1962, to undertake a study of discrimination against persons born out of wedlock, and appointed one of its members, Mr. Vieno Voitto Saario, as Special Rapporteur. On the basis of the final report examined in January 1967, the Subcommission adopted a set of draft general principles on equality and nondiscrimination in respect of persons born out of wedlock and transmitted them to the Commission on Human Rights for further consideration.

116. The Commission on the Status of Women examined the study and the draft principles later in 1967, and requested the Secretary- General to prepare a report concerning law and practice with respect to unmarried mothers. The study was presented to the Commission at its twenty-third session, in 1972. At that and the following sessions the Commission prepared a series of recommendations which were eventually adopted by the Economic and Social Council.

117. In resolution 1514 (XLVIII) of 28 May 1970, the Council noted that the number of unmarried mothers was still increasing in some countries, and that owing to

her status and the inadequacy of measures of social protection in her favour, the unmarried mother and her child were still the subject of discrimination in many countries; urged Member States to take adequate measures of social assistance in favour of the unmarried mother and the child born out of wedlock; and invited Member States, the specialized agencies and non-governmental organizations concerned to study the problems posed by the integration of the unmarried mother and her child in all spheres of society.

118. In resolution 1679 (LII) of 2 June 1972, the Council recommended to Governments of Member States a set of general principles for securing the acceptance of the unmarried mother and her child on an equal footing with other members of society. Among the principles recommended by the Council were the following:

> Maternal filiation shall be recognized in law, in all cases, automatically as a consequence of the fact of birth;
>
> Whatever the legal system applying in the case of married parents, the unmarried mother, whether paternal filiation is established or not, shall enjoy in all cases, as a parent, the fullest set of rights and duties provided for by law. In particular:
>
> If maternal filiation only is established, the surname of the mother should be transmitted to her child, if possible, in such a manner as not to reveal the fact of birth out of wedlock;
>
> If maternal filiation only is established, the nationality of the unmarried mother shall be transmitted to her child as 'a consequence of birth;
>
> The unmarried mother should be vested in law with full parental authority over her child, in all cases, as an automatic consequence of the fact of birth;

Maintenance rights and obligations as between the unmarried mother and her child should be the same as between a sole parent and a child born in wedlock;

There should be no discrimination against the offspring of unmarried mothers in all matters of inheritance;

The unmarried mother should enjoy all the measures of social assistance and social security devised for mothers in general and for single parents in particular; and

There should be no discrimination against the unmarried mother in matters of employment, education and training as well as in access to child care facilities.

119. Pursuant to Council resolution 1514 (XLVIII)r mentioned above, the Secretary-General includes information on the problems of unmarried mothers and their children in his reports on implementation of the Declaration on the Elimination of Discrimination against Women.

Legal capacity of married women

120. At its twenty-third session, in 1970, the Commission on the Status of Women initiated a programme of studies in the field of family law based on article 6 of the Declaration. The first study dealt with the legal capacity of married women and resulted in the adoption by the Economic and Social Council, on the recommendation of the Commission, of resolution 1853 (LVI) of 16 May 1974, in which the Council took note of several situations which failed to conform to the provisions of article 6 and recommended corrective measures. Among other things, the Council noted the fact that in a number of legal systems: (a) married women did not enjoy the right to engage freely in

independent work, and (b) married women who worked independently did not possess the legal capacity to manage and dispose of their earnings and were subject to other limitations which did not apply to their husbands. The Council recommended that Member States take all the measures necessary to ensure that the legal capacity of married women was equal to that of men with respect to: (a) gainful employment outside the home; (b) capacity to administer their property and the revenue of their work; (c) administration of the joint property of spouses; (d) parental authority over their children and the interests of those children; and (e) dissolution of marriage and its legal effects. The Council called upon Member States to provide adequate remedies, judicial or otherwise, to both spouses to help them solve their disagreements with respect to the questions mentioned above. It placed particular emphasis, in the case of such disagreements, upon the necessity of mediation through competent authorities with the assistance of personnel trained in all aspects of family relations.

Discrimination against women in the administration of penal law

121. In resolution 1980/40 of 2 May 1980, adopted on the recommendation of the Commission on the Status of Women, the Economic and Social Council expressed deep concern about the fact that close relatives, particularly the spouses, mothers and children, of persons accused of a penal offence are often, because of their relationship to those persons, the victims of persecution, harassment and other infringements of their rights. The Council reaffirmed the principles governing the fundamental guarantees of the individual, as set forth particularly in articles 3, 6, 7 and 10 of the Universal Declaration of Human Rights, and called upon Governments to ensure the strict application of those

provisions, and particularly to ensure that no one could be prosecuted, persecuted or harassed simply because of a family or social relationship with an accused or convicted person. The Council recommended that the competent international bodies should find ways to put an end to such action and in particular to provide effective protection for women and children to safeguard them against any reprisals.

Consent to marriage, minimum age for marriage and registration of marriages

122. After making a detailed study of marriage, with particular regard to free consent to marriage, minimum age for marriage and registration of marriages, the Commission on the Status of Women, in 1961, drafted an international convention and a recommendation on these subjects. The purpose of the proposed instruments was to eliminate such practices as child marriage, brideprice, inheritance of widows and other practices especially harmful to women.

123. The Convention on Consent to Marriage, Minimum Age for Marriage and Registration of Marriages was adopted by the General Assembly in 1962. The Recommendation on the subject, containing similar provisions but applicable to all States rather than only these States parties to the Convention, was adopted by the General Assembly in 1965.

124. The Convention contains the following provisions:

Article 1

1. No marriage shall be legally entered into without the full and free consent of both parties, such consent to be expressed by them in person after due publicity and in the presence of the authority competent to solemnize the marriage and of witnesses, as prescribed by law.

2. Notwithstanding anything in paragraph above, it shall not be necessary for one of the parties to be present when the competent authority is satisfied that the circumstances are exceptional and that the party has, before competent authority and in such manner as may be prescribed by law, expressed and not withdrawn consent.

Article 2

States Parties to the present Convention shall take legislative action to specify a minimum age for marriage. No marriage shall be legally entered into by any person under this age, except where a competent authority has granted a dispensation as to age, for serious reasons, in the interest of the intending spouses.

Article 3

All marriages shall be registered in an appropriate official register by the competent authority.

Modification or abolition of discriminatory laws, customs and practices

125. The Declaration on the Elimination of Discrimination against Women contains the following provision:

Article 2

All appropriate measures shall be taken to abolish existing laws, customs, regulations and practices which are discriminatory against women, and to establish adequate legal protection for equal rights of men and women, in particular:

(a) The principle of equality of rights shall be embodied in the constitution or otherwise guaranteed by law;

(b) The international instruments of the United Nations and the specialized agencies relating to the elimination of discrimination against women shall be ratified or acceded to and fully implemented as soon as practicable.

126. The Convention on the Elimination of All Forms of Discrimination against Women contains the following provisions:

Article 2

States Parties condemn discrimination against women in all its forms, agree to pursue by all appropriate means and without delay a policy of eliminating discrimination against women and, to this end, undertake:

(a) To embody the principle of the equality of men and women in their national constitutions or other appropriate legislation if not yet incorporated therein and to ensure, through law and other appropriate means, the practical realization of this principle;

(b) To adopt appropriate legislative and other measures, including sanctions where appropriate, prohibiting all discrimination against women,

(c) To establish legal protection of the rights of women on an equal basis with men and to ensure through competent national tribunals and other public institutions the effective protection of women against any act of discrimination;

(d) To refrain from engaging in any act or practice of discrimination against women and to ensure that public authorities and institutions shall act in conformity with this obligation;

(e) To take all appropriate measures to eliminate discrimination against women by any person, organization or enterprise;

(f) To take all appropriate measures, including legislation, to modify or abolish existing laws, regulations, customs and practices which constitute discrimination against women;

(g) To repeal all national penal provisions which constitute discrimination against women.

Article 3

States Parties shall take in all fields, in particular in the political, social, economic and cultural fields, all appropriate measures, including legislation, to ensure the full development and advancement of women, for the purpose of guaranteeing them the exercise and enjoyment of human rights and fundamental freedoms on a basis of equality with men.

Forward-looking Strategies

127. The Forward-looking Strategies for the Advancement of Women to the Year 2000,11 adopted by the World Conference to Review and Appraise the Achievements of the United Nations Decade for Women: Equality, Development and Peace, held at Nairobi from 15 to 26 July 1985,36 include the following paragraphs concerning the relationship between the law and the role, status and material circumstances of women:

Governments that have not yet done so are urged to sign the Convention on the Elimination of All Forms of Discrimination against Women and to take all the necessary steps to ensure its ratification, or their accession to it. They should consider the possibility of establishing appropriate bodies charged with reviewing the national legislation concerned and with drawing up recommendations thereon to ensure that the provisions of the Convention and of the other international instruments to which they are parties that are relevant? the role, status and material circumstances of women are complied with.

Governments that have not yet done so should

establish appropriate institutional procedures whereby the application of a revised set of laws and administrative measures may be effectively enforced from the village level up and may be adequately monitored so that individual women may, without obstruction or cost of themselves, seek to have discriminatory treatment redressed. Legislation that concerns women as a group should also be effectively enforced and monitored so that areas of systemic or *de facto* discrimination against women can be redressed. To this end, positive action policy should be developed.

Agrarian reform measures have not always ensured women's rights even in countries where women predominate in the agricultural labour force. Such reforms should guarantee women's constitutional and legal rights in terms of access to land and other means of production and should ensure that women will control the products of their labour and their income, as well as benefits from agricultural inputs, research, training, credits and other infrastructural facilities.

National research institutions, both governmental and private, are urged to undertake investigations of the problems associated with the relationship between the law and the role, status and material circumstances of women. These should be integrated into the curricula of relevant educational institutions in an attempt to promote general knowledge and awareness of the law.

In the past decade there have been significant advances in the development of statistical concepts and methods for measuring inequality between women and men. The capabilities of national institutions concerned with statistics and women's issues should be improved to implement these concepts and methods in the regular statistical programmes of countries and to make effective use of these statistics in the policy-planning process.

Training for producers and users of statistics on women should play a key role in this process.

In-depth research should be undertaken to determine instances when customary law may be discriminatory or protective of women's rights and the extent to which the interfaces between customary and statutory law may retard progress in the implementation of new legislatives measures. Particular attention should be paid to double standards in every aspect of life, with a view to abolishing them.

Law-reform committees with equal representation of women and men from Governments and from non -governmental organizations should be set up to review all laws, not only as a monitoring device but also with a view to determining research-related activities, amendments and new legislative measures.

Employment legislation should ensure equity and provide benefits for women not only in the conventional and formal]about- force but also in the informal sector, particularly with regard to migrant and service workers, by providing minimum wage standards, insurance benefits, safe working conditions and the right to organize. Opportunities for similar guarantees and benefits should also be extended to women making vital economic contributions in activities involving food production and processing, fisheries and food distribution through trade. These benefits should also pertain to women working in family enterprises and, if possible, to other self-employed women in an effort to give due recognition to the vital contribution of all these informal and invisible economic activities to the development of human resources.

Civil codes, particularly those pertaining to family law, should be revised to eliminate discriminatory practices where these exist and wherever women are considered minors. The legal capacity of married women should be reviewed in order to grant them equal rights and duties.

Such social and economic development should be encouraged as would secure the participation of women as equal partners with men in all fields of work, equal access to all positions of employment equal pay for work of equal value and equal opportunities for education and vocational training, and would coordinate the legislation on the protection of women at work with the need for women to work and be highly productive producers and managers of all political, economic and social affairs and would develop branches of the social services to make domestic duties easier for women and men.

Measures for the implementation of legislation relating to working conditions for women must be taken.

Legislative and/or other measures should be adopted and implemented to secure for men and women the same right to work and to unemployment benefits, as well as to prohibit, through, *inter alia,* the imposition of sanctions, dismissal on the grounds of pregnancy or of maternity leave and discrimination in dismissals on the grounds of marital status. Legislative and other measures should be adopted and implemented to facilitate the return to the labour market of women who have left it for family reasons and to guarantee the right of women to return to work after maternity leave.

Governments should continue to take special action to institute programmes that would inform women workers of their rights under legislation and other remedial measures. The importance of freedom of association and the protection of the right to organize should be emphasized, this being particularly relevant to the position of women in employment. Special measures should be taken to ratify and implement in national legislation the relevant conventions and recommendations of the International Labour Organisation concerning the rights of women as regards access to equal employment opportunities, equal pay for work of equal value, equal working conditions, job security and maternity protection.

Marriage agreements should be based on mutual understanding, respect and freedom of choice. Careful attention should be paid to the equal participation and valuation of both partners so that the value of housework is considered equivalent of financial contributions.

The right of all women, in particular married women, to own, ad minister, sell or buy property independently should be guaranteed as an aspect of their equality and freedom under the law. The right to divorce should be granted equally to both partners under the same conditions, and custody of children decided in a nondiscriminatory manner with full awareness of the importance of the input from both parents in the maintenance, rearing and socialization of children, Women should not forfeit their right to custody of their children or to any other benefits and freedoms simply because they have initiated a divorce. Without prejudice to the religious and cultural traditions of countries, and taking into account the *de facto* situations, legal or other appropriate provisions should be made to eliminate discrimination against single mothers and their children.

Appropriate action is necessary to ensure that the judiciary and all paralegal personnel are fully aware of the importance of the achievement by women of rights set out in internationally agreed instruments, constitutions and the law. Appropriate forms of in-service training and retraining should be designed and carried out for this purpose, with special attention given to the recruitment and training of women.

Special attention should be given in criminology training to the particular situation of women as victims of violent crimes, including crimes that violate women's bodies and result in serious physical and psychological damage. Legislation should be passed and laws enforced in every country to end the degradation of women through sexrelated crimes. Guidance should be given to law enforcement and other authorities on the need to deal sensibly and sensitively with the victims of such crimes.

Improvement of the role of women in development

128. Since their establishment the Commission on the Status of Women, the Economic and Social Council, the General Assembly and many other bodies within the United Nations system have sought to important the role of women in development and in particular to achieve their effective mobilization and integration in development programmes.

129. In a number of resolutions and decisions these bodies have repeatedly affirmed that women and men should participate and contribute on a basis of equality in the social, economic and political processes of development, including decision-making, and should share in improved conditions of life; underlined the importance of the integration and participation of women in the process of industrial development; and pointed out that accelerated development required the real an effective participation of women and men in all aspects of the development process.

(a) Advancement of women in developing countries

130. In resolution 771 H (XXX) of 25 July 1960, the Economic and Social Council requested the Secretary-General to study, in collaboration with Governments, the need for and possibilities of further United Nations

assistance specially directed towards the efforts of developing countries to advance the status of women.

131. The Secretary-General presented reports on the subject to the Commission at its sixteenth session, in 1962. On the recommendation of the Commission the Economic and Social Council adopted resolution 884 E (XXXIV) of 16 July 1962, on United Nations assistance for the advancement of women in developing countries. In the resolution the Council recommended to Governments "that they make full use, for the purpose of promoting and advancing the status of women in developing countries, of the services available under the regular programme and the Expanded Programme of Technical Assistance, as well as of the advisory services programme in human rights and the advisory social welfare services, by requesting the advisory services of experts, by promoting the attendance at seminars and other meetings, and by taking advantage of the availability of fellowships and scholarships".

132. The International Labour Organisation, the United Nations Educational, Scientific and Cultural Organization, the Food and Agriculture Organization of the United Nations, the World Health Organization and the United Nations Children's Fund were invited to strengthen and expand their programmes designed to meet the needs of women in developing countries, and to seek new methods to achieve this purpose. Women's non-governmental organizations were urged to stimulate public opinion with regard to the programmes of the United Nations which contribute to the advancement of women and by supplementing the efforts of the United Nations on the international and national levels. The Secretary-General was requested to direct his attention, when planning the various United Nations programmes of assistance, to the needs of women in developing countries, to include in these programmes projects

directed to meet such needs, and to continue to utilize the available resources of the United Nations to advance the condition of women in the developing countries.

(b) Participation of women in community development

133. In 1965 the Commission on the Status of Women called for a study on "the participation of women in community development and the possibility of increasing the scope and content of their contribution", noting at the same time "the great importance of community development in stimulating the advancement of women".

134. Community development has been defined as: "the processes by which the efforts of the people themselves are united with those of governmental authorities to improve the economic, social and cultural conditions of communities, to integrate these communities into the life of the nation, and to enable them to contribute fully to national progress. This complex of processes in then made up of two essential elements: the participation by the people themselves in efforts to improve their level of living with as much reliance as possible on their own initiative; and the provision of technical and other services in ways which encourage the initiative, self-help and mutual help, and make these more effective. It is expressed in programmes designed to achieve a wide variety of specific improvements".

135. The goals of community development may be said, therefore, to be twofold: (a) the comprehensive improvement of conditions in communities; and (b) the integration of the development of communities with national development. The methods used emphasize: a) the initiative and voluntary efforts of local people to raise their own levels of living; and (b) the provision, mainly by the Government, of the measures, services and

facilities needed for local programmes and projects Community development then is essentially a partnership between the local people and the Government.

136. The interest of the Commission on the Status of Women in community development is focused on three main points: (a) the examination of the extent to which women are participating at that present time in community development programmes, especially in rural areas; (b) the consideration of ways in which existing programmes have helped to advance the status of women; and (c) the making of recommendations that would both improve the status of women and benefit the programmes themselves.

137. In 1971 the Secretary-General completed a report on the participation of women in community development. The report was issued in printed form in 19721 at the request of the Commission in resolution 7 (XXII) of 10 February 1969.

138. The studies made for the Commission on the Status of Women on this subject have been based primarily on information furnished by Governments. It is apparent from the information received that women participate with enthusiasm and interest in community development programmes in many countries, and that their contribution is considered highly valuable. The community development programmes include activities connected with education and training, especially literacy and adult education, vocational training and civic and political education; activities in the economic and social fields aimed at raising levels of living, such as health, nutrition, social welfare, housing and home management, family planning, agriculture, small-scale industry and handicrafts and cooperatives; and activities which provide training for community development work.

Improvement of the situation of women in rural areas

139. In resolution 21, on the condition of women in rural areas, the World Conference of the international Women's Year took up a subject which had already been the concern of the World Population Conference held at Bucharest in August 1974 and the World Food Conference held in Rome in November of that year: the question of the condition of women in rural areas.

140. Bearing in mind that rural women in the developing world accounted for a substantial share of food production, that women everywhere generally played the main role in procuring and preparing food for family consumption, and that severe problems of rural unemployment, underemployment and misallocation of human resources affected women as well as men, the Conference called upon Governments:

(a) To identify needs and to formulate and implement, with greater financial and policy support, rural development programmes, particularly those which benefit women living in situations of rural poverty and of disadvantage relative to men;
(b) To carry out the statistical and information work necessary to identify and evaluate the participation of women in productive life and to measure the results of programmes for the betterment of rural life;
(c) To ensure legal parity and economic rights of women in the peasant family as an essential part of any rural development programme.

The Conference suggested

that further research should be undertaken with regard to the most effective design of systems of rural non-formal education, needed to equip women i_ rural areas with ' the necessary and additional skills relevant to their social and economic roles.

141. The General Assembly, taking Conference resolution 21 into account, adopted resolution 3523 (XXX) of 15 December 1975, on women in rural areas, in which it urged Governments to accord within their respective plans, higher priority for:

(a) Gathering relevant data on the status and role of women in rural and low-income areas;
(b) Achieving socioeconomic conditions based on the realization of the full and equal partnership of men and women in the development of society, both in law and in fact;
(c) Promoting agricultural productivity, agro-based industries and integrated rural development programmes.

Governments were also urged to develop extensive training programmes relevant to women and to make full use of all existing and proposed research institutes and centres, particularly the regional and international institutes and centres for the advancement of women in rural areas.

The Secretary-General was requested to prepare and submit "guidelines for non-formal educational programmes designed to enable rural women to use fully their capabilities and to contribute to the development of society".

142. The Secretary-General submitted a report on women in rural areas to the General Assembly at its thirty-second session in compliance with the Assembly's request for biennial reports on the progress achieved in efforts to enable rural women to use their capabilities fully and to contribute to their full integration in development. The report contained a brief account of activities undertaken by the United Nations on behalf of rural women, and clearly showed the concern of the United Nations for the improvement of the condition of

those women, both as a response to national awareness and initiatives in this regard, and as a necessary component of national and international rural development strategies and programmes.

143. At its thirty-seventh session, the attention of the General Assembly was drawn to the Declaration of Principles and the Programme of Action adopted by the World Conference on Agrarian Reform and Rural Development, organized at Rome by FAO. The Declaration called for the improvement of the legal status of women, for increasing access of women to social and economic services, for strengthening women's organization and participation, and for improving women's opportunities in formal and informal education as well as on the labour market.

144. In resolution 37/59 of 3 December 1982, the Assembly called upon Member States to take additional appropriate measures for further improving the economic and social conditions of women in rural areas; requested the Economic and Social Council, the Commission on the Status of Women, the regional commissions and other bodies of the United Nations system-in particular the Food and Agriculture Organization of the United Nations-to devote greater attention to the problems of elevating the status of rural women; and requested the Secretary-General to prepare a comprehensive report containing the observations and comments received from Governments on national experience in improving the situation of women in rural areas, paying special attention to such aspects as social insurance, mother and child care, health facilities, training, education and employment opportunities.

145. The Convention on the Elimination of All Forms of Discrimination against Women, adopted and opened for signature and ratification by General

Assembly resolution 34/180 of 18 December 1979, contains the following provisions relating to improvement of the situation of women in rural areas:

Article 14

1. States Parties shall take into account the particular problems faced by rural women and the significant roles which rural women play in the economic survival of their families, including their work in the non-monetized sectors of the economy, and shall take all appropriate measures to ensure the application of the provisions of the present Convention to women in rural areas.

2. States Parties shall take all appropriate measures to eliminate discrimination against women in rural areas in order to ensure, on a basis of equality of men and women, that they participate in and benefit from rural development and, in particular, shall ensure to such women the right:

(a) To participate in the elaboration and implementation of development planning at all levels;

(b) To have access to adequate health care facilities, including information, counselling and services in family planning;

(c) To benefit directly from social security programmes;

(d) To obtain all types of training and education, formal and nonformal, including that relating to functional literacy, as well as, *inter alia*, the benefit of all community and extension services, in order to increase their technical proficiency;

(e) To organize self-help groups and cooperatives in order to obtain equal access to economic opportunities through employment or self-employment;

(f) To participate in all community activities;

(g) To have access to agricultural credit and loans, marketing facilities, appropriate technology and equal treatment in land agrarian reform as well as in land resettlement schemes;

(h) To enjoy adequate iiving conditions, particularly in relation to housing, sanitation, electricity and water supply, transport and communications.

146. At its thirty-ninth session the General Assembly, in resolution 39/126 of 14 December 1984, reaffirmed the importance attached to the need to improve the status of women and to ensure their full participation in the development process as agents and beneficiaries of development, and noted with appreciation that an inter-regional seminar on national experience relating to the improvement of the status of women in rural areas had been held at Vienna from 17 to 28 September 1984. The Secretary-General was requested to that seminar, together with comments and observations thereon, to the Assembly at its fortieth session.

147. Later the Assembly in resolution 40/106 of 13 December 1985, considered the report of the Secretary-General on the Inter-regional Seminar on National Experience Relating to the Improvement of the Situation of Women in Rural Areas, held at Vienna from 17 to 28 September 1984, as well as the compilation of observations and comments made by Member States. In its resolution 40/106 of 13 December 1985, the Assembly called upon Governments to elaborate and implement, as a part of national development strategies, special comprehensive programmes for improving the situation of women in rural areas and to establish monitoring and evaluating mechanisms involving women themselves for these programmes; and requested the organizations and funds concerned of the United Nations system to pay greater attention to the needs of rural women and to

assist Member States, especially the developing countries, in the implementation of their national policies and programmes aimed at the advancement of rural women./The Assembly, further, requested the Secretary-General to prepare, in consultation with the Member States, a comprehensive report on the present status and perspectives for the improvement of the situation of rural women, and to submit that report to the Assembly at its forty-fourth session through the Economic and Social Council.

Effective mobilization and integration of women in development

148. The Declaration on Social Progress and Development, proclaimed by the General Assembly on 11 December 1969, provides that "Social progress and development shall aim at the continuous raising of the material and spiritual standards of living of all members of society, with respect for and in accordance with human rights and fundamental freedoms", through the attainment of certain goals. Among the goals set out in article 11 of the Declaration are: "The protection of the rights of the mother and child;... the provision of measures to safeguard the health and welfare of women and particularly of working mothers during pregnancy and the infancy of their children, as well as of mothers whose earnings are the sole source of livelihood for the family; the granting to women of pregnancy and maternity leave and allowances without loss of employment or wages.

149. Since the proclamation of the Declaration, the effective mobilization and integration of women in development has been a major concern of the United Nations system of organizations. It was expressed in the International Development Strategy for the Second United Nations Development Decade set out in General

Assembly resolution 2626 (XXV) of 24 October 1970, and reiterated in the Declaration and Programme of Action on the Establishment of a New International Economic Order, set out in Assembly resolutions 3201 and 3202 (S-VI) of 1 May 1974; the Charter of Economic Rights and Duties of States, set out in Assembly resolution 3281 (XXIX) of 12 December 1974; as well as in Assembly resolutions 3517 (XXX) of 15 December 1975, on the midterm review and appraisal of progress in the implementation of the International" Development Strategy for the Second United Nations Development Decade, and 3362 (S-VII) of 16 September 1975, on development and international economic cooperation.

150. At its thirty-first session the General Assembly, in resolution 31/175 of 21 December 1976, urged Member States to implement the recommendations it had made earlier, to facilitate the equal participation of women with men in all development efforts and, in particular, to ensure that women have equal access to political parties, trade unions, training, especially in agriculture, cooperatives, and credit and loan systems, as well as equal opportunities to participate in policy-making in the economic field, in commerce and trade and in the advanced efforts of industry. Later, in resolution 35/78 of 5 December 1980, it requested the Secretary-General to prepare a comprehensive and detailed outline for an interdisciplinary and multisectoral world survey on the role of women in overall development, taking into account the relevant recommendations of the World Conference of the United Nations Decade for Women as well as the results of the relevant United Nations conferences on development issues.

151. Pursuant to that resolution, the Secretary-General submitted the comprehensive outline of a world survey on the role of women in development, and in response to General Assembly resolution 37/60 of 3

December 1982, the survey was submitted to the World Conference to Review and Appraise the Achievements of the United Nations Decade for Women: Equality, Development and Peace. The Conference considered the survey and took it into consideration in the formulation and adoption of the Nairobi Forward-looking,,, Strategies for the Advancement of Women. It was further considered by the General Assembly at its fortieth session and in its resolution 40/204 of 17 December 1985, the Assembly invited the Commission on the Status of Women to make specific action-oriented recommendations based on the survey as a part of the overall implementation of, and follow-up to, the Nairobi Strategies; invited the Commission at its thirty-first session to make a recommendation on future updates of the survey after 1989, bearing in mind the need for effective coordination with the follow-up activities of the World Conference to Review and Appraise the Achievements of the United Nations Decade for Women: Equality, Development and Peace, and to suggest terms of reference for the first update of the survey which should contain improved data and information on the role of women in development, including, *inter alia*, their role in the informal sector of the economy. The first update should be prepared by the Secretary-General for submission to the Assembly at its forty-fourth session, in 1989.

152. The Forward-looking Strategies for the Advancement of Women to the Year 2000,44 adopted by the World Conference to Review and Appraise the Achievements of the United Nations Decade for Women: Equality, Development and Peace, held at Nairobi from 15 to 26 July 1985 set out basic strategies for the effective participation of women in development, as contained in the following paragraphs:

107. The commitment to remove obstacles to the effective participation of all women in development as intellectuals, policy-makers and decision-makers, planners, contributors and beneficiaries should be strengthened according to the specific problems of women in different regions and countries and the needs of different categories of women in them. That commitment should guide the formulation and implementation of policies, plans, programmes and projects, with the awareness that development prospects will be improved and society advanced through the full and effective participation of women.

108. Different socioeconomic and cultural conditions are to be taken into account when identifying the foremost obstacles to the advancement of women. The current- economic situation and the imbalances within the world monetary and financial system need adjustment programmes to overcome the difficulties. These programmes should not adversely affect the most vulnerable segments of society among whom women are disproportionately represented.

109. Development, being conceived as a comprehensive process, must be characterized by the search for economic and social objectives and goals that guarantee the effective participation of the entire population, especially women, in the process of development. It is also necessary to work in favour of the structural changes needed for the fulfilment of these aspirations. In line with these concerns, one should endeavour to speed up social and economic development in developing countries; accelerate the development of the scientific and technological capabilities of those countries; promote an equitable distribution of national income; and eradicate absolute poverty, experienced disproportionately by women and children, with the shortest possible delay by applying an overall strategy

that, on the one hand, eliminates hunger and malnutrition and, on the other, works towards the construction of more just societies, in which women may reach their full development.

110. As the primary objective of development is to bring about sustained improvement in the wellbeing of the individual and of society and to bestow benefits on all, development should be seen not only as a desirable goal in itself but also as an important means of furthering equality of the sexes and the maintenance of peace.

111. Women should be an integral part of the process of defining the objectives and modes of development, as well as of developing strategies and measures for their implementation. The need for women to participate fully in political processes and to have an equal share of power in guiding development efforts and in benefiting from them should be recognized. Organizational and other means of enabling women to bring their interests and preferences into the evaluation and choice of alternative development objectives and strategies should be identified and supported. This would include special measures designed to enhance women's autonomy, bringing women into the mainstream of the development process on an equal basis with men, or other measures designed to integrate women fully in the total development effort.

112. The actual and potential impact on women of macroeconomic processes operating at the international and national levels, as well as of financial spatial and physical development policies, should be assessed and appropriate modifications made to ensure that women are not adversely affected. Initial emphasis should be placed on employment, health and education. Priority should be given to the development of human resources,

bearing in mind the need to avoid further increases in the workload of women, particularly when alternative policies are formulated to deal with the economic and debt crisis

113. With due recognition of the difficulties involved, Governments, international and regional organizations, and non-governmental organizations should intensify their efforts to enhance the self-reliance of women in a viable and sustained fashion. Because economic independence is a necessary pre-condition for self-reliance, such efforts should above all be focused on increasing women's access to gainful activities. Grassroots participatory processes and planning approaches using local talent, expertise and resources are vital and should be supported and encouraged.

114. The incorporation of women's issues in all areas and sectors and at the local, national, regional and international levels should be institutionalized. To this end, appropriate machinery should be established or strengthened, and further legislative action taken. Sectoral policies and plans should be developed, and the effective participation of women in development should be integrated both in those plans and in the formulation and implementation of mainstream programmes and projects and should not be confined solely to statements of intent within plans or to small-scale, transitory projects relating to women.

115. The gender bias evident in most development programmes should be eliminated and the prejudices hindering the solution of women's problems removed. Particular attention should be given to the restructuring of employment, health and education systems and to ensuring equal access to land, capital and other productive resources. Emphasis should be placed on strategies to assist women in generating and keeping

income, including measures designed to improve women's access to credit. Such strategies must focus on the removal of legal, customary and other barriers and on strengthening women's capacity to use existing credit systems.

116. Governments should seek means to increase substantially the number of women who are decision-makers, policy-makers, managers, professionals and technicians in both traditional and non-traditional areas and sectors. Women should be provided with equal opportunities for access to resources, especially education and training, in order to facilitate their equal representation at higher managerial and professional levels.

117. The role of women as a factor of development is in many ways linked to their involvement in various forms and levels of decision-making and management in economic and social structures, such as worker participation in management, industrial democracy, worker self-management, trade unions and cooperatives. The development of these forms of participation, which have an impact on the development and promotion of working and living conditions, and the inclusion of women in these forms of participation on an equal footing with men is of crucial importance.

118. The relationships between development and the advancement of women under specific sociocultural conditions should be studied locally to permit the effective formulation of policies, programmes and projects designed for stable and equitable growth. /_p

The findings should be used to develop social awareness of the need for effective participation of women in development and to create realistic images of women in society.

119. It is vital that the link between the advancement of women and socioeconomic and political development be emphasized for the effective mobilization of resources for women.

120. The remunerated and, in particular, the unremunerated contributions of women to all aspects and sectors of development should be recognized, and appropriate efforts should be made to measure and reflect these contributions in national accounts and economic statistics and in the gross national product. Concrete steps should be taken to quantify the unremunerated contributions of women to agriculture, food production, reproduction and household activities.

121. Concerted action should be directed towards the establishment of a system of sharing parental responsibilities by women and men in the family and by society. To this end, priority should be given to the provision of a social infrastructure that will enable society to share these responsibilities with families and, simultaneously, to bring about changes in social attitudes so that new or modified gender roles will be accepted, promoted and become exercisable. Household tasks and parental responsibilities, including decision-making regarding family size and child spacing, should be re-examined with a view to a better sharing of responsibilities between men and women and therefore, be conducive to the attainment of women's and men's self-reliance and to the development of future human resources.

122. Monitoring and evaluation efforts should be strengthened and directed specifically towards women's issues and should be based on a thorough review and extensive development of improved statistics and indicators on the situation of women as compared with men, over time and in all fields.

123. Appropriate national machinery should be established and should be utilized to integrate women effectively in the development process. To be effective, this machinery should be provided with adequate resources, commitment and authority to encourage and enhance development efforts.

124. Regional and international cooperation, within the framework of technical cooperation among developing countries, should be strengthened and extended to promote the effective participation of women in development.

Improvement of the economic status of women

153. The Commission on the Status of Women, the Economic and Social Council and the General Assembly have on numerous occasions considered questions and adopted measures aimed at improving the economic status of women. They have been assisted by the extensive work of the International Labour Organisation in this field, and by the reports on ILO activities of special interest from the standpoint of the employment of women which are submitted to the Commission at each session.

154. In resolution 587 F III (XX) of 3 August 1955, adopted on the initiative of the Commission, the Council recommended that all States should adopt legislative and other Measures to provide women with suitable economic opportunities by granting them equal rights with men to employment, pay, education, rest and material security in case of old age, illness or loss of capacity to work," and "encourage such action as will secure for women, in the economic field, equal rights with men in all countries, including the Trust and Nonself-Governing Territories." In the same resolution the Council urged non-governmental organizations to

work for the eradication of all possible obstacles in the way of economic emancipation of women.

(a) ILO instruments concerning the economic status of women

155. Even before the establishment of the United Nations, the International Labour Organisation was actively engaged in activities aimed at improving the economic status of women. Between 1919 and 1935 the ILO General Conference adopted such international conventions as the Maternity Protection Convention 1919 (No. 3); the Night Work (Women) Convention, 1919 (No. 4); the White Lead (Painting) Convention, 1921 (No. 13); the Night Work (Women) Convention (Revised), 1934 (No. 41); and the Underground Work (Women) Convention, 1935 (No. 45).45

156. Later, the General Conference adopted the Night Work (Women) Convention (Revised), 1948 (No. 89); the Equal Remuneration Convention, 1951 (No. 100); the Maternity Protection Convention (Revised), 1952 (No. 103); the Plantations Convention, 1958 (No. 110) (Part VII: Maternity Protection); the Discrimination (Employment and Occupation) Convention, 1958, (No. 111); the Equality of Treatment (Social Security) Convention, 1962 (No. 118) (articles 2 and 4, where they refer to maternity benefit); the Social Policy (Basic Aims and Standards) Convention, 1962 (No. 117) (Part V: Non-Discrimination on Grounds of... Sex...); the Maximum Weight Convention, 1967 (No. 127); and the Human Resources Development Convention, 1975 (No. 142) (article 1, paragraph 5, where it refers to nondiscrimination).

157. In 1975, the General Conference proclaimed the Declaration on Equality of Opportunity and Treatment for Women Workers. In 1981 it adopted the Workers with Family Responsibilities Convention (No. 156),

providing that men and women with family responsibilities should be able to exercise their right to work without being discriminated against because of those responsibilities; and in 1982 it adopted the Maintenance of Social Security Rights Convention (No. 157), providing for the establishment of an international system for the maintenance of acquired social security rights.

(b) Equal pay for work of equal value

158. The question of equal pay for work of equal values has been a concern of the Commission on the Status of Women, the Economic and Social Council and the International Labour Organisation for many years.

159. The Council, in resolution 121 (VI) of 10 March 1948, adopted on the initiative of the Commission, reaffirmed the principle of equal rights of men and women laid down in the preamble of the Charter of the United Nations, approved the principle of equal remuneration for work of equal value for men and women workers, and called upon Member States to implement that principle in every way, irrespective of nationality, race, language and religion.

160. The Council at the same time transmitted a memorandum of the World Federation of Trade Unions on the subject to the International Labour Organisation -inviting the latter to proceed as rapidly as possible with the further consideration of the subject-and to the Commission on the Status of Women for its consideration and any suggestions it might wish to make to the Council.

161. The International Labour Conference, as result of its consideration of the matter, adopted the above-mentioned Equal Remuneration Convention (No. 100) and a supplementary Recommendation (No. 90) in 1951. By the Convention, States parties undertake, "by

means appropriate to the methods in operation for determining rates of remuneration, to promote and, in so far as is consistent with such methods, to ensure the application to all workers of the principle of equal remuneration for men and women workers for work of equal value" (article 2). This principle may be applied by means of national laws or regulations, legally established or recognized machinery for wage determination, collective agreements between employers and workers or a combination of these various measures. Differential rates between workers, which correspond, without regard to sex, to differences, as determined by objective appraisal, in the work to be performed, shall not be considered as being contrary to this principle. The Recommendation lays down more detailed rules concerning the measures and methods for implementing the equal remuneration principle, and also calls for action to facilitate the application of this principle through measures in regard to vocational guidance and training, vocational placement, the provision of social welfare services to meet the needs of women workers, particular those with family responsibilities, and promotion of equality as regards access to employment and posts.

162. On the initiative of the Commission on the Status of Women, the Economic and Social Council reviewed on many occasions the progress achieved towards implementation of the principle of equal remuneration for work of equal value. In a number of resolutions, the Council urged Member States to ratify the Equal Remuneration Convention or otherwise to implement its provisions, and to apply and promote consistently the principle of equal pay for equal work in accordance with the Convention. It also called upon ILO "to continue to follow the introduction of the principle of equal pay for equal work on a world scale, and to bear this principle in mind in considering working and social questions on an international level."

163. The International Labour Conference in 1975, and again in 1986, reviewed a worldwide survey based on reports submitted by Governments under articles 19 and 22 of the ILO Constitution, on the position of their law and practice respecting the equal pay principle contained in the Equal Remuneration Convention, 1951 (No. 100). As mentioned above, the Conference adopted in 1975 a Declaration on Equality of Opportunity and Treatment for Women Workers and two resolutions, one concerning a plan of action with a view to promoting equality of opportunity and treatment for women workers and the other calling for a study of the need for new international instruments to supplement the provisions of the Equal Remuneration Convention, 1951 (No. 100), and the Discrimination (Employment and Occupation) Convention, 1958 (No. 111).

164. A significant early development in this field was the unanimous adoption by the International Labour Conference in 1965 of the Employment (Women with Family Responsibilities) Recommendation (No. 123), providing that the competent national authorities should, in cooperation with the public and private organizations concerned, in particular employers' and workers' organizations and in accordance with national and local needs and possibilities, (a) pursue an appropriate policy with a view to enabling women with family responsibilities who work outside their home to exercise their right to do so without being subject to discrimination and in accordance with the principles laid down in the Discrimination (Employment and Occupation) Convention, 1958, as well as in other standards adopted by the International Labour Conference relating to women; and (b) encourage, facilitate or themselves undertake the development of services to enable women to fulfil their various responsibilities at home and at work harmoniously.

Other provisions are intended to facilitate women's entry into employment, or re-entry after a comparatively long absence, so that they may enjoy equality of opportunity and training to enable them to become integrated into the labour force on a footing of equality.

165. A second significant development occurred in 1981 with the adoption of the Workers with Family Responsibilities Convention (No. 156) and Recommendation (No. 165). These instruments apply to both men and women workers who have responsibilities in relation to their dependent children and other members of their immediate family who clearly need their care and support. The Convention includes the following substantive provisions:

(c) Workers with family responsibilities

Article I

1. This Convention applies to men and women workers with responsibilities in relation to their dependent children, where such responsibilities restrict their possibilities of preparing for, entering, participating in or advancing in economic activity.
2. The provisions of this Convention shall also be applied to men and women workers with responsibilities in relation to other members of their immediate family who clearly need their care or support, where such responsibilities restrict their possibilities of preparing for, entering, participating in or advancing in economic activity.
3. For the purposes of this Convention, the terms "dependent child" and "other member of the immediate family who clearly needs care or support" mean persons defined as such in each country by one of the means referred to in article 9 of this Convention.

4. The workers covered by virtue of paragraphs 1 and 2 of this article are hereinafter referred to as "workers with family responsibilities".

Article 2

This Convention applies to all branches of economic activity and all categories of workers.

Article 3

1. With a view to creating effective equality of opportunity and treatment for men and women workers, each member shall make it an aim of national policy to enable persons with family responsibilities who are engaged or wish to engage in employment to exercise their right to do so without being subject to discrimination and, to the extent possible, without conflict between their employment and family responsibilities.
2. For the purposes of paragraph 1 of this article, the term "discrimination" means discrimination in employment and occupation as defined by articles 1 and 5 of the Discrimination (Employment and Occupation) Convention, 1958.

Article 4

With a view to creating effective equality of opportunity and treatment for men and women workers, all measures compatible with national conditions and possibilities shall be taken-

(a) to enable workers with family responsibilities to exercise their right to free choice of employment; and

(b) to take account of their needs in terms and conditions of employment and in social security.

Article 5

All measures compatible with national conditions and possibilities shall further be taken-

(a) to take account of the needs of workers with family responsibilities in community planning; and

(b) to develop or promote community services, public or private, such as child-care and family services and facilities.

Article 6

The competent authorities and bodies in each country shall take appropriate measures to promote information and education which engender broader public understanding of the principle of equality of opportunity and treatment for men and women workers and of the problems of workers with family responsibilities, as well as a climate of opinion conducive to overcoming these problems.

Article 7

All measures compatible with national conditions and possibilities, including measures in the field of vocational guidance and training, shall be taken to enable workers with family responsibilities to become and remain integrated in the labour force, as well as to re-enter the labour force after an absence due to those responsibilities.

Article 8

Family responsibilities shall not, as such, constitute a valid reason for termination of employment.

Article 9

The provisions of this Convention may be applied by laws or regulations, collective agreements, works rules, arbitration awards, court decisions or a combination of these methods, or in any other manner consistent with national practice which may be appropriate, account being taken of national conditions.

Article 10

1. The provisions of this Convention may be applied by stages if necessary, account being taken of national conditions: Provided that such measures of implementation as are taken shall apply in any case to all the workers covered by article 1, paragraph 1.

(d) Age of retirement and social security benefits

166. Two subjects studied by the Commission on the Status of Women at several sessions between the years 1958-1963 were the age of retirement and pension rights, which in many countries are not the same for men and women workers. After preliminary consideration of the question on the basis of information furnished by the United Nations Secretariat and by ILO, the Commission recognized that the question was one of some complexity on which differences of opinion existed; and it decided in 1960 to recommend that the Economic and Social Council invite ILO to make a complete study of the subject. The Council endorsed this recommendation in resolution 771 F (XXX) of 25 July 1960. ILO submitted a comprehensive report to the Commission, which was first discussed in 1963.[1] The Commission noted, in resolution 9 (XVII) of 25 March 1963, that although there was a trend towards equal provisions in retirement for men and women, a divergence of views existed among Governments and women's organizations in various countries about the pensionable ages for men and women. It recommended that the provisions on age of retirement and right to a pension "should be sufficiently flexible to meet varied and changing circumstances, individual needs and reasonable individual preferences as regards effective retirement, bearing in mind the encouraging trend towards equal economic conditions for the work of men and women, including equal provisions in the matter of the age of retirement and the right to pension".

167. The Declaration on Equality of Opportunity and Treatment for Women (Workers, adopted by the ILO General Conference in 1975, specified that there should be no discrimination against women in respect of social security and provisions concerning retirement and pensions, and that differences in the treatment of men and women under such schemes should be reviewed and revised. The Declaration also called for special measures to be taken, as necessary and appropriate, to ensure equality of treatment for workers employed regularly on a part-time basis, the majority of whom were women, with respect to *pro rata* fringe benefits.

168. With regard to maternity benefits and protection, part VII (Maternity Benefit) of the ILO Social Security (Minimum Standards) Convention, 1952 (No. 102) requires women in prescribed classes of employees or of the economically active population to be protected against contingencies including pregnancy and confinement and their consequences and suspension of earnings. More generally, under ILO Conventions Nos. 3, 103 and 110 (part VII) and the supplementary Recommendations, appropriate arrangements affecting the economic status of women workers in case of maternity include the provision of medical care, the granting of leave before and after childbirth, the provision of cash benefits during such leave, the right to be given other suitable work in case of otherwise harmful employment, safeguarding of remuneration or means of subsistence where they are unable to perform their normal work during pregnancy or after confinement, protection against termination of employment or diminution of connected rights, and adaptation of working hours for working mothers.

(e) Repercussions of scientific and technical progress

169. In resolution 1136 (XLI) of 26 July 1966, the Economic and Social Council invited the International

Labour Organisation "to study the repercussions of scientific and technical progress on the position of women in the matter of labour and employment", and to submit a report to the Commission on the Status of Women, covering the results of its study and the measures taken by ILO with regard to such repercussions. The reports prepared by ILO were considered by the Commission and the Council. The Council, in resolution 1513 (XLVIII) of 28 May 1970, noted that certain unfavourable consequences of scientific and technical progress weighed more heavily upon the status of women workers, due in part to the low degree of skill of most women workers and the difficulty in changing occupations resulting therefrom, and also to women's limited geographical mobility, resulting usually from their family responsibilities.

170. The Council requested Member States:

(a) To make provision in school programmes for appropriate general education that prepares the ground for a flexible vocational training which can be adjusted at all times to the structure of employment, and to which girls and boys have equal access under the same conditions;

(b) To ensure that lifelong adult education, accelerated vocational training and vocational and other retraining are available to men and women under the same conditions;

(c) To see to it that new opportunities or employment are accorded on the basis of individual ability and 'aptitudes, irrespective of sex and without division of work into men's and women's work;

(d) To see to it that no reduction is permitted in the employment of women, in particular in skilled work;

(e) To pay special attention to the problems of environment, social installations, hygiene and occupational safety associated with scientific and technological progress.

171. The Council requested the Secretary-General and the specialized agencies concerned, in particular ILO, as well as Member States, to continue to study the question and to submit reports to the Commission on the Status of Women. ILO was also requested to continue its review of international conventions from the point of view of changes that occurred as a result of scientific and technical progress. X

(f) Access of women to financial assistance

172. Recognizing the difficulties encountered by women in many countries of the world in securing credit and loans for activities which enhanced their productive capacities and thus the contribution of their full share to the development of their families and communities and to their consequent full integration into development, the World Conference of the International Women's Year adopted resolution 10, on access of women to financial assistance, in which it recommended that Governments in the countries concerned:

(a) Establish mechanisms to facilitate the extension of credit to meet the special needs of women of low-income groups in rural and urban areas.
(b) Facilitate also the access of women in low-income groups to existing financial institutions;
(c) Encourage and commend the initiatives taken by non-governmental and voluntary women's organizations to establish their own financial institutions and banks.

173. Reaffirming the above-mentioned resolution, the General Assembly in resolution 3522 (XXX) of 15 December 1975 urged "Governments and governmental

and non-governmental organizations to support more vigorously official and private efforts to extend to women the facilities now being offered only to men by financial and lending institutions"; and requested "Governments to encourage all efforts by women's organizations, cooperatives and lending institutions which will enable women at the lowest level in rural and urban areas to obtain credit and loans to improve their economic activities and integration in national development". The Assembly further urged "Governments and the organizations of the United Nations development system, including specialized agencies and non-governmental organizations, to incorporate, in their training programmes, workshops and seminars, courses designed to improve the efficiency of women in business and financial management".

(g) Participation of women in rural development

174. The Declaration of Principles and Programme of Action adopted in July 1979 by the World Conference on Agrarian Reform and Rural Development, meeting at Rome, stresses the basic principle that "Women should participate and contribute on an equal basis with men in the social, economic and political process of rural development and share fully in improved conditions of life in rural areas". The Declaration further states that "Recognition of the vital role of women in socioeconomic life, in both agricultural and non-agricultural activities,... is a prerequisite for successful rural development planning and implementation. Rural development based on growth with equity will require full integration of women..."

(h) Provisions of international instruments

175. The question of discrimination against women in employment and in other areas of economic and social life has been dealt with in a number of international

instruments, mentioned in section (a) above, including the ILO Discrimination (Employment and Occupation) Convention, 1958 (No. 111), adopted by the International Labour Conference on 25 June 1958; the Declaration on the Elimination of Discrimination against Women, proclaimed by General Assembly resolution 2263 (XXII) of 7 November 1967; and the Convention on the Elimination of All Forms of Discrimination against Women, adopted by General Assembly resolution 34/180 of 18 December 1979.

Article I

1. For the purpose of this Convention the term "discrimination"
   (a) any distinction, exclusion or preference made on the basis of race, colour, sex, religion, political opinion, national extraction or social origin, which has the effect of nullifying or impairing equality of opportunity or treatment in employment or occupation;
   (b) such other distinction, exclusion or preference which has the effect of nullifying or impairing equality of opportunity or treatment in employment or occupation as may be determined by the Member concerned after consultation with '-/representative employers' and workers' organisations, where such exist, and with other appropriate bodies.
2. Any distinction, exclusion or preference in respect of a particular job based on the inherent requirements thereof shall not be deemed to be discrimination.
3. For the purpose of this Convention the terms employment and occupation include access to vocational training, access to employment and to particular occupations, and terms and conditions of employment.

Article 2

Each Member for which this Convention is in force undertakes to declare and pursue a national policy designed to promote, by methods appropriate to national conditions and practice, equality of opportunity and treatment in respect of employment and occupation, with a view to eliminating any discrimination in respect thereof.

Article 3

Each Member for which this Convention is in force undertakes, by methods appropriate to national conditions and practice:

(a) to seek the cooperation of employers' and workers organisations and other appropriate bodies in promoting the acceptance and observance of this policy;

(b) to enact such legislation and to promote such educational programmes as may be calculated to secure the acceptance and observance of the policy;

(c) to repeat any statutory provisions and modify any administrative!, instructions or practices which are inconsistent with the policy;

(d) to pursue the policy in respect of employment under the direct control of a national authority;

(e) to ensure observance of the policy in the activities of vocational guidance, vocational training and placement services under the direction of a national authority;

(f) to indicate in its annual reports on the application of the Convention the action taken in pursuance of the policy and the results secured by such action.

Article 4

Any measures affecting an individual who is

justifiably suspected of, or engaged in, activities prejudicial to the security of the State shall not be deemed to be discrimination, provided that the individual concerned shall have the right to appeal to a competent body established in accordance with national practice.

Article 5

1. Special measures of protection or assistance provided for in other Conventions or Recommendations adopted by the International Labour Conference shall not be deemed to be discrimination.
2. Any Member may, after consultation with representative employers' and workers' organisations, where such exist, determine that other special measures designed to meet the particular requirements of persons who, for reasons such as sex, age, disablement, family responsibilities or social or cultural status, are generally recognised to require special protection or assistance shall not be deemed to be discrimination.

177. The Declaration on the Elimination of Discrimination against Women contains the following provision:

Article 10

1. All appropriate measures shall be taken to ensure to women, married or unmarried, equal rights with men in the field of economic and social life, and in particular:
   (a) The right, without discrimination on grounds of marital status or any other grounds, to receive vocational training, to work, to free choice of profession and employment, and to professional and vocational advancement;

(b) The right to equal remuneration with men and to equality of treatment in respect of work of equal value;

(c) The right to leave with pay, retirement privileges and provision for security in respect of unemployment, sickness, old age or other incapacity to work;

(d) The right to receive family allowances on equal terms with men.

2. In order to prevent discrimination against women on account of marriage or maternity and to ensure their effective right to work, measures shall be taken to prevent their dismissal in the event of marriage or maternity and to provide paid maternity leave, with the guarantee of returning to former employment, and to provide the necessary social services, including child-care facilities.

3. Measures taken to protect women in certain types of work, for reasons inherent in their physical nature, shall not be regarded as discriminatory.

178. The Convention on the Elimination of All Forms of Discrimination against Women contains the following provisions:

Article 11

1. States Parties shall take all appropriate measures to eliminate discrimination against women in the field of employment in order to ensure, on a basis of equality of men and women, the same rights, in particular:

(a) The right to work as an inalienable right of all human beings;

(b) The right to the same employment opportunities, including the application of the same criteria for selection in matters of employment;

(c) The right to free choice of profession and employment, the right to promotion, job security and all benefits and conditions of service and the right to receive vocational training and retraining, including apprenticeships, advanced vocational training and recurrent training;

(d) The right to equal remuneration, including benefits, and to equal treatment in respect of work of equal value, as well as equality of treatment in the evaluation of the quality of work;

(e) The right to social security, particularly in cases of retirement, unemployment, sickness, invalidity and old age and other incapacity to work, as well as the right to paid leave;

(f) The right to protection of health and to safety in working conditions, including the safeguarding of the function of reproduction.

2. In order to prevent discrimination against women on the grounds of marriage or maternity and to ensure their effective right to work, States Parties shall take appropriate measures:

(a) To prohibit, subject to the imposition of sanctions, dismissal on the grounds of pregnancy or of maternity leave and discrimination in dismissals on the basis of marital status;

(b) To introduce maternity leave with pay or with comparable social benefits without loss of former employment, seniority or social allowances;

(c) To encourage the provision of the necessary supporting social services to enable parents to combine family obligations with work responsibilities and participation in public life, in particular through promoting the establishment and development of a network of childcare facilities;

(d) To provide special protection to women during pregnancy 1 types of work proved to be harmful to them.

3. Protective legislation relating to matters covered in this article shall be reviewed periodically in the light of scientific and technological knowledge and shall be revised, repealed or extended as necessary.

Article 13

States Parties shall take all appropriate measures to eliminate discrimination against women in other areas of economic and social life in order to ensure, on a basis of equality of men and women, the same rights, in particular:

(a) The right to family benefits;

(b) The right to bank loans, mortgages and other forms of financial credit;

(c) The right to participate in recreational activities, sports and all aspects of cultural life.

Forward-looking Strategies

179. The Forward-looking Strategies for the Advancement of Women to the Year 2000, adopted by the World Conference to Review and Appraise the Achievements of the United Nations Decade for Women: Equality, Development and Peace, held at Nairobi from 15 to 26 July 1985, include measures for specific action in the area of employment, as contained in the following paragraphs:

> 132. Special measures aimed at the advancement of women in all types of employment should be consistent with the economic and social policies promoting full productive and freely chosen employment.

133. Policies should provide the means to mobilize public awareness, political support, and institutional and financial resources to enable women to obtain jobs involving more skills and responsibility, including those at the managerial level, in all sectors of the economy. These measures should include the promotion of women's occupational mobility, especially in the middle and lower levels of the workforce, where the majority of women work.

134. Governments that have not yet done so should ratify and implement the Convention on the Elimination of All Forms of Discrimination against Women and other international instruments relating to the improvement of the conditions of women workers.

135. Measures based on legislation and trade union action should be taken to ensure equity in all jobs and avoid exploitative trends in part-time work, as well as the tendency towards the feminization of part-time, temporary and seasonal work.

136. Flexible working hours for all are strongly recommended as a measure for encouraging the sharing of parental and domestic responsibilities by women and men, provided that such measures are not used against the interests of employees. Re-entry programmes, complete with training and stipends, should be provided for women who have been out of the labour force for some time. Tax structures should be revised so that the tax liability on the combined earnings of married couples does not constitute a disincentive to women's employment.

137. Eliminating all forms of employment discrimination, *inter alia* through legislative measures, especially wage differentials between women and men carrying out work of equal value,

is strongly recommended to all parties concerned. Additional programmes should help to overcome still existing disparities in wages between women and men. Differences in the legal conditions of work of women and men should also be eliminated, where there are disadvantages to women, and privileges should be accorded to male and female parents. Occupational desegregration of women and men should be promoted.

138. The public and private sectors should make concerted efforts to diversify and create new employment opportunities for women in the traditional, non-traditional and high productivity areas and sectors in both rural and urban areas through the design and implementation of incentive schemes for both employers and women employees and through widespread dissemination of information. Gender stereotyping in all areas should be avoided and the occupational prospects of women should be enhanced.

139. The working conditions of women should be improved in all formal and informal areas by the public and private sectors. Occupational health and safety and job security should be enhanced and protective measures against work-related health hazards effectively implemented for women and men. Appropriate measures should be taken to prevent sexual harassment on the job or sexual exploitation in specific jobs, such as domestic service. Appropriate measures for redress should be provided by Governments and legislative measures guaranteeing these rights should be enforced. In addition, Governments and the private sector should put in place mechanisms to identify and correct harmful working conditions.

140. National planning should give urgent consideration to the development and strengthening of social security and health schemes and maternity protection schemes in keeping with the principles laid down in the ILO maternity protection convention and maternity protection recommendation and other relevant ILO conventions and recommendations as a prerequisite to the hastening of women's effective participation in production, and all business and trade unions should seek to promote the rights and 'compensations of working women and to ensure that appropriate infrastructures are provided. Parental leave following the birth of a child should be available to both women and men and preferably shared between them. Provision should be made for accessible childcare facilities for working parents

141. Governments and non-governmental organizations should recognize the contribution of older women and the importance of their input in those areas that directly affect their wellbeing. Urgent attention should be paid to the education and training of young women in all fields. Special retraining programmes including technical training should also be developed for young women in both urban and rural sectors, who lack qualifications and are ill-equipped to enter productive employment. Steps should be taken to eliminate exploitative treatment of young women at work, in line with ILO Convention No. 111 concerning discrimination in respect of employment and occupation, 1958 and ILO Convention No. 122 concerning employment policy, 1964.

142. National planning, programmes and projects should launch a twofold attack on poverty and unemployment. To enable women to gain access to

equal economic opportunities, Governments should seek to involve and integrate women in all phases of the planning, delivery and evaluation of multi-sectoral programmes that eliminate discrimination against women, provide required supportive services and emphasize income generation. An increased number of women should be hired in national planning mechanisms. Particular attention should be devoted to the informal sector since it will be the major employment outlet of a considerable number of underprivileged urban and rural women. The cooperative movement could play an indispensable role in this area.

143. Recognition and application should be given to the fact that women and men have equal rights to work and, on the same footing, to acquire a personal income on equal terms and conditions, regardless of the economic situation. They should be given opportunities in accordance with the protective legislation of each country and especially in the labour market, in the context of measures to stimulate economic development and to promote employment growth.

144. In view of the persistence of high unemployment levels in many countries, Governments should endeavour to strengthen the efforts to cope with this issue and provide more job opportunities for women. Given that in many cases women account for a disproportionate share of total unemployment, that their unemployment rates are higher than those of men and that, owing to lower qualifications, geographical mobility and other barriers, women's prospects for alternative jobs are mostly limited, more attention should be given to unemployment as it affects women. Measures should be taken to alleviate the consequences of

unemployment for women in declining sectors and occupations. In particular, training measures must be instituted to facilitate the transition.

145. Although general policies designed to reduce unemployment or to create jobs may benefit both men and women, by their nature they are often of greater assistance to men than to women. For this reason, specific measures should be taken to permit women to benefit equally with men from national policies to create jobs.

146. As high unemployment among youth wherever it exists, is a matter of serious concern, policies designed to deal with this problem should take into account that unemployment rates for young women are often much higher than those for young men. Moreover, measures aimed at mitigating unemployment among youth should not negatively affect the employment of women in other age groups-for example, by lowering minimum wages. Women should not face any impediment to employment opportunities and benefits in cases where their husbands are employed.

147. Governments should also give special attention to women in the peripheral or marginal labour market, such as those in unstable temporary work or unregulated part-time work, as well as to the increasing number of women working in the informal economy.

180. The Forward-looking Strategies also outline measures for action to enhance the role of women in science and technology for development and to deal with repercussions of scientific and technical progress, as contained in the following paragraphs:

200. The full and effective participation of women in the decision making and implementation process related

to science and technology, including planning and setting priorities for research and development, and the choice, acquisition, adaptation, innovation and application of science and technology for development should be enhanced. Governments should reassess their technological capabilities and monitor current processes of change so as to anticipate and ameliorate any adverse impact on women, particularly adverse effects upon the quality of job.

201. The involvement of women in all of the peaceful uses of outer space should be enhanced, and effective measures should be undertaken to integrate women into all levels of decision-making and the implementation of such activities. In all countries special efforts should be made by Governments and non-governmental organizations to provide women and women's organizations with information on the peaceful uses of outer space. Special incentives should be provided to enable women to obtain advanced education and training in areas related to outer space in order to expand their participation in the application of outer space technology for peaceful uses, especially in the high-priority development areas of water, health, energy, food production and nutrition. To achieve these goals, increased opportunities and encouragement should be given to women to study science, mathematics and engineering at the university levels and to girls to study mathematics and science the pre-university level.

202. Women with appropriate skills should be employed at managerial and professional levels and not restricted to service-level jobs. Special measures should be taken to improve working conditions for women in the science and technology fields, to eliminate discriminatory classification of jobs and to protect the right of women to promotion. Efforts should be made to

ensure that women obtain their fair share of jobs at all levels in new technology industries.

203. Major efforts should be undertaken and effective incentives created to increase the access of women to both scientific and technological education and training. To achieve these goals, efforts should be made by Government and women themselves to enhance, where necessary, the change of attitudes towards women's performance in scientific fields.

204. The potential and actual impact of science and technology on the developments that affect women's integration into the various sectors of the economy, as well as on their health, income and status, should be assessed. Relevant findings should be integrated in policy formulation to ensure that women benefit fully from available technologies and that any adverse effects are minimized.

205. Efforts in the design and delivery of appropriate technology to women should be intensified, and attention should be given to the achievement of the best possible standard in such technologies. In particular, the implications of advances in medical technology for women should be carefully examined.

Improvement of the Status and Role of Women in Education, Science and Culture

181. Improvement of the status and role of women in education, science and culture, and the elimination of discrimination against women in the field of education, are questions which have been considered on many occasions by the Commission on the Status of Women, the Economic and Social Council and the General Assembly.

182. The Council, on the recommendation of the Commission, requested Members of the United Nations

"to grant women equal educational rights with men and to ensure that they are afforded genuine educational opportunities, irrespective of nationality, race or religion", in resolution 154 F (VII) of 23 August 1948. In the same resolution, the Council suggested that UNESCO include in its reports information on progress achieved and plans for improving educational opportunities for women.

183. A few years later, in resolution 547 K (XVIII) of 12 July 1954, the Council recommended that States should:

(a) Take the necessary steps to ensure that women have equal access with men to all types of education, without any of the distinctions mentioned in article 2 of the Universal Declaration of Human Rights;

(b) Enact the necessary laws and regulations to eliminate all forms of discrimination against women in education and to ensure access for women to all types of education, including vocational and technical education, and equal opportunities to obtain State scholarships for education in any field and in preparation for all careers;

(c) Take the necessary measures to institute free, compulsory primary education and take full advantage of the facilities and resources of UNESCO in developing additional educational opportunities for girls and women, as needed.

184. In the following years, the Commission on the Status of Women and the Economic and Social Council have examined at regular intervals reports prepared by UNESCO on particular aspects of the education of girls and women, and adopted recommendations to Member States on such subjects as the access of girls and women to primary, secondary and higher education; to technical and vocational education; and to the teaching profession.

(a) Programme for the advancement of women through access to education, science and culture

185. A development of considerable importance in UNESCO's activities to improve the access of girls and women to education is its elaboration of a long-term programme for the advancement of women through access to edcuation, science and culture. The programme was approved by the General Conference of UNESCO at its fourteenth session in 1996.

186. The Director-General of UNESCO was authorized by the General Conference, in cooperation with the United Nations and the appropriate specialized agencies, to intensify long-term action to achieve full equality for women and, consequently, to hasten the advancement of women and their full participation in the economic and social development of their countries through access to education, science and culture, and to assist Member States at their request in their efforts to elaborate and apply a general policy directed to this end, in particular:

(a) to implement a study, research and training programme carried out in cooperation with Member States in the field of education, the social and natural sciences and communication;

(b) to aid government projects within UNESCO's sphere of activity which are designed to meet the need for the advancement of women and girls in various regions both rural and urban and to participate, in cooperation with a Member State, the implementation of an experimental project, and to this end to participate in the activities of Member States;

(c) to give technical and financial support to activities planned and carried out by international non-governmental organizations working within the field of UNESCO's activities to facilitate the full participation of women and girls in the economic and social development of their countries.

187. United Nations organs welcomed the initiative taken by UNESCO and expressed their support for the programme. Since 1969, UNESCO has submitted a report on its activities of special interest to women to the Commission on the Status of Women at each session. Members of the Commission have commented upon UNESCO's programme and activities and have pointed out areas where, in their view, either too much or too little emphasis was being given.

188. In recent years UNESCO's action-while still comprising an important educational element-has increasingly broadened to include other concerns, notably the promotion of the role of women in decision-making processes and in the promotion of peace, the teaching of women's studies as an integral part of human rights teaching, the improvement of the access of women to science and technology, and the study of the structure of the mass media in society and their relationship to the status of women.

Provisions of international instruments

189. The question of discrimination against women in education has been dealt with, on the international level, in the Convention and Recommendation against Discrimination in Education, adopted by the General Conference of UNESCO on 14 December 1960; the Declaration on the Elimination of Discrimination against Women, proclaimed by the General Assembly in resolution 2263 (XXII) of 7 November 1967; and the Convention on the Elimination of All Forms of Discrimination against Women, adopted by General Assembly resolution 34/180 of 18 December 1979.

Article I

1. For the purpose of this Convention, the term "discrimination" includes any distinction, exclusion, limitation or preference which, being based on race, colour, sex, language, religion, political or other opinion, national or social origin, economic condition or birth, has the purpose or effect of nullifying or impairing equality of treatment in education and in particular:

   (a) Of depriving any person or group of persons of access to education of any type or at any level;

   (b) Of limiting any person or group of persons to education of an inferior standard;

   (c) Subject to the provisions of article 2 of this Convention, of establishing or maintaining separate educational systems or institutions for persons or groups of persons; or

   (d) Of inflicting on any person or group of persons conditions which are incompatible with the dignity of man.

2. For the purposes of this Convention, the term "education" refers to all types and levels of education, and includes access to education, the standard and quality of education, and the conditions under which it is given.

Article 2

When permitted in a State, the following situations shall not be deemed to constitute discrimination, within the meaning of article 1 of this Convention.

(a) The establishment or maintenance of separate educational systems or institutions for pupils of the two sexes, if these systems or institutions offer equivalent access to education, provide a teaching staff with qualifications of the same standard as well as school premises and equipment of the same quality, and afford the opportunity to take the same or equivalent courses of study;

191. The Convention entered into force on 22 May 1962. The Recommendation contains similar substantive provisions. Implementation of the Convention is monitored by the Conciliation and Good Offices Commission established in accordance with the Protocol Instituting a Conciliation and Good Offices Commission to be responsible for seeking a settlement of any disputes which may arise between States parties to the Convention, adopted by the General Conference of UNESCO on 10 December 1962. The Protocol entered into force on 24 October 1968.

192. The Declaration on the Elimination of Discrimination against Women contains the following provision:

Article 9

All appropriate measures shall be taken to ensure to girls and women, married or unmarried, equal rights with men in education at all levels, and in particular:

(a) Equal conditions of access to, and study in, educational institutions of all types, including universities and vocational, technical and professional schools;

(b) The same choice of curricula, the same examinations, teaching staff with qualifications of the same standard, and school premises and equipment of the same quality, whether the institutions are coeducational or not;

(c) Equal opportunities to benefit from scholarships and other study grants;

(d) Equal opportunities for access to programmes of continuing education, including adult literacy programmes;

Article 10

States Parties shall take all appropriate measures to eliminate discrimination against women in order to ensure to them equal rights with men in the field of education and in particular to ensure, on a basis of equality of men and women:

(a) The same conditions for career and vocational guidance, for access to studies and for the achievement of diplomas in educational establishments of all categories in/rural as well as in urban areas; this equality shall be ensured in preschool, general, technical, professional and higher technical education, as well as in all types of vocational training;

(b) Access to the same curricula, the same examinations, teaching staff with qualifications of the same standard and school premises and equipment of the same quality;

(c) The elimination of any stereotyped concept of the roles of men and women at all levels and in all forms of education by encouraging coeducation and other types of education which will help to achieve this aim and, in particular, by the revision of textbooks and school programmes and the adaptation of teaching methods;

(d) The same opportunities to benefit from scholarships and other study grants;

(e) The same opportunities for access to programmes of continuing education, including adult and functional literacy programmes, particularly those aimed at reducing, at the earliest possible time, any gap in education existing between men and women;

(f) The reduction of female student dropout rates and the organization of programmes for girls and women who have left school prematurely;

(g) The same opportunities to participate actively in sports and physical education;

(h) Access to specific educational information to help to ensure the health and wellbeing of families, including information and advice on family planning V

194. Implementation of the provisions of the Convention is monitored by the Committee on the Elimination of Discrimination against Women.

Forward-looking Strategies

195. The Forward-looking Strategies for the Advancement of Women to the Year 2000,50 adopted by the World Conference to Review and Appraise the Achievements of the United Nations Decade for Women: Equality, Development and Peace, held at Nairobi from 15 to 26 July 1985, outline measures for action relating to education as the basis for the improvement of the status of women, as contained in the following paragraphs:

> 163. Education is the basis for the full promotion- and improvement of the status of women. It is the basic tool that should be given to women in order to fulfil their role as full members of society. Governments should strengthen the participation of women at all levels of national educational policy and in formulating and implementing plans, programmes and projects. Special measures should be adopted to revise and adapt women's education to the realities of the developing world. Existing and new services should be directed to women as intellectuals, policy-makers, decision-makers, planners, contributors and beneficiaries, with particular attention to the UNESCO Convention

against Discrimination in Education (1960). Special measures should also be adopted to increase equal access to scientific, technical and vocational education, particularly for young women, and evaluate progress made by the poorest women in urban and rural areas.

164. Special measures should be taken by Governments and the unanimous adoption by the international organizations, especially UNESCO, to eliminate the high rate of illiteracy by the year 2000, with the support of the international community. Governments should establish targets and adopt appropriate measures for this purpose. While the elimination of illiteracy is important to all, priority programmes are still required to overcome the special obstacles that have generally led to higher illiteracy rates among women than among men. Efforts should be made to promote functional literacy, with special emphasis on health, nutrition and viable economic skills and opportunities, in order to eradicate illiteracy among women and to produce additional material for the eradication of illiteracy. Programmes for legal literacy in low-income urban and rural areas should be initiated and intensified. Raising the level of education among women is important for the general welfare of society and because of its close link to child survival and child spacing.

165. The causes of high absenteeism and dropout rates of girls in the educational system must be addressed. Measures must be developed, strengthened and implemented that will, *inter alia*, create the appropriate incentives to ensure that women have an equal opportunity to acquire education at all levels, as well as to apply their education in a work or career context. Such

measures should include the strengthening of communication and information systems, the implementation of appropriate legislation and the reorientation of educational personnel. Moreover, Governments should encourage and finance adult education programmes for those women who have never completed their studies or were forced to interrupt their studies, owing to family responsibilities, lack of financial resources or early pregnancies.

166. Efforts should be made to ensure that available scholarships and other forms of support from governmental, non-governmental and private sources are expanded and equitably distributed to girls and boys and that boarding and lodging facilities are equally accessible to them.

167. The curricula of public and private schools should be examined, textbooks and other educational materials reviewed an educational personnel retrained in order to eliminate all discriminatory gender stereotyping in education. Educational institutions should be encouraged to expand their curricula to include studies on women's contribution to all aspects of development.

168. The Decade has witnessed the rise of centres and programmes of women's studies in response to social forces and to the need for developing a new scholarship and a body of knowledge on women's studies from the perspective of women. Women's studies should be developed to reformulate the current models influencing the constitution of knowledge and sustaining a value system that reinforces inequality. The promotion and application of women's studies inside and outside conventional institutions of learning will help to create a just and equitable society in which men and women enjoy equal partnership.

169. Encouragement and incentives, as well as counselling services, should be provided for girls to study scientific, technical and managerial subjects at all levels, in order to develop and enhance the aptitudes of women for decision-making, management and leadership in these fields.

170. All educational and occupational training should be flexible and accessible to both women and men. It should aim to improve employment possibilities and promotion prospects for women including those areas where technologies are improving rapidly, and vocational training programmes, as well as workers' educational schemes dealing with cooperatives, trade unions and work associations, should stress the importance of equal opportunity for women at all levels of work and work-related activities.

171. Extensive measures should be taken to diversify women's vocational education and training in order to extend their opportunities for employment in occupations that are non-traditional or are new to women and that are important to development. The present educational system, which in many countries is sharply divided by sex, with girls receiving instruction in home economics and boys in technical subjects, should be altered. Existing vocational training centres should be opened to girls and women instead of continuing a segregated training system.

172. A fully integrated system of training, having direct linkages with employment needs, pertinent to future employment and development trends should be created and implemented in order to avoid wastage of human resources.

173. Educational programmes to enable men to

assume as much responsibility as women in the upbringing of children and the maintenance of the household should be introduced at all levels of the educational system.

Improvement of the status and role of women in the field of health care

196. Because women are the main providers of primary health care in their capacity as wives, mothers and community health workers, the Commission on the Status of Women, in close co-operation with the World Health Organization and the United Nations Children's Fund, has given special attention to the health needs of women, the utilization of health services by women, and women's role in the promotion of health. In recent years the Commission has placed increased emphasis upon the occupational health and safety of women, the ability of women to control their own fertility and to take decisions about their desired number of children, and the access of women to adequate nutrition and health care for themselves and their children. Meanwhile the Sub-Commission on Prevention of Discrimination and Protection of Minorities has completed a study of traditional practices affecting the health of women and children.

Traditional practices affecting the health of women and children

197. The question of traditional practices affecting the health of women and children was first discussed by the Commission on Human Rights in 1952, in connection with its study of human rights in Trust and Non-Self-Governing Territories. At that time the Commission expressed the view that certain practices are not only dangerous to health but also seriously impair the human dignity of women; and noted that some of the Governments concerned were working towards the elimination of these practices. On the initiative of the Commission the Economic and Social Council, in

resolution 680 B II (XXVI) of 10 July 1958, invited the World Health Organization to undertake a study "of the persistence of customs which subject girls to ritual operations" and of the measures adopted or planned to put an end to these practices.

198. The question was also discussed at the United Nations Seminar on the Participation of Women in Public Life, held at Addis Ababa in 1960 for African participants. In resolution 82 II (XXXII) of 19 July 1961 the Council drew the attention of the World Health Organization to this report and asked the agency whether it would undertake a study of the medical aspects of operations based on customs to which many women were still being subjected. Noting this request, the WHO Executive Board stated, in resolution EB 29.R.50 of 25 January 1962, that "a study of the medical aspects of this subject could not be undertaken in isolation but must be related to the cultural and socio-economic background of the countries concerned". The Board authorized the Director-General, "in the event that the wide socio-economic study indicated is undertaken.... to provide any information of a medical character he may have available which is related to the question in its socio-economic context".

199. The 1975 World Health Assembly gave particular attention to traditional practices and their effects on the health of women and children. A seminar on the subject, organized by the WHO Regional Office for the Eastern Mediterranean, was held at Khartoum, Sudan, from 10 to 15 February 1979.

200. The World Conference of the United Nations Decade for Women, held at Copenhagen in July 1980, appealed to African Governments and women's organizations to search for a solution to the problem of female circumcision and infibulation. The question was

also raised during a meeting of the Association of African Women for Research and Development, held at Addis Ababa in 1981 under the aegis of the Economic Commission for Africa.

201. The Working Group on Slavery of the Sub-Commission on Prevention of Discrimination and Protection of Minorities considered information on traditional practices affecting the health of women and children at its session in 1981, and recommended that this information be drawn to the attention of the competent intergovernmental organizations. In 1982 the Working Group recommended that a study on female circumcision should be undertaken with a view to examining all aspects of the problem.

202. The Sub-Commission, in resolution 1982/15 of 7 September 1982, requested two of its members, Mr. Mudawi and Mrs. Warzazi, to carry out such a study. Later, the Commission on Human Rights, in resolution 1984/48 of 13 March 1984, recommended that the Economic and Social Council should request the Secretary-General "to entrust a working group composed of experts designated by the Sub-Commission on Prevention of Discrimination and Protection of Minorities, the United Nations Children's Fund and the United Nations Educational, Scientific and Cultural Organization with the task of conducting a comprehensive study on the phenomenon of traditional practices affecting the health of women and children". The Council endorsed the recommendation by resolution 1984/34.

203. A Seminar on Traditional Practices Affecting the Health of Women and Children in Africa was held at Dakar, Senegal, in February 1984 under the sponsorship of the Working Group on Traditional Practices, WHO, UNICEF, UNFPA and the Government of Senegal. The

Seminar created the Inter-African Committee on Traditional Practices to follow up the implementation of its recommendations. The Inter-Africa Committee, which has a co-ordinating office at Addis Ababa and a liaison office at Geneva, has set up national committees to deal with the problem in a number of countries, including Djibouti, Egypt, Ethiopia, Gambia, Ghana, Liberia, Mali, Nigeria, Senegal, Sudan and Togo.

204. The problem was further considered at the Khartoum Workshop, "African Women Speak on Female Circumcision," organized by the Babiker Badri Scientific Association for Women's Studies in October 1984, and at the Afro-Arab International Conference on the Condition of Women, organized by the Arab Lawyers Union at Cairo in February 1985. The World Health Assembly, meeting at Geneva in May 1985, adopted a resolution (38/27) recognizing the problem of harmful traditional practices and calling for concrete action to eradicate them.

205. The report of the Working Group on Traditional Practices Affecting the Health of Women and Children, on which Mrs. Halima Embarek Warzazi and Mr. Murlidhar C. Bhandare served as experts designated by the Sub-Commission on Prevention of Discrimination and Protection of Minorities, was examined and noted by the Commission on Human Rights in resolution 1986/28 of 11 March 1986.

206. In the study, the Working Group gave priority consideration to three traditional practices adversely affecting the health of women and children: (a) female circumcision, (b) traditional birth practices, and (c) preferential treatment for male children. Other adverse practices studied included forced feeding, early marriage and adolescent child-bearing, other taboos or practices which prevent women from controlling their own

fertility, such as nutritional taboos and differential feeding patterns (for example, withholding certain nutritious foods from women and children); traditional birth practices, including the work of untrained traditional birth attendants; and the application of contaminated substances or the use of dangerous medicaments during childbirth. At the same time, it also studied certain beneficial practices, such as breast-feeding and the use of traditional methods of birth-spacing.

207. After examining the report, the Commission on Human Rights requested the Secretary-General to transmit it to Governments, the competent organizations and the specialized agencies, drawing their attention to the recommendations which it contained; and called upon the specialized agencies and the interested non-governmental organizations, in their respective fields of competence, to provide the necessary assistance to the Governments which request it to help them combat such practices.

Provisions of an international instrument

The question of discrimination against women in the field of health care is dealt with in the Convention on the Elimination of All Forms of Discrimination against Women, which contains the following provision:

Article 12

1. States Parties shall take all appropriate measures to eliminate discrimination against women in the field of health care in order to ensure, on a basis of equality of men and women, access to health care services, including those related to family planning.
2. Notwithstanding the provisions of paragraph I of this article, States Parties shall ensure to women appropriate services in connexion with pregnancy, confinement and the post-natal period, granting free

services where necessary, as well as adequate nutrition during pregnancy and lactation.

Forward-looking Strategies

209. The Forward-looking Strategies for the Advancement of Women to the Year 2000,51 adopted by the World Conference to Review and Appraise the Achievements of the United Nations Decade for Women: Equality, Development and Peace, held at Nairobi from 15 to 26 July 1985 outline measures for action relating to the improvement of the status and role of women in health, as contained in the following paragraphs:

> 148. The vital role of women as providers of health care both inside and outside the home should be recognized, taking into account the following: the creation and strengthening of basic services for the delivery of health care, with due regard to levels of fertility and infant and maternal mortality and the needs of the most vulnerable groups and the need to control locally prevalent endemic and epidemic diseases. Governments that have not already done so should undertake, in co-operation with the World Health Organization, the United Nations Children's Fund and the United Nations Fund for Population Activities, plans of action relating to women in health and development in order to identify and reduce risks to women's health and to promote the positive health of women at all stages of life, bearing in mind the productive role of women in society and their responsibilities for bearing and rearing children. Women's participation in the achievement of Health for All by the Year 2000 should be recognized, since their health knowledge is crucial in their multiple roles as health providers and health brokers for the family and community, and as informed consumers of adequate and appropriate health care.

149. The participation of women in higher professional and managerial positions in health institutions should be increased through appropriate legislation; training and supportive action should be taken to increase women's enrolment at higher levels of medical training and training in health-related fields. For effective community involvement to ensure the attainment of the World Health Organization's goal of Health for All by the Year 2000 and responsiveness to women's health needs, women should be represented in national and local health councils and committees. The employment and working conditions of women health personnel and health workers should be expanded and improved at all levels. Female traditional healers and birth attendants should be more fully and constructively integrated in national health planning.

150. Health education should be geared towards changing those attitudes and values and actions that are discriminatory and detrimental to women's and girls' health. Steps should be taken to change the attitudes and health knowledge and composition of health personnel so that there can be an appropriate understanding of women's health needs. A greater sharing by men and women of family and health-care responsibilities should be encouraged. Women must be involved in the formulation and planning of their health education needs. Health education should be available to the entire family not only through the health care system, but also through all appropriate channels and in particular the educational system. To this end, Governments should ensure that information meant to be received by women is relevant to women's health priorities and is suitably presented.

151. Promotive, preventive and curative health measures should be strengthened through combined measures and a supportive health infrastructure which, in accordance with the International Code of Marketing of Breast Milk Substitutes, should be free of commercial pressure. To provide immediate access to water and sanitary facilities for women, Governments should ensure that women are consulted and involved in the planning and implementation of water and sanitation projects, trained in the maintenance of water-supply systems, and consulted with regard to technologies used in water and sanitation projects. In this regard, recommendations arising from the activities generated by the International Drinking Water Supply and Sanitation Decade and other public health programmes should be taken into account.

152. Governments should take measures to vaccinate children and pregnant women against certain endemic local diseases as well as other diseases as recommended by the vaccination schedule of the World Health Organization and to eliminate any differences in coverage between boys and girls (cf. WHO report EB 75/22). In regions where rubella is prevalent, vaccinations should preferably be given to girls before puberty. Governments should ensure that adequate arrangements are made to preserve the quality of vaccines. Governments should ensure the quality of vaccines. Governments should also ensure the full and informed participation of women in programmes to control chronic and communicable diseases.

153. The international community should intensify efforts to eradicate the trafficking, marketing and distribution of unsafe and ineffective drugs and to disseminate information on their ill effects. Those

efforts should include educational programmes to promote the proper prescription and informed use of drugs. Efforts should also be strengthened to eliminate all practices detrimental to the health of women and children. Efforts should be made to ensure that all women have access to essential drugs appropriate to their specific needs and as recommended in the WHO List of Essential Drugs as applied in 1978. It is imperative that information on the appropriate use of such drugs is made widely available to all women. When drugs are imported or exported Governments should use the WHO Certification Scheme on the Quality of Pharmaceutical Products Moving in International Commerce.

154. Women should have access to and control over income to provide adequate nutrition for themselves and their children. Also, Governments should foster activities that will increase awareness of the special nutritional needs of women; provide support to ensure sufficient rest in the last trimester of pregnancy and while breast-feeding; and promote interventions to reduce the prevalence of nutritional diseases such as anaemia in women of all ages, particularly young women, and promote the development and use of locally produced weaning food.

155. Appropriate health facilities should be planned, designed, constructed and equipped to be readily accessible and acceptable. Services should be in harmony with the timing and patterns of women's work, as well as with women's needs and perspectives. Maternal and child-care facilities, including family planning services, should be within easy reach of all women. Governments should also ensure that women have the same access as men to

affordable curative preventive and rehabilitative treatment. Wherever possible, measures should be taken to conduct general screening and treatment of women's common diseases and cancer. In view of the unacceptably high levels of maternal mortality in many developing countries, the reduction of maternal mortality from now to the year 2000 to a minimum level should be a key target for Governments and non-governmental organizations, including professional organizations.

156. The ability of women to control their own fertility forms an important basis for the enjoyment of other rights. As recognized in the World Population Plan of Action and reaffirmed at the International Conference on Population, 1984, all couples and individuals have the basic human right to decide freely and informedly the number and spacing of their children; maternal and child health and family-planning components of primary health care should be strengthened; and family-planning information should be produced and services created. Access to such services should be encouraged by Governments irrespective of their population policies and should be carried out with the participation of women's organizations to ensure their success.

157. Governments should make available, as a matter of urgency, information, education and the means to assist women and men to take decisions about their desired number of children. To ensure a voluntary and free choice, family-planning information, education and means should include all medically approved and appropriate methods of family planning. Education for responsible parenthood and family-life education should be widely available and should be directed towards

both men and women. Non-governmental organizations, particularly women's organizations, should be involved in such programmes because they can be the most effective media for motivating people at that level.

158. Recognizing that pregnancy occurring in adolescent girls, whether married or unmarried, has adverse effects on the morbidity and mortality of both mother and child, Governments are urged to develop policies to encourage delay in the commencement of child-bearing. Governments should make efforts to raise the age of entry into marriage in countries in which this age is still quite low. Attention should also be given to ensuring that adolescents, both girls and boys, receive adequate information and education.

159. All Governments should ensure that fertility-control methods and drugs conform to adequate standards of quality, efficiency and safety. This should also apply to organizations responsible for distributing and administering these methods. Information on contraceptives should be made available to women. Programmes of incentives and disincentives should be neither coercive nor discriminatory and should be consistent with internationally recognized human rights, as well as with changing individual and cultural values.

160. Governments should encourage local women's organizations to participate in primary health-care activities including traditional medicine, and should devise ways to support women, especially underprivileged women, in taking responsibility for self-care and in promoting community care, particularly in rural areas. More emphasis should be placed on preventive rather than curative measures.

161. The appropriate gender-specific indicators for

monitoring women's health that have been or are being developed by the World Health Organization should be widely applied and utilized by Governments and other interested organizations in order to develop and sustain measures for treating low-grade ill health and for reducing high morbidity rates among women, particularly when illnesses are psychosomatic or social and cultural in nature. Governments that have not yet done so should establish focal points to carry out such monitoring.

162. Occupational health and safety should be enhanced by the public and private sectors. Concern with the occupational health risks should cover female as well as male workers and focus among other things on risks endangering their reproductive capabilities and unborn children. Efforts should equally be directed at the health of pregnant and lactating women, the health impact of new technologies and the harmonization of work and family responsibilities.

Improvement of the status and role of women in society

210. The Commission on the Status of Women examined a preliminary report of the Secretary-General on the influence of mass communication media on the formation of new attitudes towards the roles of women in present-day society at its twenty-fourth session, in 1972, and expressed concern that in several countries those media perpetuated the traditional deep-rooted attitudes held by women and men about their respective roles in present-day society, and that the influence of those media in the determination of cultural patterns hindered efforts to promote equal rights of women and men and the integration of women in the development effort. On the recommendation of the Commission the Economic and Social Council, in resolution 1862 (LVI) of 16 May 1974, noted that the report substantiated the

Commission's concern and invited all organizations of the United Nations system, and particularly UNESCO, to make a special effort to increase their audiovisual material and to develop their programmes in such a way as to promote the integration of women in development; and invited Governments to urge the mass media, with due regard to freedom of expression, to adapt their programmes in order to provide for men as well as women a continuing education as to their economic and professional prospects and opportunities for leisure, family life and broadening horizons.

211. The World Conference of the International Women's Year, held in Mexico City from 19 June to 2 July 1975, condemned, in resolution 19, "the degrading exploitation of women as a sex symbol and instrument of economic interests by certain media of social communication", and requested "Governments and responsible organizations, as appropriate, to promote and encourage, in the mass communication media of their countries, the projection of a dignified and positive image of women, divesting them of their role as vehicles for publicity and as targets for the sale of consumer goods, with a view to bringing about changes in the attitudes and ways of thinking of both men and women that will be conducive to securing the equality and integrity of women and their full participation in society". The Conference likewise requested "those in charge of the mass communication media to cease projecting and gradually eliminate commercialized, tasteless and stereotyped images of women, particularly in pornographic publications, the use of such images in depicting sexual crimes and crimes of violence, and the dissemination of any material tending to create prejudices and negative attitudes with regard to the changes necessary for the revaluation of the role of women and to transmit an image of men's and women's

roles that is as varied as possible". The Conference called for "the critical and creative participation of women in all systems of mass communication, at the programming, production, distribution, reception and consumer levels".

(a) Media perpetuation of traditional attitudes held by women and men about their respectives roles in society

212. The Secretary-General submitted a progress report on the subject of the influence of the mass communication media on attitudes towards the roles of women and men in present-day society to the Commission on the Status of Women at its twenty-sixth session, in 1976. The report indicated that little information was available on the images of women projected by the more traditional types of mass communication media or on their influence on the perpetuation of sex-role stereotypes, and that there was a need for research in this area.

213. On the recommendation of the Commission the Economic and Social Council, in resolution 2063 (LXII) of 12 May 1977, decided to appoint a special rapporteur to prepare a study on the impact of the mass communication media on the changing roles of men and women, including action taken by the public and private sectors at national, regional and international levels to remove prejudices and sex-role stereotyping, to accelerate the acceptance of women's new and expanded roles in society and to promote their integration into the development process as equal partners with men.

214. The Special Rapporteur, Mrs. Esmeralda Arboleda Cuevas, submitted her report on the influence of the mass communication media on attitudes towards the roles of women and men in present-day society to the Commission on the Status of Women at its twenty-eighth session, in 1980. The report included a brief history of relevant United Nations efforts, a chapter

dealing with the pervasive social obstacles which maintained image-stereotyping, summaries of measures taken in the field by Governments and non-governmental organizations, and a series of recommendations.

215. On the recommendation of the Commission, the Council in resolution 1980/5 of 17 April 1980, took note of the report and of the importance of the problems which it raised. Regretting a tendency in mass communication media to present women in stereotyped roles and pointing to the need to correct that tendency, the Council called upon those responsible for the content and presentation of material by mass communication media to make additional efforts to present in a more comprehensive and balanced way the right of women to enjoy equal rights and equal opportunities with men, and encouraged all relevant organizations, institutions and other associations to exercise their influence on those responsible in order to achieve that goal.

216. As suggested by the Commission and the Council, the report served as a background document for the World Conference of the United Nations Decade for Women.

(b) Forward-looking Strategies

217. The Nairobi Forward-looking Strategies for the Advancement of Women to the Year 2000,61 adopted by the World Conference to Review and Appraise the Achievements of the United Nation Decade for Women: Equality, Development and Peace, held at Nairobi from 15 to 26 July 1985, outline measures for action to enhance the role of mass communications in promoting the advancement of women and the role of women in this sector, including decision-making relating to communications, as contained in the following paragraphs:

206. In view of the critical role of this sector in

eliminating stereotyped images of women and providing women with easier access to information, the participation of women at all levels of communications policy and decision-making and in programme design, implementation and monitoring should be given high priority. The media's portrayal of stereotyped images of women and also that of the advertising industry can have a profoundly adverse effect on attitudes towards and among women. Women should be made an integral part of the decision-making concerning the choice and development of alternative forms of communication and should have an equal say in the determination of the content of all public information efforts. The cultural media, involving ritual, drama, dialogue, oral literature and music, should be integrated in all development efforts to enhance communication. Women's own cultural projects aimed at changing the traditional images of women and men should be promoted and women should have equal access to financial support. In the field of communication, there is ample scope for international co-operation regarding information related to the sharing of experience by women and to projecting activities concerning the role of women in development and peace in order to enhance the awareness of both accomplishments and the tasks that remain to be fulfilled.

207. The enrolment of women in publicly operated mass communication networks and in education and training should be increased. The employment of women within the sector should be promoted and directed towards professional, advisory and decision-making positions.

208. Organizations aimed at promoting the role of women in development as contributors and beneficiaries should be assisted in their efforts to establish effective communications and information networks.

Integration of women in society

218. In resolution 42/64 of 30 November 1987, the General Assembly expressed its awareness of the fact that efforts to promote the status of women in all its aspects and their complete integration in society go beyond the problem of legal equality and that deeper structural transformations of society and changes in present-day economic relations, as well as elimination of traditional prejudices through education and dissemination of information, are required to create conditions for women to develop fully their intellectual and physical capacities and to participate actively in the decision-making process in political, economic, social and cultural development.

219. Mindful of the necessity to enlarge the possibilities for both men and women to combine parental duties and household work with paid employment and social activities and to ensure that the role of women in child-bearing should not be the cause of inequality and discrimination and that childrearing demands shared responsibilities among women, men and society as a whole, the Assembly appealed to all Governments, international organizations and intergovernmental and non-governmental organizations to pay due attention in their activities to the importance of the role of women in society in all its interrelated aspects-as mothers, as participants in political, economic, social and cultural development and as participants in public life.

220. The Assembly invited all Governments to encourage such social and economic development as will ensure the equal participation of women in all spheres of work, equal pay for work of equal value and equal opportunities for education and vocational training, taking into consideration the necessity of combining all

aspects of the role of women in society as well as the challenges faced by women in all countries when seeking to combine parental duties and family responsibilities with their full involvement in political, social, economic and cultural development. It appealed to them to promote conditions that will enable women to participate as equal partners with men in public and political life, in the decision-making process at all levels and in the management of different spheres of life in society.

221. Further, the Assembly urged all Governments to recognize the special status and social importance of child-bearing and childrearing and to take all necessary measures to encourage the support of parenthood, including paid maternity and parental and child-care leave, and to provide women with security for their jobs as long as necessary with a view to allowing them, if they so wish, to fulfil their role as mothers without prejudice to their professional and public activities; and appealed to them to promote the establishment of appropriate facilities for the care and education of children as a means of combining parenthood with economic, political, social, cultural and other activities, and thus to assist women towards full integration in society.

222. Finally, it called upon Member States to adopt the necessary effective measures with a view to implementing the Nairobi Forward-looking Strategies as a matter of priority, including the establishment or strengthening of appropriate mechanisms for the advancement of women in order to ensure the full participation of women in all spheres of life in their countries; requested the Secretary-General to pay due attention to all the interrelated aspects of the role of women in society when preparing surveys on the role of women in development as well as reports on the world

social situation and other relevant surveys; and invited the Commission on the Status of Women to pay due attention to the provisions of the present resolution during the consideration at its next sessions of the priority themes under the heading "Equality", with a view to formulating recommendations for appropriate action by concerned United Nations organs and bodies.

Protection of women and children in emergency and armed conflict

223. At its twenty-fourth session, in 1972, the Commission on the Status of Women considered a report on the protection of women in emergency situations prepared by the Secretary-General in accordance with its resolution 4 (XXII) of 3 February 1969. On the recommendation of the Commission, the Economic and Social Council adopted resolution 1515 (XLVIII) of 28 May 1970, in which it requested the Secretary-General to submit to the Commission a report on the conditions of women and children in emergency and armed conflicts in the struggle for peace, self-determination, national liberation and independence. The Council also requested the General Assembly to consider the possibility of drafting a declaration on the protection of women and children in emergency or wartime.

224. At its twenty-fifth session, in 1974, the Commission proposed for adoption by the General Assembly a draft declaration on the protection of women and children in emergency and armed conflict in the struggle for peace, self-determination, national liberation and independence. The Economic and Social Council endorsed this decision in resolution 1861 (LVI) of 16 May 1974. The General Assembly, in resolution 3318 (XXIX) of 14 December 1974, adopted and proclaimed the Declaration on the Protection of Women and Children in Emergency and Armed Conflict, and called for its strict observance by all Member States.

225. The Declaration states, in article 1, that attacks and bombings on the civilian population shall be prohibited and such acts condemned, since they inflict incalculable suffering, especially on women and children, who are the most vulnerable members of the population. It also condemns the use of chemical and bacteriological weapons in the course of military operations as constituting one of the most flagrant violations of the Geneva Protocol of 1925,13 the Geneva Conventions of 194964 and the principles of international humanitarian law.

226. The Declaration provides that "all efforts shall be made by States involved in armed conflicts... to spare women and children from the ravages of war"; and that "all the necessary steps shall be taken to ensure the prohibition of measures such as persecution, torture, punitive measures, degrading treatment and violence, particularly against that part of the civilian population that consists of women and children". It specifies that "all forms of repression and cruel and inhuman treatment of women and children, including imprisonment, torture, shooting, mass arrests, collective punishment, destruction of dwellings and forcible eviction, committed by belligerents in the course of military operations or in occupied territories shall be considered criminal". Finally, it provides that "women and children belonging to the civilian population and finding themselves in circumstances of emergency and armed conflict in the struggle for peace, self-determination, national liberation and independence, or who live in occupied territories, shall not be deprived of shelter, food, medical aid or other inalienable rights, in accordance with the provisions of the Universal Declaration of Human Rights, the International Covenant on Economic, Social and Cultural Rights, the Declaration of the Rights of the Child or other instruments of international law".

227. At its twenty-seventh session, in 1978, the Commission was informed by the Secretary-General that two Protocols additional to the Geneva Conventions of 1949,66 dealing with the protection of victims of international armed conflicts and non-international armed conflicts respectively, had been adopted at the fourth session of the Diplomatic Conference on the Reaffirmation and Development of International Humanitarian Law Applicable in Armed Conflicts, in 1977. These Protocols contain provisions with respect to the protection of women and children, which strengthen those of the Geneva Conventions and include provisions for the evacuation of children and the protection of women and children against rape, enforced prostitution and any form of indecent assault.

228. In resolution 7 (XXVII) of 31 March 1978, the Commission called upon all States and all parties to armed conflicts, in emergency situations in the struggle for peace, self-determination, national liberation and independence, to accord special protection to women and children in accordance with the relevant international provisions applicable in armed conflicts and to give every possible support to the work of international humanitarian organizations to alleviate the suffering of the civilian population, especially women and children, in these conflicts; called upon relevant international humanitarian organizations such as the International Committee of the Red Cross to continue to do their utmost for the protection of the civilian population, especially women and children, in emergency and armed conflicts, including those in the struggle for peace, self-determination, national liberation and independence; and requested international humanitarian organizations helping the civilian population in armed conflicts to give special care to pregnant women and mothers with small children and to orphans.

229. The Nairobi Forward-looking Strategies for the Advancement of Women to the Year 2000,61 adopted by the World Conference to Review and Appraise the Achievements of the United Nations Decade for Women: Equality, Development and Peace, held at Nairobi from 15 to 26 July 1985, reiterated the need to implement measures proposed in the 1974 Declaration on the Protection of Women and Children in Emergency and Armed Conflict for the protection of women and children in emergency and armed conflict, as contained in the following paragraphs:

261. Armed conflicts and emergency situations impose a serious threat to the lives of women and children, causing constant fear, danger of displacement, destruction, devastation, physical abuse, social and family disruption, and abandonment. Sometimes these result in complete denial of access to adequate health and educational services, loss of job opportunities and overall worsening of material conditions.

262. International instruments, ongoing negotiations and international discussions aimed at the limitation of armed conflicts, such as the Fourth Geneva Convention of 1949 and the First Additional Protocol to the Geneva Conventions of 1949, adopted in 1977, provide a general framework for the protection of civilians in times of hostilities and the basis of provisions of humanitarian assistance and protection to women and children. Measures proposed in the 1974 Declaration on the Protection of Women and Children in Emergency and Armed Conflict (General Assembly resolution 3318 (XXIX)) should be taken into account by Governments.

Additional areas of special concern

230. The Nairobi Forward-looking Strategies for the Advancement of Women to the Year 200068 refer to an increasing number of categories of women who, because

of their special characteristics, are experiencing not only the common problems dealt with above but also specific difficulties due to their socio-economic and health condition, age, minority status or a combination of these factors. These special groups of women are extremely diverse, and their problems vary tremendously from one country to another; accordingly no single strategy or group of measures can apply adequately to all cases. The basic strategy must remain one of fundamentally changing the economic conditions that produce such deprivation and of upgrading women's low status in society, which accounts for their extreme vulnerability to such conditions, especially to poverty. It is suggested in the Strategies that:

280. The economic, social, cultural and political conditions of those groups of women should be improved basically by the implementation of the measures proposed for the attainment of equality, development and peace for women in general. Additional efforts should be directed towards ensuring the gainful and productive inclusion of these women in mainstream development and in political activities. Priority emphasis should be placed upon income-generating opportunities and for the independent and sustained improvement of their condition and by the full integration and active participation of women as agents and beneficiaries of development.

231. The categories of women concerned, and the Strategies recommended for the improvement of their condition, are as follow:

Women in areas affected by drought

283. During the Decade, the phenomenon of drought and desertification grew and developed incessantly, no longer affecting merely some localities in a single country but several entire countries. The scale

and persistence of drought constitutes a grave threat, particularly for the countries of the Sahel, in which famine and a far-reaching deterioration of the environment set in as a result of the desertification process. Hence, despite the considerable efforts of the international community, the living conditions of the peoples, particularly those of women and children, which were already precarious, have become particularly miserable.

In view of that situation steps should be taken to promote concerted programmes between the countries concerned for combating drought and desertification. Efforts should be intensified for the formulation and implementation of programmes aimed at food security and self-sufficiency, in particular by the optimum control and exploitation of hydro-geological resources.

A distinction should be made between emergency aid and productive activities. Emergency aid should be intensified when necessary and as far as ever possible directed towards development aid.

Measures should be adopted to take into account women's contribution to production, involve them more closely in the design, implementation and evaluation of the programmes envisaged and ensure ample access for them to the means of production and processing and preservation techniques.

Urban poor women

284. Urbanization has been one of the major socio-economic trends over the past few decades and is expected to continue at an accelerating rate. Although the situation varies considerably from one region to another, it can generally be expected that by the year 2000 close to half the number of women in the world will be living in urban areas. In developing countries, the number of

urban women could nearly double by the year 2000, and it is envisaged that there could be a considerable increase in the number of poor women among them.

285. To deal effectively with the issue, Governments should organize multi-sectoral programmes with emphasis on economic activities, elimination of discrimination and the provision of supportive services and, *inter alia,* adequate child-care facilities and, where necessary, workplace canteens to enable women to gain access to economic, social and educational opportunities on an equal basis with men. Particular attention should be devoted to the informal sector, which constitutes a major outlet for employment of a considerable number of urban poor women.

Elderly women

286. The International Plan of Action on Aging adopted by the World Assembly on Aging in 1982 emphasized both the humanitarian and developmental aspects of aging. The recommendations of the Plan of Action are applicable to women and men with a view to providing them with protection and care, and ensuring their involvement and participation in social life and development. However, the Plan of Action recognizes a number of specific areas of concern for elderly women since their longer life expectancy frequently means an old age aggravated by economic need and isolation for both unmarried women and widows, possibly with little or no prospect of paid employment. This applies particularly to those women whose lifetimes were spent in unpaid and unrecognized work in the home with little or no access to a pension. If women have an income, it is generally lower than men's, partly because their former employment status has in the majority of cases been broken by maternity and family responsibilities. For this reason, the Plan of Action also noted the need for

long-term policies directed towards providing social insurance for women in their own right. Governments and non-governmental organizations should, in addition to the measures recommended, explore the possibilities of employing elderly women in productive and creative ways and encouraging their participation in social and recreational activities.

It is also recommended that the care of elderly persons, including women, should go beyond disease orientation and should include their total well-being. Further efforts, in particular primary health care, health services and suitable accommodation and housing as strategies should be directed at enabling elderly women to lead a meaningful life as long as possible, in their own home and family and in the community.

Women should be prepared early in life, both psychologically and socially, to face the consequences of longer life expectancy. Although, while getting older, professional and family roles of women are undergoing fundamental changes, aging, as a stage of development, is a challenge for women. In this period of life, women should be enabled to cope in a creative way with new opportunities. The social consequences arising from the stereotyping of elderly women should be recognized and eliminated. The media should assist by presenting positive images of women, particularly emphasizing the need for respect because of their past and continuing contributions to society.

Attention should be given to studying and treating the health problems of aging, particularly in women. Research should also be directed towards the investigation and slowing down of the process of premature aging due to a lifetime of stress, excessive work-load, malnutrition and repeated pregnancy.

Young women

287. Initiatives begun for the 1985 International Youth Year should be extended and expanded so that young women are protected from abuse and exploitation and assisted to develop their full potential. Girls and boys must be provided with equal access to health, education and employment to equip them for adult life. Both girls and boys should be educated to accept equal responsibilities for parenthood.

Urgent attention should be paid to the educational and vocational training of young women in all fields of occupation, giving particular emphasis to those who are socially and economically disadvantaged. Self-employed young women and girls should be assisted to organize co-operatives and ongoing training programmes to improve their skills in production, marketing and management techniques. Special retraining programmes should also be developed for teenage mothers and girls who have dropped out of school and are ill equipped to enter productive employment.

Steps should be taken to eliminate exploitative treatment of young women at work in line with ILO Convention No. 111 concerning discrimination in respect of employment and occupation, 1958 and ILO Convention No. 122 concerning employment policy, 1964. Legislative measures guaranteeing young women their rights should be enforced.

Governments should recognize and enforce the rights of young women to be free from sexual violence, sexual harassment and sexual exploitation. In particular, Governments should recognize that many young women are victims of incest and sexual abuse in the family, and should take steps to assist the victims and to prevent such abuse by education, by improving the status of women and by appropriate action against offenders.

Young women should be educated to assert their rights. Particular attention should also be given to sexual harassment and exploitation in employment, especially those areas of employment such as domestic service, where sexual harassment and exploitation are most prevalent.

Governments must also recognize their obligation to provide housing for young women who, because of unemployment and low incomes, suffer special problems in obtaining housing. Homeless young women are particularly vulnerable to sexual exploitation.

In the year 2000, women aged 15-24 will constitute over 8 per cent of both rural and urban populations in developing countries. The great majority of these women will be out of school and in search of jobs. For those employed, frequent exploitation, long working hours and stress have serious implications for their health. Low nutritional levels and unplanned and repeated pregnancies are also aggravating factors.

Abused women

288. Gender-specific violence is increasing and Governments must affirm the dignity of women, as a priority action.

Governments should therefore intensify efforts to establish or strengthen forms of assistance to victims of such violence through the provision of shelter, support, legal and other services. In addition to immediate assistance to victims of violence against women in the family and in society, Governments should undertake to increase public awareness of violence against women as a societal problem, establish policies and legislative measures to ascertain its causes and prevent and eliminate such violence, in particular by suppressing degrading images and representations of women in society, and finally encourage the development of educational and re-educational measures for offenders.

Destitute women

289. Destitution is an extreme form of poverty. It is estimated that its effects on large segments of the population in developing and developed countries are on the increase. Forward-looking Strategies to promote the objectives of the United Nations Decade for Women: Equality, Development and Peace at the national and international levels are the basis for dealing with this problem. In addition strategies already specified for the implementation of the International Development Strategy for the Third United Nations Development Decade and the new international economic order are suggested in these recommendations. Governments should therefore ensure that the special needs and concerns of destitute women are given priority in the above-mentioned strategies. Moreover, efforts being undertaken for the International Year of Shelter for the Homeless (1987) should focus attention on the particular situation of women commensurate with their relative needs.

Women victims of trafficking and involuntary prostitution

290. Forced prostitution is a form of slavery imposed on women by procurers. It is, *inter alia,* a result of economic degradation that alienates women's labour through processes of rapid urbanization and migration resulting in underemployment and unemployment. It also stems from women's dependence on men. Social and political pressures produce refugees and missing persons. Often these include vulnerable groups of women who are victimized by procurers. Sex tourism, forced prostitution and pornography reduce women to mere sex objects and marketable commodities.

291. States parties to the United Nations Convention for the Suppression of the Traffic in Persons and of the-Exploitation of the Prostitution of Others should implement the provisions dealing with the exploitation of women as prostitutes. Urgent consideration should also be given to the improvement of international measures to combat trafficking in women for the purposes of prostitution. Resources for the prevention of prostitution and assistance in the professional, personal and social reintegration of prostitutes should be directed towards providing economic opportunities, including training, employment, self-employment and health facilities for women and children. Governments should also endeavour to co-operate with non-governmental organizations to create wider employment possibilities for women. Strict enforcement provisions must also be taken at all levels to stem the rising tide of violence, drug abuse and crime related to prostitution. The complex and serious problems of the exploitation of and violence against women associated with prostitution call for increased and co-ordinated efforts by police agencies internationally.

Women deprived of their traditional means of livelihood

292. The excessive and inappropriate exploitation of land by any party for any purpose, *inter alia,* by transnational corporations, as well as natural and man-made disasters are among the predominant causes of deprivation of traditional means of livelihood. Droughts, floods, hurricanes and other forms of environmental hazards, such as erosion, desertification and deforestation, have already pushed poor women into marginal environments. At present the pressures are greatest in drought-afflicted and semi-arid areas. Urban slums and squatter settlements are also seriously affected. "Critically low levels of water supplies, shortage of fuel, over-utilization of grazing and arable lands, and

population density are all factors that deprive women of their livelihood.

293. National and international emphasis on ecosystem management should be strengthened, environmental degradation should be controlled and options provided for alternative means of livelihood. Measures should be established to draw up national conservation strategies aimed at incorporating women's development programmes, among which are irrigation and tree planting and also orientation in the area of agriculture, with women constituting a substantial part of the wage-earning labour force for those programmes.

Women who are the sole supporters of families

294. Recent studies have shown that the number of families in which women are the sole supporters is on the increase. Owing to the particular difficulties (social, economic and legal) which they face, many such women are among the poorest people concentrated in urban informal labour markets and they constitute large numbers of the rural unemployed and marginally employed. Those with very little economic, social and moral support face serious difficulties in supporting themselves as well as in bringing up their children alone. This has serious repercussions for society in terms of the quality, character, productivity and human resource capabilities of its present and future citizenry.

295. The assumptions that underlie a large part of the relevant legislation, regulations and household surveys that confine the role of supporter and head of household to men hinder women's access to credit, loans and material and non-material resources. Changes are needed in these areas to secure for women equal access to resources. There is a need to eliminate terms such as "head of household" and introduce others that are comprehensive enough to reflect women's role

appropriately in legal documents and household surveys to guarantee the rights of these women. In the provision of social services, special attention has to be given to the needs of these women. Governments are urged to ensure that women with sole responsibility for their families receive a level of income and social support sufficient to enable them to attain or maintain economic independence and to participate effectively in society. To this end, the assumptions that underlie policies, including research used in policy development, and legislation that confines the role of supporter or head of household to men should be identified and eliminated. Special attention, such as accessible, quality child care, should be given to assisting those women in discharging their domestic responsibilities and to enabling them to participate in and benefit from education, training programmes and employment. The putative father should be made to assist in the maintenance and education of those children born out of wedlock.

Women with physical and mental disabilities

296. It is generally accepted that women constitute a significant number of the estimated 500 million people who are disabled as a consequence of mental, physical or sensory impairment. Many factors contribute to the rising numbers of disabled persons, including war and other forms of violence, poverty, hunger, nutritional deficiencies, epidemics and work-related accidents. The recognition of their human dignity and human rights and the full participation by disabled persons in society is still limited, and this presents additional problems for women who may have domestic and other responsibilities. It is recommended that Governments should adopt the Declaration on the Rights of Disabled Persons (1975) and the World Programme of Action concerning Disabled Persons (1982) which provide an overall framework for action and also refer to problems

specific to women that have not been fully appreciated by society because they are still not well known or understood. Community-based occupational and social rehabilitation measures, support services to help them with their domestic responsibilities, as well as opportunities for the participation of such women in all aspects of life should be provided. The rights of intellectually disabled women to obtain health information and advice and to consent to or refuse medical treatment should be respected; similarly, the rights of intellectually disabled minors should be respected.

Women in detention and subject to penal law

297. One of the major areas of current concern in the field of crime prevention and criminal justice is the need for equal treatment of women by the criminal justice system. In the context of changing socio-economic and cultural conditions some improvements have taken place but more need to be made. The number of women in detention has increased over the Decade and this trend is expected to continue. Women deprived of freedom are exposed to various forms of physical violence, sexual and moral harassment. The conditions of their detention are often below acceptable hygienic standards and their children are deprived of maternal care.

The recommendations of the Sixth United Nations Congress on the Prevention of Crime and the Treatment of Offenders, held at Caracas, in 1980, and the principles of the Caracas Declaration with special reference to the "fair and equal treatment of women", should be taken into account in designing and implementing concrete measures at the national and international levels. The proportions of indigenous women imprisoned in some countries is a matter of concern.

Refugee and displaced women and children

298. The international community recognizes a humanitarian responsibility to protect and assist refugees and displaced persons. In many cases refugee and displaced women are exposed to a variety of difficult situations affecting their physical and legal protection as well as their psychological and material well-being. Problems of physical debility, physical safety, emotional stress and socio-psychological effects of separation or death in the family, as well as changes in women's roles, together with limitations often found in the new environment including lack of adequate food, shelter, health care and social services call for specialized and enlarged assistance. Special attention has to be offered to women with special needs. Furthermore, the potential and capacities of refugee and displaced women should be recognized and enhanced.

299. It is recognized that a lasting solution to the problems of refugees and displaced women and children should be sought in the elimination of the root causes of the flow of refugees and durable solutions should be found leading to their voluntary return to their homes in conditions of safety and honour and their full integration in the economic, social and cultural life of their country of origin in the immediate future. Until such solutions are achieved, the international community, in an expression of international solidarity and burden sharing, should continue providing relief assistance and also launching special relief programmes taking into account the specific needs of refugee women and children in countries of first asylum. Similarly, relief assistance and special relief programmes should also continue to be provided to returnees and displaced women and children. Legal, educational, social, humanitarian and moral assistance should be offered as well as opportunities for their voluntary repatriation, return or

resettlement. Steps should also be taken to promote accession by Governments to the 1951 Convention relating to the Status of Refugees and to implement, on a basis of equity for all refugees, provisions contained in this Convention and its 1987 Protocol.

Migrant women

300. The Decade has witnessed the increasing involvement of women in all forms of migration, including rural-rural, rural-urban and international movements of a temporary, seasonal or permanent nature. In addition to their lack of adequate education, skills and resources, migrant women may also face severe adjustment problems due to differences in religion, language, nationality, and socialization as well as separation from their original families. Such problems are often accentuated for international migrants as a result of the openly "pressed prejudices and hostilities, including violation of hum~ rights in host countries. Thus recommendations of the World Population Plan of Action and the Programme of Action for the Second Half of the United Nations Decade for Women pertaining to migrant women should be implemented and expanded in view of the anticipated increase in the scope of the problem. It is also urgent to conclude the elaboration of the draft International Convention on the Protection of the Rights of All Migrant Workers and their Families, as agreed by the General Assembly in the relevant resolutions.

301. The situation of migrant women, who are subject to double discrimination as women and as migrants, should be given special attention by the Governments of host countries, particularly with respect to protection and maintenance of family unity, employment opportunities and equal pay, equal conditions of work, health care, benefits to be provided

in accordance with the existing social security rights in the host country, and racial and other forms of discrimination. Particular attention should also be given to the second generation of migrant women, especially with regard to education and professional training, to allow them to integrate themselves in their countries of adoption and to work according to their education and skills. In this process, loss of cultural values of their countries of origin should be avoided.

Minority and "indigenous" women

302. Some women are oppressed as a result of belonging to minority groups or populations which have historically been subjected to domination and suffered dispossession and dispersal. These women suffer the full burden of discrimination based on race, colour, descent, ethnic and national origin and the majority experience serious economic deprivation. As women, they are therefore doubly disadvantaged. Measures should be taken by Governments in countries in which there are minority and indigenous populations to respect, preserve and promote all of their human rights, their dignity, ethnic, religious, cultural and linguistic identity and their full participation in societal change.

303. Governments should ensure that the fundamental human rights and freedoms as enshrined in relevant international instruments are fully guaranteed also to women belonging to minority groups and indigenous populations. Governments in countries in which there are indigenous and minority populations should ensure respect for the economic, social and cultural rights of these women and assist them in the fulfilment of their family and parental responsibilities. Specific measures should address dietary deficiencies, high levels of infant and maternal mortality and other health problems, lack of education, housing and child

care. Vocational, technical, professional and other training should be provided to enable these women to secure employment or to participate in income-generating activities and projects, and to secure adequate wages, occupational health and safety and their other rights as workers. As far as possible, Governments should ensure that these women have access to all services in their own languages.

304. Women belonging to minority groups or indigenous populations should be fully consulted and should participate in the development and implementation of programmes affecting them. The Governments of countries where minorities and indigenous populations exist should take proper account of the work of bodies such as the Committee on the Elimination of Racial Discrimination and the Sub-Commission on Prevention of Discrimination and Protection of Minorities, in particular its Working Group which is developing a set of international standards to protect the rights of indigenous populations. The General Assembly should consider the advisability of designating an international year of indigenous and traditional cultures in order to promote international understanding and to emphasize the distinctive role of women in sustaining the identity of their people.

Involvement of women in strengthening international peace and co-operation

232. The World Conference of the International Women's Year, held at Mexico City in 1975, examined a report on the involvement of women in strengthening international peace and eliminating racism and racial discrimination.

233. In resolution 29, on women's participation in the strengthening of international peace and security and in the struggle against colonialism, racism, racial

discrimination and foreign domination, the Conference called upon "all Governments, intergovernmental and non-governmental organizations, women's organizations and women's groups to intensify their forces in order to strengthen peace, to expand and deepen the process of detente and to implement its irreversible character, to eliminate completely and definitely all forms of colonialism, to put an end to the policy and practice of *apartheid* and racism, and to foreign domination and aggression". Further, it urged all Governments "to take effective measures towards bringing about general and complete disarmament".

234. In the Declaration of Mexico on the Equality of Women and Their Contribution to Development and Peace, the Conference pointed out that "Women have a vital role to play in the promotion of peace in all spheres of life: in the family, the community, the nation and the world. Women must participate equally with men in the decision-making processes which help to promote peace at all levels." It further stated that "Peace requires that women as well as men should reject any type of intervention in the domestic affairs of States, whether it be openly or covertly carried on by other States or by transnational corporations. Peace also requires that women as well as men should also promote respect for the sovereign right of a State to establish its own economic, social and political system without undergoing political and economic pressures or coercion of any type."

235. After considering the report of the Conference the General Assembly, in resolution 3519 (XXX) of 15 December 1975, called upon "all Governments, intergovernmental and non-governmental organizations and women's groups, to intensify their efforts to strengthen peace, to expand and deepen the process of international detente and make it irreversible, to

eliminate completely and definitely all forms of colonialism and to put an end to the policy and practice of *apartheid,* all forms of racism, racial discrimination, aggression, occupation and foreign domination".

Declaration on the participation of the women in promoting international peace and cooperation

236. Two years later, in resolution 32/142 of 16 December 1977, the General Assembly requested the Commission on the Status of Women to consider the elaboration of a draft declaration on the participation of women in the struggle for the strengthening of international peace and security and against colonialism, racism, racial discrimination, foreign aggression and occupation and all forms of foreign domination. The Economic and Social Council expressed the hope, in resolution 1978/29 of 5 May 1978, that the Commission would make every effort to elaborate such a draft, and invited all Governments, specialized agencies and organizations to transmit their views and/or proposals concerning the nature and content of the draft, to the Secretary-General.

237. The Economic and Social Council, at it first regular session in 1978, expressed the hope, in resolution 1978/29 of 5 May 1978, that the Commission on the Status of Women would make every effort to consider elaborating the draft declaration on the participation of women in the struggle for the strengthening of international peace and security and against colonialism, racism, racial discrimination, foreign aggression and occupation and all forms of foreign domination requested by the Assembly in resolution 32/142; and invited all Governments, the specialized agencies and other intergovernmental organizations, as well as concerned non-governmental organizations in consultative status, to transmit to the Secretary-General their views and/or

proposals concerning the nature and content of the proposed declaration.

238. The Secretary-General's report to the Commission contained the text of a draft declaration submitted by the German Democratic Republic, as well as excerpts from replies received from 19 Governments and a brief summary of replies received from specialized agencies and non-governmental organizations. .

239. The Commission set up a Working Group at its twenty-eighth session to consider the elaboration of the draft declaration. When it became apparent that the work could not be completed rapidly, the Commission recommended, and the Economic and Social Council agreed, in resolution 1980/36 of 2 May 1980, that the question should be referred to the General Assembly.

240. At its thirty-fifth session, the General Assembly considered a proposal submitted to its Third Committee entitled "Draft Declaration on the Participation of Women in the Struggle for the Strengthening of International Peace and Security and against Colonialism, Racism, Racial Discrimination, Foreign Aggression, Occupation and All Forms of Foreign Domination". After extensive discussion in the Committee, the Assembly, by decision 35/429 of 11 December 1980, requested the Secretary-General to seek, and report on, the views of Governments.

241. The draft declaration was again discussed extensively in the Third Committee at the thirty-sixth session of the Assembly, but again the Committee was unable to conclude the discussions or even to examine fully the various proposals before it. The Assembly accordingly requested the Secretary-General, by decision 36/428 of 14 December 1981, to seek and to report further comments from Member States.

242. At the thirty-seventh session of the General Assembly, the Third Committee received and considered a draft resolution sponsored by 20 Member States 74 and adopted it as orally revised. On the recommendation of the Committee the General Assembly proclaimed, in resolution 37/63 of 3 December 1982, the Declaration on the Participation of Women in Promoting International Peace and Co-operation.

243. The Declaration contains a preamble and 14 articles. The preamble recalls that the Convention on the Elimination of All Forms of Discrimination against Women affirms that the strengthening of international peace and security, the relaxation of international tension, mutual co-operation among all States irrespective of their social and economic systems, general and complete disarmament and in particular, nuclear disarmament under strict and effective international control, the affirmation of the principles of justice, equality and mutual benefit in relations among countries and the realization of the right of peoples under alien and colonial domination and foreign occupation to self-determination and independence, as well as respect for national sovereignty and territorial integrity, will promote social progress and development, and as a consequence, will contribute to the attainment of full equality between men and women.

244. The articles of a general nature, contained in part I of the Declaration, include:

Article 1, which states that women and men have an equal and vital interest in contributing to international peace and co-operation, and that, to this end, women must be enabled to exercise their right to participate in the economic, social, cultural, civil and political affairs of society on an equal footing with men;

Article 2, which points out that the full participation of women in the economic, social, cultural, civil and political affairs of society and in the endeavour to promote international peace and co-operation is dependent on a balanced and equitable distribution of roles between men and women in the family and in society as a whole;

Article 3, which states that the increasing participation of women in the economic, social, cultural, civil and political affairs of society will contribute to international peace and co-operation;

Article·4, which concludes that the full enjoyment of the rights of women and men and the full participation of women in promoting international peace and co-operation will contribute to the eradication of *apartheid,* of all forms of racism, racial discrimination, colonialism, neo-colonialism, aggression, foreign occupation and domination and interference in the internal affairs of States; and

Article 5, which indicates that special national and international measures are necessary to increase the level of women's participation in the sphere of international relations so that women can contribute, on an equal basis with men, to national and international efforts to secure world peace and economic and social progress and to promote international co-operation.

245. Articles 6 to 13, in part II of the Declaration, enumerate measures to be taken to improve the participation of women in promoting international peace and cooperation, including measures to ensure the equal participation of women in the economic, social, cultural, civil and political affairs of society through a balanced and equitable distribution of roles between men and women in the domestic sphere and in society as a whole, to promote the exchange of experience at the national

and international levels for the purpose of furthering the involvement of women in promoting international peace and co-operation and in solving other vital national and international problems, to encourage women to participate in non-governmental and intergovernmental organizations aimed as the strengthening of international peace and security, and to establish adequate legal protection of the rights of women on an equal basis with men in order to ensure effective participation of women in the activities referred to above.

246. Article 14, which concludes the Declaration, urges Governments, non-governmental and international organizations, including the United Nations and the specialized agencies, and individuals, to do all in their power to promote the implementation of the principles contained in the Declaration.

Forward looking strategies

247. The Nairobi Forward-looking Strategies for the Advancement of Women to the Year 2000,75 adopted by the World Conference to Review and Appraise the Achievements of the United Nations Decade for Women: Equality, Development and Peace, held at Nairobi from 15 to 26 July 1985, outlined basic strategies for the participation of women in promoting international peace and co-operation, as contained in the following paragraphs:

239. The main principles and directions for women's activities aimed at strengthening peace and formulated in the Declaration on the Participation of Women in Promoting International Peace and Co-operation should be put into practice. The Declaration calls for Governments, the United Nations system, non-governmental organizations, relevant institutions and individuals to strengthen women's participation in this sphere and it provides the overall framework for such activities.

240. Women and men have an equal right and the same vital interest in contributing to international peace and co-operation. Women should participate fully in all efforts to strengthen and maintain international peace and security and to promote international co-operation, diplomacy, the process of detente, disarmament in the nuclear field in particular, and respect for the principles of the Charter of the United Nations, including respect for the sovereign rights of States, guarantees of fundamental freedoms and human rights, such as recognition of the dignity of the individual and self-determination, and freedom of thought, conscience, expression, association, assembly, communication and movement without distinction as to race, sex, political and religious beliefs, language or ethnic origin. The commitment to remove the obstacles to women's participation in the promotion of peace should be strengthened.

241. In view of the fact that women are still very inadequately represented in national and international political processes dealing with peace and conflict settlement, it is essential that women support and encourage each other in their initiatives and action relating either to universal issues, such as disarmament and the development of confidence-building measures between nations and people, or to specific conflict situations between or within States.

242. There exist situations in several regions of the world where the violation of principles of non-use of force, non-intervention, noninterference, non-aggression and the right to self-determination endangers international peace and security and creates massive humanitarian problems which constitute an impediment to the advancement of women and hence to the full implementation of the Forward-looking Strategies. In regard to these situations strict adherence to and respect

for the cardinal principles enshrined in the Charter of the United Nations and implementation of relevant resolutions consistent with the principles of the Charter are an imperative requirement with a view to seeking solutions to such problems; thereby ensuring a secure and better future for the people affected, most of whom are invariably women and children.

243. Since women are one of the most vulnerable groups in the regions affected by armed conflicts, special attention has to be drawn to the need to eliminate obstacles to the fulfilment of the objectives of equality, development and peace and the principles of the Charter of the United Nations.

244. One of the important obstacles to achieving international peace is the persistent violation of the principles and objectives of the Charter of the United Nations and the lack of political will of Governments of some countries to promote constructive negotiations aimed at decreasing international tension on the issues that seriously threaten the maintenance of international peace and security. For this reason, the strategies in this field should include the mobilization of women in favour of all acts and actions that tend to promote peace, in particular, the elimination of wars and danger of nuclear war.

245. Immediate and special priority should be given to the promotion and the effective enjoyment of human rights and fundamental freedoms for all without distinction as to sex, the full application of the rights of peoples to self-determination and the elimination of colonialism, neo-colonialism, *apartheid*, of all forms of racism and racial discrimination, oppression and aggression, foreign occupation, as well as domestic violence and violence against women.

246. In South-West Asia women and children have endured serious suffering owing to the violation of the Charter of the United Nations, leading, among other things, to the vast problem of refugees in neighbouring countries.

247. The situation of violence and destabilization that exists in Central America constitutes the most serious obstacle to the achievement of peace in the region and thus hinders the fulfilment of the Forward-looking Strategies vital to the advancement of women. In this regard and to promote conditions favourable to the objectives of the Strategies, it is important to reiterate the principles of non-intervention and self-determination, as well as the non-use of force or rejection of the threat of use of force in the solution of conflicts in the region. Therefore, the validity of the United Nations resolutions that establish the right of all sovereign States in the area to live in peace, free from all interference in their internal affairs, should be reaffirmed. It is necessary to support the negotiated political solutions and the peace proposals that the Central American States adopt under the auspices of the Contadora Group, as the most viable alternative for the solution of the crisis in Central America for the benefit of their people. In this sense it is important that the five Central American Governments speed up their consultations with the Contadora Group with the aim of bringing to a conclusion the negotiation process with the early signing of the Contadora Act on Peace and Cooperation in Central America.

248. Women have played and continue to play an important role in the self-determination of peoples, including through national liberation, in accordance with the United Nations Charter. Their efforts should be recognized and commanded and used as one basis for their full participation in the construction of their countries, and in the creation of humane and just social

and political systems. Women's contribution in this area should be ensured by their equal access to political power and their full participation in the decision-making process.

249. Strategies at the national, regional and the global levels should be based on a clear recognition that peace and security, self-determination and national independence are fundamental for the attainment of the three objectives of the Decade: equality, development and peace.

250. Safeguarding world peace and averting a nuclear catastrophe is one of the most important tasks today in which women have an essential role to play, especially by supporting actively the halting of the arms race followed by arms reduction and the attainment of a general and complete disarmament under effective international control, and thus contributing to the improvement of their economic position. Irrespective of their socio-economic system, the States should strive to avoid confrontation and to build friendly relations instead, which should be also supported by women.

251. Peace requires the participation of all members of society' women and men alike, in rejecting any type of intervention in the domestic affairs of States, whether it is openly or covertly carried out by other States or by transnational corporations. Peace also requires that women and men alike should promote respect for the sovereign right of a State to establish its own economic, social and political system without undergoing political and economic pressures or coercion of any type.

252. There exists a relationship between the world economic situation, development and the strengthening of international peace and security, disarmament and the relaxation of international tension. All efforts should be made to reduce global expenditures on armaments and

to reach an agreement on the internationally agreed disarmament goals in order to prevent the waste of immense material and human resources, some part of which might otherwise be used for development, especially of the developing countries, as well as for the improvement of standards of living and well-being of people in each country. In this context, particular attention should be given to the advancement of women, including to the participation of women in the promotion of international peace and co-operation and the protection of mothers and children who represent a disproportionate share of the most vulnerable group, the poorest of the poor.

253. Women's equal role in decision-making with respect to peace and related issues should be seen as one of their basic human rights and as such should be enhanced and encouraged at the/national, regional and international levels. In accordance with the Convention on the Elimination of All Forms of Discrimination against Women, all existing impediments to the achievement by women of equality with men should be removed. To this end, efforts should be intensified at all levels to overcome prejudices, stereotyped thinking, denial to women of career prospects and appropriate educational possibilities, and resistance by decision-makers to the changes that are necessary to enable equal participation of women with men in the international and diplomatic service.

254. Mankind is confronted with a choice: to halt the arms race and proceed to disarmament or face annihilation. The growing opposition of women to the danger of war, especially a nuclear war, which will lead to a nuclear holocaust, and their support for disarmament must be respected. States should be encouraged to ensure unhindered flow and access to information, including to women, with regard to various aspects of disarmament to avoid dissemination of false and

tendentious information concerning armaments and to concentrate on the danger of the escalation of the arms race and on the need for general and complete disarmament under effective international control. The resources released as a result of disarmament measures should be used to help promote the well-being of all peoples and improve the economic and social conditions of the developing countries. Under such conditions, States should pay increased attention to the urgent need to improve the situation of women.

255. Peace education should be established for all members of society, particularly children and young people. Values, such as tolerance, racial and sexual equality, respect for and understanding of others, and good-neighbourliness should be developed, promoted and strengthened.

256. Women of the world, together with men, should, as informal educators and socialization agents, play a special role in the process of bringing up younger generations in an atmosphere of compassion, tolerance, mutual concern and trust, with an awareness that all people belong to the same world community. Such education should be part of all formal and informal educational processes as well as of communications, information and mass-media systems.

257. Further action should be taken at family and neighbourhood levels, as well as at national and international levels, to achieve a peaceful social environment compatible with human dignity. The questions of women and peace and the meaning of peace for women cannot be separated from the broader question of relationships between women and men in all spheres of life and in the family. Discriminatory practices and negative attitudes towards women should be eliminated and traditional gender norms changed to enhance women's participation in peace.

258. Violence against women exists in various forms in everyday life in all societies. Women are beaten, mutilated, burned, sexually abused and raped. Such violence is a major obstacle to the achievement of peace and the other objectives of the Decade and should be given special attention. Women victims of violence should be given particular attention and comprehensive assistance. To this end, legal measures should be formulated to prevent violence and to assist women victims. National machinery should be established in order to deal with the question of violence against women within the family and society. Preventive policies should be elaborated, and institutionalized forms of assistance to women victims provided.

Long-term programme of work for the advancement of women

248. In resolution 1985/46 of 31 May 1985, the Economic and Social Council urged all United Nations bodies, including the regional commissions, and the specialized agencies which had not then done so, to develop and implement comprehensive policies for women and development and to incorporate them into their medium-term plans, statements of objectives, programmes and other major policy statements. The Council, further, requested the Secretary-General, in his capacity as Chairman of the Administrative Committee on Co-ordination, to take the initiative in formulating a system-wide, medium-term plan for women and development. The World Conference to Review and Appraise the Achievements of the United Nations Decade for Women also called for a system-wide, medium-term plan in order to achieve greater coherence and efficiency of the policies and programmes of the United Nations system related to women and development.

249. A report on the proposed framework of the

plan (E/1986/8) was submitted to the Economic and Social Council at its second regular session of 1986 through the Commission on the Status of Women and the Committee for Programme and Co-ordination. The Council, in resolution 1986/71 of 23 July 1986, took note of the proposed framework and arranged for it to be analysed and reviewed by the Committee for Programme and Co-ordination and the Commission on the Status of Women.

250. A draft of the system-wide, medium-term plan for women and development (E/CN.6/1987/2) was submitted by the Secretary-General to the Commission on the Status of Women at its session held from 12 to 16 January 1987. The draft was revised, taking into account the recommendations of the Commission, and submitted by the Administrative Committee on Co-ordination to the Council (E/1987/52).

251. When the Council considered the plan, it recommended, in paragraph 5 of its resolution 1987/86 of 8 July 1987, that the Administrative Committee on Coordination should report to it, through the Commission on the Status of Women, on arrangements to implement the system-wide plan.

Long-term programme of work of the commission on the status of women

252. The Commission on the Status of Women at its 1987 session made significant progress and self-reform. It restructured its agenda along functional lines, developed a systematic long-term programme of work and urged improvements in the system of reporting, monitoring and appraising the implementation of the Forward-looking Strategies; it strengthened and rationalized its role and functions in the mobilization of the resources of the United Nations system as a whole towards the advancement of women, by integrating this objective in

the programme planning and budgeting processes of the Organization; it agreed to hold annual sessions until the year 2000.

253. In resolution 1987/24 of 26 May 1987, the Economic and Social Council endorsed the long-term programme of work of the Commission, including an annual consideration of three themes, one under each of the three objectives-equality, development and peace -beginning with its thirty-second session in 1988, in the order listed below:

Equality

1. National machinery for monitoring and improving the status of women;
2. Equality in economic and social participation;
3. Equality in political participation and decision-making;
4. Vulnerable women, including migrant women;

Development

1. Problems of rural women, including food, water resources, agricultural technology, rural employment, transportation and environment;
2. Women and education, eradication of illiteracy, employment, health and social services, including population issues and child care;
3. Negative effects of the international economic situation on the improvement of the status of women;
4. National, regional and international machinery for the effective integration of women in the development process, including non-governmental organizations; Integration of women in the process of development.

Peace

1. Access to information, education for peace, and efforts to eradicate violence against women within the family and society;
2. Full participation of women in the construction of their countries and in the creation of just social and political systems;
3. Women in areas affected by armed conflicts, foreign intervention, alien and colonial domination, foreign occupation and threats to peace;
4. Refugee and displaced women and children;
5. Equal participation in all efforts to promote international co-operation, peace and disarmament.

254. The Council further decided that the work of the Commission in relation to the priority themes should be closely related to the relevant provisions of the Forward-looking Strategies and other policy documents, the programmes elaborated in the system-wide, medium-term plan for women and development and the relevant chapters of the World *"Survey on the Role of Women in Development,"* with a view to ensuring the effective implementation of the Forward-looking Strategies women.

Bibliography

Ahuja, R (1986) *Crime Against Women,* Rawat, Jaipur.

An attempt was made to achieve the purpose of eradicating the evil of dowry by introducing amendments in the Dowry Prohibition Act in 1984 were still inadequate. Therefore, a bill to make the Provisions of the Dowry Prohibition Act more stringent and effective was passed by Parliament on 23rd August, 1986.

Bunch C., "Transforming Human Rights from a Feminist Perspective."

Carlson, E. (1987) Wife Battering: A Social Deviance Analysis; in Figueira, J. Mcdonough and Sarri, R (eds), *The Trapped Women,* Sage, London.

Convention for the Protection of Human Rights and Fundamental Freedoms, 213 U.N.T.S. 221, reprinted in Brownile, *supra note* 18, at 391.

Friedman E., Women's Human Rights: the Emergence of a Movement".

Emancipation of Women -S. Lalitha, the Academy Law Review, Vol. 13:2. 1989.

Fighting Female Foeticide- A long way to go- Ravinder R.P., The Lawyers Collective, Aug. 1991.

Human Rights Watch Global Report on Women's Human Rights. New York of 1993 & 1995.

Indian Evidence Act, Section 113-A. A presumption has also been incorporated in the Indian Evidence Act to enable the court ton draw an inference of abetment of suicide when the question is whether the commission of suicide by a woman was abetted by her husband or any relative, the complainant has been freed from that onus to prove that the accused had indeed abetted the offence.

International Convention on the suppression and Punishment of the Crime of Apartheid, opened for signature Nov. 30, 1973, G.A. res. 3068, 28 U.N. GAOR Supp. (No.30) 75 U.N Dec. A/9030.

Law Commission of India, *Eighty-fourth Report on Rape and Allied Offences* (1980).

Lewis, O. (1983) See Finkelhor, et. al. *The Dark Side of Families, Sage,* California.

Mayer A. E., "Cultural Particularism as a Bar to Women's Rights: Reflections on the Middle Eastern Experience".

Nandy, A.C (1980) 'women versus Womanliness in India; An Essay in Cultural and Political Psychology' in *At the Edge of Psychology; Essays in Politics and Culture.* Oxford Univ. Press, Delhi.

Rao A. "The Politics of Gender and Culture in International Human Rights Discourse."

Rape, as perceived under the Indian Penal Code, 1860 (IPC), in essence, involves a coercive non-consensual (as well as consensual in a set of specified circumstances) sexual intercourse with a Woman. [See sec. 375, IPC] A perpetrator is also subjected to serve punitive sanctions [See sec. 376, IPC].

Singh (1990) *Indian women;* The Captured Beings, Intellectual, New Delhi.

Stamatopoulou E., "Women's Rights and the United Nations."

The Criminal Law (Amendment) Act of 1983, among others, increased punishment for rape; distinguished gang rape and custodial rape and laid down stiffer penalties; distinguished rape on a pregnant woman and reversed the burden of proof in case of gang rape, custodial rape, rape on a pregnant woman.

The Dowry Prohibition (Amendment) Act, 1966, Section 8-B.

Youssef N. H., "Women's Access to Productive Resources; the Need for Legal Instruments to Protect Women's Development Rights."

Index